THE PROCESS OF SME GROWTH

Integrating
the resource-based
and transaction cost
approaches

THE PROCESS OF SME GROWTH

Marta Gancarczyk

Integrating
the resource-based
and transaction cost
approaches

Jagiellonian
University
Press

ENGLISH LANGUAGE EDITOR
Frederic Widlak

REVIEWER
Dr. Hab. Krzysztof Wach, Professor of Cracow University of Economics

COVER DESIGN
Magdalena Warzecha

This publication is a result of the project financed by Polish National Science Centre (Narodowe Centrum Nauki) – Decision no. DEC-2013/09/B/HS4/01938.

ISBN 978-83-233-4377-6
ISBN 978-83-233-9766-3 (e-book)

www.wuj.pl

Jagiellonian University Press
Editorial Offices: Michałowskiego 9/2, 31-126 Kraków, Poland
Phone: +48 12 663 23 80, +48 12 663 23 82, Fax: +48 12 663 23 83
Distribution: Phone: +48 12 631 01 97, Fax: +48 12 631 01 98
Cell Phone: +48 506 006 674, e-mail: sprzedaz@wuj.pl
Bank: PEKAO SA, IBAN PL 80 1240 4722 1111 0000 4856 3325

TABLE OF CONTENTS

Introduction 7

1. Firm growth as a phenomenon and an object of research 19
    1.1. The uniqueness and importance of firm growth at the macro-
    and micro-economic levels 19
    1.2. The measures and criteria of identification of high-growth firms 24
    1.3. The methods of identifying high-growers 27
    1.4. Theoretical approaches to firm growth and their relevance for SME
    expansion 32
    1.5. Approaches to systemizing the research on small firm growth 39
    1.6. The established streams of research in firm growth 40
    1.7. The emerging streams of research in firm growth 43
    1.8. A cross-fertilization among the established and emerging research
    streams in firm growth 47
    1.9. The core of the firm growth process 49

**2. The Resource-Based View (RBV) and Transaction Cost Theory (TCT)
as alternative approaches to the growth process of firms** 55
    2.1. The rationale for adopting the RBV and TCT to explain the growth
    process of SMEs 55
    2.2. The structural elements of the growth process 59
    2.3. The structural elements of the growth process according to the RBV 61
    2.4. The structural elements of the growth process according to TCT 65
    2.5. The RBV and TCT as alternative views on the structural elements
    of company growth 70
    2.6. Empirical tests, theoretical advancements, and the convergence
    of the foci of the RBV and TCT 72

3. The integrative RBV-TCT approach to the SME growth process 79
    3.1. Methodology for developing an integrative RBV-TCT framework
    of the growth process of SMEs 79
    3.2. The overview of the methodologies and results of the integrative
    RBV-TCT studies 84
    3.3. The logics of integrating the RBV and TCT and the choice of the logic
    relevant for explaining the SME growth process 96

3.4. The "why" dimension of the SME growth process: behavioral motives
and rationale 106
3.5. The "how" dimension of growth: mechanisms and modes 111
3.6. Contextual influences and moderators of the RBV and TCT variables
on the process of growth 114
3.7. Theoretical framework of the SME growth process 116

4. Methodology of empirical research on the growth process of SMEs 121
4.1. Empirical research framework 121
4.2. Methods and sources of data 123
4.3. Variables 130
4.4. Case selection criteria, characteristics of the research sample, and data
collection procedure 134
4.5. Scientific validity of the research methodology 140

**5. Patterns of the SME growth process: results of the multi-case study
research** 143
5.1. Results of the cross-case study analysis 143
5.2. Results of the within-case study analysis 159
5.3. A model of the SME growth process 162

Discussion and conclusion 165
Contribution and implications of the research 165
Limitations 172

Bibliography 175

List of tables... 203

List of figures... 205

INTRODUCTION

The micro- and macro-economic importance and the research challenges make the growth of the firm one of the focal topics in entrepreneurship, economics, and strategic management studies. At the micro-economic level and from the perspective of an individual entrepreneur, growth ensures efficiency gains, return on investment, and self-fulfillment (Storey, 1994; Achtenhagen, Naldi, & Melin, 2010). Expansion is also evidence of success in innovation activities that broaden the firm's scope by generating new products, services, and markets. Increasing the size and scope improves the survival prospects for start-ups and young firms, since non-growers were found to be more vulnerable to failure (Stam et al., 2006).

However, the phenomenon of fast-growing firms is even better recognized from the macro-economic perspective. This macro-economic impact was recognized in the 1980s as the disproportionally large input of so-called *gazelles* on job creation (Birch, 1979, 1987; Birch & Medoff, 1994; Birch, Haggerty & Parsons, 1995). High-growth firms, i.e., those capable of considerable size increase within a short time, form a small share of the firm population, ranging from 2% to 6% (Coad, 2009, p. 6; OECD, 2007; 2010). However, they strongly contribute both to employment and value-added (Storey, 1994; Coad, 2009; Acs, Parsons, & Tracy, 2008; Stam et al. 2006). Moreover, they are also more likely to increase their scope by providing radical product innovations that accelerate technological progress (Coad, 2009; Schreyer, 2000; Storey, 1994; Smallbone, Leigh, & North, 1995). Research on rapid expansion predominantly focuses on young and small and medium-sized enterprises (SMEs) based on the evidence of their major share among fast-growers. This attention is strengthened by the evidence that large, established, non-growth enterprises are the primary generators of job losses (Stam et al., 2006; Storey, 1994; Acs, Parsons, & Tracy, 2008).

The challenging nature of rapid growth as a research problem consists in its importance and rarity among enterprises, as well as in its heterogeneity that leaves wide unexplored areas for research. The heterogeneity of this phenomenon is seen in a variety of expansion drivers and causal relationships that remain unexplained (Achtenhagen, Naldi, & Melin, 2010; Shepherd & Wiklund, 2009). Moreover, it can be argued that growth is worth discussing only in the context of fast-growing firms (Coad, 2009). While these companies significantly increase in size and scope, the remaining population grows incrementally or not at all (Acs, Parsons, & Tracy, 2008; Coad, 2009; Stam et al., 2006; Storey, 1994).

Therefore, it is justified to focus the research on high growth and on the major representation of rapid growers, which are predominantly SMEs. Consequently, *in this book, the growth or expansion phenomenon is treated as synonymous with high-growth, understood to be intense size and scope increases (usually at least doubling in size) within a relatively short period (such as three to four years)* (Moreno & Casillas, 2007; Davidsson, Delmar, & Wiklund, 2006). The expansion of scope and size is inseparable from learning and competence development, which represents both the driving force and outcome of growth (Penrose, 1959; Macpherson & Holt, 2007).

The economic importance and challenging nature of firm growth attracted a broad stream of empirical studies to explore this phenomenon. However, extant research demonstrates some gaps and under-explored areas. This research is predominantly aimed at discovering distinctive features of high-growth firms with the adoption of quantitative, survey-based methods, to formulate recommendations for company management and public policies (McKelvie & Wiklund, 2010; Dobbs & Hamilton, 2007). Empirical evidence in this field identified several distinctive characteristics (Storey, 1994; Barringer, Jones, & Neubaum, 2005; Gilbert, McDougall, & Audretsch, 2006; Dobbs & Hamilton, 2007). Yet, there remains some ambiguity in understanding the content, impact, and cause-effect relationships among the factors identified as determinants and predictors of expansion (Achtenhagen, Naldi, & Melin, 2010; Shepherd & Wiklund, 2009). It is argued that pursuing this deterministic stream will not be a fruitful pathway, since different research questions and methodologies are needed to fully understand the causes of growth (Davidsson, Achtenhagen, & Naldi, 2010).

Instead of investigating isolated growth determinants with static methods, it is more beneficial to learn about growth as a process and explain why and how it is accomplished (Dobbs & Hamilton, 2007; Wright & Stigliani, 2013; Selden & Fletcher, 2015; Muñoz & Dimov, 2015). Growth is a dynamic and idiosyncratic phenomenon that requires adequate theoretical and methodological approaches (Davidsson, Delmar, & Wiklund, 2006; Leitch, Hill, & Neergaard, 2010; McKelvie & Wiklund, 2010; Stam, 2010; Hansen & Hamilton 2011; Wright & Stigliani, 2013; Koryak et al., 2015). However, the research on the growth process is scarce both in empirical and theoretical terms (Hansen & Hamilton, 2011; Wright & Stigliani, 2013; Koryak et al., 2015).

Expanding the range of theoretical perspectives on firm growth has been recently called for to explain the complexity of this phenomenon, including processes and modes of its implementation (Dobbs & Hamilton, 2007; McKelvie & Wiklund, 2010). It is natural to adopt the entrepreneurial process perspective for such an area of study (Steyaert, 2007). From this point of view, the entrepreneurship process is a flow of events, i.e., decisions and actions (Selden & Fletcher, 2015; Muñoz & Dimov, 2015). Consequently, the question emerges about how this flow of events is organized. The structuring of this process to produce a sequence of events needs to be investigated with a theoretical background that is relevant to the phenomenon under study.

Penrose's work (1959), as a dominant theoretical perspective on firm expansion, laid the foundations for the resource-based view (the RBV) focused on the company's performance and competitive advantage. Recently, the RBV has advanced to become a theory of firm nature and boundaries (scope and size), including a specific area of firm expansion as well (Tsang, 2000; Pitelis & Teece, 2009; Foss & Foss, 2008). By extending its scope, the RBV challenged transaction cost theory (TCT) as a dominant approach to firm boundaries and proposed alternative assumptions. The value- and capability-oriented approach of the RBV has been increasingly confronted and integrated with TCT that emphasizes uncertainty and the costs of economic exchange (Argyres & Zenger, 2012; Leiblein & Miller, 2003; Silverman, 1999). The integrative approach is supported by empirical evidence that demonstrates the legitimacy of both perspectives. This evidence calls for investigating conditions under which the two seemingly contradictory approaches hold and combine in the decisions regarding a firm's scope and size (Combs et al., 2011; Leiblein, 2003).

Deterministic studies on growth drivers usually adopted the RBV orientation towards value and competitive advantage through capability development (Storey, 1994; Wiklund & Shepherd, 2003; Barringer, Jones, & Neubaum, 2005; Macpherson & Holt, 2007). However, they rarely utilized the RBV theoretical assumptions in a systematic way. On the other hand, considering the rarity and uncertainty associated with expansion, this process is also challenged by transaction costs that impede the entrepreneurial opportunity pursuit (Foss & Foss, 2008), rent creation and appropriation (Alvarez, 2007), as well as innovation (Michael, 2007). The integrative RBV-TCT studies developed predominantly in strategic management and economics literature (Williamson, 1999; Pitelis & Pseiridis, 1999; Argyres & Zenger, 2012). However, one can observe a few successful applications of these theories in entrepreneurship studies (Davidsson, Steffens, & Fitzsimmons, 2009; Garnsey, Stam, & Heffernan, 2006; Chandler, McKelvie, & Davidsson, 2009; Verwaal et al., 2010) to explain such aspects of growth as measures, performance, and governance modes. Still, none of the studies confront the issue of growth process with the use of the both perspectives.

The studies in firm scope and size that adopt the integrative RBV and TCT approach address such strategies of expansion as vertical integration and diversification, market development and penetration, as well as hybrid modes of growth, including joint ventures, franchising, alliances, outsourcing, and licensing (Leiblein & Miller, 2003; Mayer & Salomon, 2006; Safizadeh et al., 2008; Ray, Xue, & Barney, 2013). However, these studies are rarely conducted in the context of high-growth firms, leaving a research gap for testing their theoretical assumptions on this group of enterprises.

In response to the above research challenges, *the major aim of this book is to conceptualize a model of the growth process of SMEs based on the integration of the resource-based view of the firm and transaction cost theory.*

Detailed objectives were formulated as follows:
1. *Identifying the specificity of SME growth and the core of the process perspective on the firm's expansion.*
2. *Systemizing the RBV and TCT concepts and the assumptions relative to SME growth.*
3. *Assessing the relevance of the assumptions of the RBV and TCT as competing perspectives on the SME growth process.*
4. *Combining the RBV and TCT approaches to the SME growth process into one theoretical framework.*
5. *Assessing the relevance of the integrated RBV-TCT framework for the growth process of SMEs.*

Corresponding with the aim and the indicated research gaps, *the major research questions* were:
1. *What are the characteristics of the SME growth process, including its motives, rationale, mechanisms, and modes?*

2. *Does the integration of the resource-based view and transaction cost theory enable explaining the SME growth process?*

The integrated RBV-TCT model of the SME growth process will consist of motives, rationale, mechanisms, and modes derived from these two theories as structural elements of the process of growth. The motives refer to behavioral assumptions about the attitudes of entrepreneurs and other economic agents in making decisions (such as opportunism versus trust and mutuality). The growth rationale consists of reasons and goals for enlarging the company size. The mechanisms involve interdependencies among growth determinants (cause-effect relationships). Growth modes denote different governance structures of achieving growth in terms of internal (organic), external (acquisitive), or hybrid options. This approach to modeling firm growth sets the entrepreneur's perceptions about structural elements of the growth process at the center and intends to explain his or her decisional rules with the use of those elements. Namely, the entrepreneur's perceptions about motives, rationale, mechanism, and modes are treated as enabling constraints (Juarrero, 2000; Selden & Fletcher, 2015) that limit the range of accessible options but at the same time lay the foundations for specific decisions and actions. Therefore, the perceptions about motives affect how contractual relationships with business partners are governed. The growth rationale influences the choice of new activities to pursue expansion (products, services, markets) and thus the type of company portfolio. Mechanisms determine the sources of new activities, i.e., new products and services are either capability-driven (adjusted to capabilities) or driven by the requirements from customers and suppliers (adjusted to transaction requirements). The adjustment type is associated with specific modes to pursue expansion through internalization or hybrids, or via internal or external governance.

The *general hypothesis* established for the research is:

The integration of the resource-based view and transaction cost theory enables building a model of the SME growth process, including its motives, rationale, mechanisms, and modes.

Considering the current state of the art in theoretical and empirical terms, the following specific hypotheses have been formulated:

Hypothesis 1. *In the process of growth, entrepreneurs perceive trust as the major motive of exchange partners, limited by the perceived opportunism.*

Hypothesis 2. *In the process of growth, entrepreneurs perceive value as the major rationale for growth, supplemented by transaction cost considerations.*

Hypothesis 3. *In the process of growth, entrepreneurs perceive the mechanism of growth as based on aligning the new activity and its mode (hierarchy or hybrid, organic or acquisitive) with transaction characteristics and with the firm's capabilities. Namely, the choice between hierarchy and hybrid modes depends on transaction characteristics, while the choice between organic and acquisitive modes depends on relatedness with the firm's core competence.*

Hypotheses 1, 2, and 3 test the alternative assumptions of the RBV and TCT and, at the same time, they combine them into one framework of entrepreneurial perceptions of motives, rationale, mechanisms, and modes as structural elements in the process of SME growth.

Hypotheses 4 and 5 include the assumptions about the influence of contextual factors on the entrepreneurial perceptions of the structural elements in the growth process. The contextual factors are specified as the major variables of the RBV and TCT. Therefore, their influence will positively or negatively verify the validity of these theories.

Hypothesis 4. *The characteristics of motives, rationale, mechanisms, and modes of growth are affected by moderators during the growth process. Namely, the levels of resource advantage over competitors and transaction asset specificity have moderating effects on how entrepreneurs perceive motives in business exchange, rationales for growth, mechanisms, and modes of growth.*

Hypothesis 5. *The explanatory power of the RBV and TCT towards the SME growth process depends on the contextual characteristics of the SMEs' capabilities and transactional environment.*

Hypothesis 5.1. *In the conditions of a limited company potential (low resource advantage) and unfavorable transactional environment (high asset specificity), entrepreneurs conform to the principles of TCT.*

Hypothesis 5.2. *In the favorable conditions of company potential (high resource advantage) and transactional environment (low asset specificity), entrepreneurs make choices consistent with the assumptions of the RBV.*

A general methodological idea for building the model of the SME growth process consists in 1) confronting and empirically testing the RBV and TCT theoretical perspectives on firm growth and then 2) integrating them to build a new theoretical framework, a descriptive model of the SME growth process. The methodology involves desk research (meta-analysis of conceptual and empirical research in the field), empirical experiment, and conceptual work.

A qualitative meta-analysis (meta-synthesis) was conducted to synthesize theoretical and empirical studies related to the SME growth process and to testing the RBV and TCT assumptions (Hoon, 2013; Sandelowski,

Docherty, & Emden, 1997; Paterson et al., 2001; Weed, 2005). The meta-synthesis not only generalized the findings from the research, but also the methodologies used specifically for operationalizing the major constructs of the RBV and TCT. This qualitative meta-analysis resulted in the RBV-TCT integrative framework of the growth process of SMEs to be adopted in the empirical research. The argumentation was based on a systematic, innovative literature review of the RBV-TCT integrative studies, since extant reviews focus on only one of the approaches. To synthesize the findings, theory pruning (reducing) was adopted (Leavitt, Mitchell, & Peterson, 2010; Shareff, 2007; Davis, 2006).

The empirical research combines an exploratory and under-explored theme of the SME growth process with a deductive approach to explain this phenomenon and to build theory. The deductive approach may bias explorative findings towards the extant theory. This bias has been avoided by confronting and combining two alternative theories, by validating data during two-staged interviews, and by data triangulation with the use of natural observation and analysis of secondary sources. The deductive approach offers more structured and better-recognized assumptions and variables than the inductive approach that is associated with the idiosyncrasy of concepts and methodologies. The inductive approach, which dominates the extant research on entrepreneurial growth, is one of the causes of ambiguous interpretations of findings. Moreover, deductive theory building is useful at the start of exploratory research to pave the way for further, inductive and grounded theory-based investigations.

The explorative theme and deductive approach establish special methodological requirements to cope with complex, under-researched phenomena and simultaneously match it to well-established theoretical assumptions.

Responding to these challenges, the explorative nature of the SME growth process was addressed with *a multiple-case study as the major research method*. The adoption of an innovative case study design, namely, *the prospective case study*, enabled testing the RBV and TCT (Hoon, 2013). The prospective case study is an advancement of qualitative deductive testing (Yin, 2009), alternate template approach and pattern-matching (Langley, 1999; Lee, 1989) in the case study method. It consists of formulating hypotheses at the start of the research and testing them through falsification (Popper, 1968) instead of generating proposals *ex-post*, as the research outcome. The prospective case study represents an advancement in the case study methodology towards more systematic and structured conceptual background, analysis, and interpretation of a complex problem.

The multiple-case study was implemented by using complementary research methods, such as two-staged, structured, and semi-structured interviews with entrepreneurs, natural observation, and content analysis. The analytical methods and tools included Qualitative Comparative Analysis and text-mining, among others.

The research presented in this book offers three *contributions* relevant to explaining the growth process. *First*, it contributes to the entrepreneurial process perspective *by developing a model of the SME growth process with the use of the deductive approach.* The model builds upon the RBV and TCT approaches and extends the structuration view of the entrepreneurial process (Sarason, Dean, & Dillard, 2006; Selden & Fletcher, 2015). The deductive approach is useful at the initial stage of growth process studies. It ensures a well-recognized and coherent basis for problem conceptualization and choosing empirical research methods. Thus, it helps to limit the ambiguity of interpretations that might arise from inductive, empirically-driven theory development.

This model is not only a theoretical construct, but it has been verified in the empirical research that acknowledged the criteria of scientific validity. The empirical verification of the model enabled identifying three patterns of the SME growth process, namely a capability-based process of growth, a transactional process of growth, and a capability- and-market opportunity-oriented process of growth. Thus, the model responds to the calls for a broader theoretical and conceptual basis to study the process of entrepreneurial growth and for more empirical verification of these theoretical approaches (McKelvie & Wiklund, 2010; Dobbs & Hamilton, 2007; Koryak et al., 2013; Wright & Stigliani, 2013).

The second contribution of the research is a theoretical and methodological framework for further studying the growth process of firms, whether focused on SMEs or other types of enterprises and for future investigation of the entrepreneurial process. The general theoretical framework offered in this book can be complemented with the use of other theoretical approaches that a researcher finds relevant for the enterprises under study. Entrepreneurial process perspectives offer general models focused predominantly on venture creation and the development stages that follow. However, to our knowledge, none of them has been designed for and focuses on the specificity of the growth process. We address this gap in the entrepreneurial process modeling by addressing the growth process with a focus on SMEs. However, the general framework can serve future empirical studies on firm growth as a deductive, theory-driven approach.

Third, the research broadens the integrative RBV-TCT studies by the inclusion of the specific context of the entrepreneurial growth process, both in theoretical and empirical terms. Although addressing growth issues, integrative RBV-TCT studies in firm boundaries (scope and size) hardly refer to the context of high-growth companies and entrepreneurial growth. In the entrepreneurship literature, the framework linking both theories to investigate expansion has been represented by only individual studies (Chandler, McKelvie, & Davidsson, 2009; Verwaal et al., 2010). Moreover, none of them investigated the process dimension of expansion. The present research tests the integrative RBV-TCT assumptions in the context of high-growth firms and thus adds a new dimension to the extant integrative research. Moreover, it proposes a configurational view on the validity of both theories and the possibilities of their integration within the reality of small business growth. Namely, the empirical evidence shows that both theories may prove valid individually or they can be combined in different contexts of firm potential and environment.

The book *draws upon three fields of academic research, namely entrepreneurship literature on firm growth as well as microeconomics and strategic management literature on firm boundary decisions related to scope and size issues.* This broader perspective supports the *accumulation of knowledge on the growth phenomenon.* Moreover, it responds to the recommendation that the boundary literature in vertical integration, diversification, and governance modes should be included in the research on entrepreneurial growth due to an overlapping focus (Davidsson, Achtenhagen, & Naldi, 2010). Similarly, in the studies on firm boundaries, it supplements the entrepreneurial perspective in setting up firm scope and size (Jacobides & Winter, 2007).

This monograph is structured into five chapters, which lead to the elaboration of the model of the SME growth process and implementation of the detailed objectives of the research. Figure 1 presents the phases of the development of the model of the SME growth process, the detailed objectives addressed, and the structure of the book.

The first chapter discusses firm growth as a phenomenon and object of research with an emphasis on the process perspective on growth. This chapter clarifies the understanding of firm growth, specifically SME growth. The focus on intense growth as uncommon but vitally important at the micro- and macro-economic levels is emphasized. The review of extant theoretical approaches and research streams provides the arguments for the present interest in the process perspective on growth. Moreover, it enables the assessment of the suitability of extant theoretical approaches to study SME growth process. The outcome of the first chapter is a general theoretical framework of the firm growth process as a first stage of building the model of the SME growth process. This general framework required structural elements stemming from an adequate theoretical background.

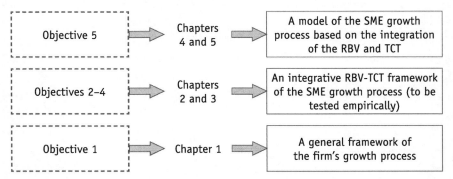

Figure 1. The phases of the elaboration of the model of SME growth process and the structure of the book

Source: own work.

The second chapter presents the RBV and TCT as alternative approaches to the firm's growth process and justifies their adoption to specify the structural elements of the SME growth process. The analysis of both theories enabled the identification of these key elements, namely, motives, rationale, mechanisms, and modes. Conceptual and empirical advancements of both theories were synthesized to show the convergence of their focus and comparability of their assumptions about firm scope and size. The comparability and validity confirmed through a literature review were recognized as arguments for combining the RBV and TCT into one theoretical framework.

In the third chapter, the methodology of integrating the RBV and TCT to develop a theoretical framework of the SME growth process was elaborated, and qualitative meta-analysis of theoretical and empirical studies that integrate these approaches was performed. Upon the assessment of three logics of integrating the RBV and TCT, we selected the one most suitable for further development of hypotheses about entrepreneurs' perceptions of the structural elements of the growth process. The entrepreneur's perceptions about these elements are proposed as enabling constraints that both limit and form a basis for decisions and actions. Qualitative meta-analysis enabled the formulation of research hypotheses. Finally, an integrative RBV-TCT framework of the SME growth process was proposed, as a second stage of building the final model. The framework complements the first-stage general framework of the firm growth process (Chapter 1) with hypotheses regarding the specificity of the SME growth process. This conceptual framework will be tested in the empirical research.

The fourth chapter presents the methodology of empirical research to test the RBV-TCT framework of SME growth process. The empirical research framework, methods, data collection, operationalization of variables, and case selection criteria were explained.

The fifth chapter encompasses the findings from the cross-case and within-case study analyses. Three patterns of SME growth are proposed, each of them demonstrating distinctive characteristics of motives, rationale, mechanisms, and modes of growth. Moreover, it is shown how these elements act as enabling constraints. Namely, how differing entrepreneurial perceptions about motives in business exchange impact the way that contractual arrangements are governed, how rationale affects the type of portfolio development, how mechanisms explain the sources of new activities that drive growth, and how the hierarchy or hybrid, organic or acquisitive governance modes for growth emerge. Finally, the contextual influences of firm capabilities and the contractual environment on how entrepreneurs perceive structural elements of growth process were analyzed and assessed. These findings complemented the earlier integrative RBV-TCT framework of the SME growth process with three patterns of the growth of small and medium sized enterprises. Based on these findings, the final model of the SME growth process grounded on the RBV-TCT approach was proposed.

The Discussion and conclusion section summarizes the project by presenting its contribution to the field of study and the limitations of the research.

1. FIRM GROWTH AS A PHENOMENON AND AN OBJECT OF RESEARCH

1.1. The uniqueness and importance of firm growth at the macro- and micro-economic levels

Although firm growth and development are often treated as synonymous and interchangeable in the literature and business vocabulary, it is wise to differentiate these phenomena (Wach, 2012, p. 23). Development denotes predominantly a qualitative phenomenon that implies progress in company competence, and that is not necessarily associated with size increases. It can merely be a step to keep up with the competition, to survive, or to maintain operations in response to customer requirements. Growth consists in enlarging the company size, which is reflected in quantitative measures such as employment, sales, value of assets, market share, or level of diversification (Davidsson & Wiklund, 2000; Davidsson, Delmar, & Wiklund, 2006). Growth or expansion unavoidably invokes development, either as a driver of expansion, i.e., introducing new products, services, or marketing practices that result in sales and employment increases, or as its outcome, e.g., expanding sales to international markets that brings learning effects (Stawasz, 2011; Wach, 2012; Lisowska, 2012; Lachiewicz & Matejun, 2011). Therefore, in this book the term of growth is a phenomenon that includes the size and scope increase as a necessary component, and that is associated with a qualitative development.

The distinctiveness of firm growth compared to firm development stems from the empirical research at the macroeconomic level that has been intensely developing since the 1980s (Birch, 1979; 1987; Birch & Medoff, 1994). In the European Union, small and medium-sized enterprises (SMEs) form 99,8% of all firms, while large entities represent only

0,2% of the population (Muller et al., 2016). More in-depth and dynamic investigations provide insights about the special nature of growth that matters for the economy and about the rarity of this kind of expansion. These findings emphasize the special importance of a firms' rapid size increase within a limited time, i.e., the importance of high growth. Policy-makers and researchers focus on high-growers because they contribute disproportionally to the economy by increasing employment and innovation development. The remaining enterprises expand only marginally or not at all (Acs, Parsons & Tracy, 2008; Coad, 2009; Stam et al., 2006; Storey, 1994). Therefore, there is no justification to focus on the growth of an average firm, but rather on the small fraction of high-growers that represent only 2% to 6% of all companies (Coad, 2009, p. 6; OECD, 2007; 2010). Consequently, the focus of this book is on rapid or high-growth instead on normal or average growth. Explaining the characteristics, determinants, and pathways of achieving expansion by rapidly growing firms facilitates managing these organizations and aids policy-making at the regional and macro-levels of the economy.

Despite being an enterprise-level phenomenon, growth became a major focus of research on economic policy due to the macroeconomic importance of creating new jobs and innovation leading to the increased value added and economic growth (Storey, 1994; Audretsch, 2012).

Rapidly growing firms generate a disproportionately large share of all new jobs and are predominantly of small size (Autio, Arenius, & Wallenius, 2000; Schreyer, 2000; Fritsch & Mueller, 2004). In the 1970s, Birch pioneered the stream of research on the input of young, small, high-growth firms into job creation (Birch, 1979; 1987; Giaoutzi, Nijkamp, & Storey, 2016). When investigating the change in employment in the population of 5.6 million SMEs, he found that about 50% of new jobs were generated by existing firms, while 50% were delivered by a small fraction of newly established companies that demonstrated high growth. Moreover, in the period studied, enterprises with less than 20 employees provided 66% of net new employment. Following Birch's investigations, Acs, Parsons, and Tracy (2008) focused on the so-called *high-impact firms* as job generators. They confirmed the rarity of these enterprises forming 2–3% of all the USA firms, as well as their small size and young age. Namely, 93% of this group employed less than 20 people while firms employing from 20 to 499 people represented only 5,9%. Almost all job losses were due to employment cuts in large, established, non-growth enterprises, called *low-impact* firms, i.e., those hiring more than 500 people.

Birch (1979, 1987) coined the term *gazelles* to describe young (pre-dominantly up to five years old) enterprises that are capable of rapid size increases within a limited time, suggesting their extraordinary dynamics relative to the remaining population. Other research confirmed that growth firms have a more positive impact on job creation than the average firm (Storey, 1994; Davidsson & Delmar, 2003; Henrekson & Johansson, 2010). The employment growth can be observed in high-growth firms rather than in the entire population (Littunen & Tohmo, 2003). More evidence of the input from growing firms is that only a small fraction of companies established in a specific point of time, namely 4% of them, were responsible for 50% of the employment generated by the entire population after 10 years (Birch, Haggerty, & Parsons, 1995; Storey, 1994). According to Birch and Medoff (1994), 4% of the sampled high-growth firms generated 70% of new jobs in the USA economy annually, while Davidsson and Delmar (2003) noted that young high-growth firms demonstrated 80% of organic employment growth. The importance of growth firms to generating employment was also reported by Smallbone, Leigh, and North (1995), however, they studied incumbent firms of which 23% were responsible for 70% of employment in the population studied. Similar results were yielded by Piasecki, Rogut, and Smallbone (1997), who investigated the contribution of the established high-growth enterprises to generating jobs in Poland.

The importance of entrepreneurial activity is emphasized since growth firms are predominantly in the early phases of their life cycles. Namely, they provide the strongest effect on employment when entering the market, while later, this impact weakens (Thwaites & Wynarczyk, 1996; Acs & Mueller, 2008). The short-term effect on employment was partially supported by the research of van Stel, Dielbandhoesing, van den Heuvel, and Storey (2002) in the UK regions. They found a long-term effect of start-ups on employment growth in the first part of the 18-year period studied, while a short-term, immediate effect was reported in the second phase of that time span. This research provides the evidence of discontinuity and irregularity of the expansion of young firms. Moreover, the employment effect revealed in this study was due to young rather than established enterprises. Also, the research by Acs, Parsons, and Tracy (2008) finds high-impact firms to be younger than the remaining, low-impact firms.

The research investigating the relationship between entrepreneurship and economic growth proves a strong positive correlation between economic growth and the activity of gazelles (Stam et al., 2006). Such an impact was not observed for self-employed individuals or for start-up firms in general. Therefore, entrepreneurship, understood as establishing new ventures, is linked to economic growth through the phenomenon of gazelles, i.e., fast-growing new companies, and not to the entire group of start-ups. On the other hand, there is evidence that high-growers are not only young firms, but also established companies (OECD, 2007; 2010; Henrekson & Johansson, 2010, p. 1; Audretsch, 2012), supporting the earlier findings by Smallbone, Leigh, and North (1995).

Another widely discussed contribution from gazelles comes from their innovative activities that result in new products and services, which, in turn, increase the value-added generated by enterprises in the economy (Tatum, 2007; Okoń-Horodyńska & Zachorowska-Mazurkiewicz, 2007). A strong relationship was found among job creation, young age, and innovativeness of organizations (Storey, 1994; Barth, 2003; Stam, 2008, p. 25). It can be argued that a firm's growth is driven by product innovation, at least new to the firm's market (Smallbone, Leigh, & North, 1995; Schreyer, 2000; Barth, 2003). This innovativeness is often associated with operating in high-technology sectors with substantial research and development (R&D) intensity (Hölzl & Friesenbichler, 2008; Okoń-Horodyńska, Wisła, & Sierotowicz, 2011). Although high-growers are not limited to high-technology sectors, these sectors are overrepresented among rapidly expanding firms (Acs, Parsons, & Tracy, 2008; Audretsch, 1995; Geroski, 1995; Almus & Nerlinger, 1999). Innovation is an important contribution of rapidly growing firms to the economy; however, it is at the same time a determinant and a condition for their success (Coad & Rao, 2008).

Considering the empirical evidence reviewed, growth is rare and difficult to accomplish, as well as idiosyncratic (heterogeneous) in terms of determinants, outcomes, processes, and modes (Garnsey, Stam, & Heffernan, 2006; Stam, 2010).

Characteristics of high-growers that are usually considered to be determinants of growth, such as age, industry, size, the features of the entrepreneur, firm capabilities, and environment have generally been confirmed by empirical research (Storey, 1994; Barringer, Jones, & Neubaum, 2005; Gilbert, McDougall, & Audretsch, 2006; Dobbs & Hamilton, 2007). However, even these predominant factors have been challenged (Davidsson, Achtenhagen, & Naldi, 2010; Garnsey, Stam, & Heffernan, 2006; Storey, 1994).

The outcomes of growth (employment, value added, and innovation) might considerably depend on the measures of growth adopted (Achtenhagen, Naldi, & Melin, 2010). If these measures are independent, there is the possibility of jobless growth with only sales enlargement, which increases value-added but not employment at the macroeconomic level. Some researchers report a correlation among measures of growth, such as employment, sales, and assets value (Smallbone, Leigh, & North, 1995; Baum, Locke, & Smith, 2001; Lumpkin & Dess, 2001; Delmar, Davidsson, & Gartner, 2003). While others find them unrelated (Weinzimmer, Nystrom, & Freeman, 1998; Shepherd & Wiklund, 2009).

Like determinants and outcomes, processes and modes of expansion appear to be heterogeneous as well. A firm can expand its size and scope with the adoption of different modes, including the organic mode, based on the company resources, or the external mode, such as mergers and acquisitions, or the hybrid mode, in the form of joint ventures, licensing, and franchising (McKelvie & Wiklund, 2010; Gancarczyk & Gancarczyk, 2011). The modes differ in their macro-economic importance. Namely, the organic and hybrid modes increase value-added and possibly employment, which leads to the growth of the entire economy. External modes predominantly consist of regrouping resources and ownership instead of generating new value, resulting in efficiency gains at the enterprise level rather than impacting the economy at large (Davidsson, Delmar, & Wiklund, 2006).

From the point of view of a small, newly established company, expansion is needed to achieve an efficient scale of operations and a satisfactory return on investment, as well as limiting the risk of failure, which is a threat at this development stage (Piasecki, 1997; Almus & Nerlinger, 1999). While the vulnerability of start-ups to failure has been widely documented in all market economies, the likelihood of new entrants' survival is positively related to firm size (Audretsch, 1995; Geroski, 1995; Wagner 2001). From the perspective of established companies, expansion is critical for competitive improvement through strategic changes in products, markets, and processes, among others (Smallbone, Leigh, & North, 1995; Bednarczyk, 2006).

In Europe, the importance of growth is also emphasized due to the lower average size of firms compared to the USA and Japan (Muller et al., 2015, p. 22). At the same time, there are positive correlations among firm size and productivity, the gross national product *per capita,* and real value added (Muller et al., 2016). Small size is one of the reasons for high mortality among the population of SMEs at large, particularly during economic downturns.

Entrepreneurs' perceptions of growth focus on its outcomes rather than growth itself and emphasize the increase in profitability, firm value, knowledge, and experience, as well as a general sense of success (Achtenhagen,

Naldi, & Melin, 2010). Consequently, they use such measures of growth as net profitability, book value, and other efficiency indicators rather than scope and size, especially, size measured by the number of employees. This distinguishes entrepreneurs from managers for whom the sense of power stems from the number of employees supervised and the amount of resources controlled (Marris, 1963, 1964; Baumol, 1959; Williamson 1964; Jensen & Meckling, 1976). From the micro-economic point of view, both entrepreneurs and private investors acknowledge the importance of growth. However, there are practical limits to enlarging the firm, including internal coordination costs, the firm's core competence, the costs of market transactions, and the costs of information and communication technologies.

1.2. The measures and criteria of identification of high-growth firms

The essence of growth (understood as high-growth) is the increase in firm size associated with learning and competence development. However, as earlier claimed, development is unavoidably associated with growth, while growth does not necessarily accompany development. This suggests a quantitative approach to understanding growth, with the adoption of size measures. Among these, the dominant variables are employment and total sales, due to their objectivity and accessibility (Coad, 2009; Achtenhagen, Naldi, & Melin, 2010). The disadvantages of using sales as a measure of growth include the need to correct it for depreciation in the long run and to acknowledge currency differences in international comparative research. Moreover, sales do not reveal value added in the enterprise, which is a drawback often emphasized by entrepreneurs (Coad, 2009).

However, hiring new employees is considered an adequate sign of sustainable and purposeful rather than casual or accidental growth. Some studies emphasize the high correlation of this measure with sales and asset value that support a positive assessment of long-term market perspectives and a capacity to compete based on the developed resource base (Coad, 2009; Smallbone, Leigh, & North, 1995; Baum, Locke, & Smith, 2001; Lumpkin & Dess, 2001; Delmar, Davidsson, & Gartner, 2003; Zbierowski, 2012). Other studies find this correlation weak for all popular measures of expansion (Weinzimmer, Nystrom, & Freeman, 1998; Shepherd & Wiklund, 2009). The explanation may be that this correlation appears in the long-run, since, for instance, the study by Smallbone, Leigh, and North (1995) considered a 10-year period of growth. The limitation of employment as a growth indicator is its lower importance for entrepreneurs who are more interested in sales, profits, and firm value than hiring new people. On the other hand, the employment effect is critical for policy-makers.

Other less popular measures of growth include asset value and profits or profitability (Coad, 2009; Achtenhagen, Naldi, & Melin, 2010). Asset value is questionable when a research sample includes firms from industries with differing capital intensity (Coad, 2009). When referring to profits (e.g., operating profits) and profitability, the important question arises whether we should measure the size of the firm or rather the outcomes that result from size increases. Profits and profitability should be treated as indicators of the efficiency expected from size increases. Size increase by itself is not the ultimate goal, but it is rather a requisite for the profitability, survival, sustainability, and competitiveness of the firm and for the dynamics of employment and value-added in the economy. Therefore, it is vital to distinguish between growth (size increase) and the outcomes of profit and profitability as measures of the efficiency of growth.

This delimitation is also relevant for empirical research methods directed at explaining causes, stimuli, and predictors of expansion. To pursue this stream of inquiry, a coherent understanding of dependent and independent variables is obligatory, otherwise causes turn into outcomes and vice versa. Discriminating between size and efficiency is relevant, even if we acknowledge some feedback loops in growth causality. Steffens, Davidsson, and Fitzsimmons (2009) find that profits are expected outcomes but also are conditions for further profitable and sustainable expansion. Many studies of firm growth do not differentiate between growth and development, treating them interchangeably or as synonyms. Therefore, in this broad research, we find expansion measures including both size and efficiency criteria, as well as some qualitative indicators, such as development strategies including diversification, product development, and internationalization, among others (Achtenhagen, Naldi, & Melin, 2010). The latter approaches are not only qualitative, but they denote modes of growth or enablers, determinants of growth rather than measures of growth. The fuzziness of understanding the essence of growth affects the clarity of its measures in the empirical research, causing some inconsistencies in results and the explanations of growth determinants and predictors. Table 1 summarizes the discussion about growth measures by pointing to their major types and to implications of adopting them in empirical research.

Table 1. The major measures of growth and implications of using them in empirical research

Type of measure	Advantages	Limitations
Size (e.g., sales, employment, assets)	Reflects the uniqueness of firm expansion relative to firm development	Does not embrace all dimensions of growth, specifically those relating to learning and development
Sales as a size measure	Objective and accessible measure; considered important and adequate by entrepreneurs	Necessity to use deflators in the long-run (to correct for depreciation) and deal with different currencies in international research; does not inform about value-added
Employment as a size measure	Objective and accessible measure; does not require deflating and acknowledging currency differences in international research; represents sustainable and firm and not occasional growth; valued especially by policy-makers	Less important from entrepreneurs' point of view
Asset value as a size measure	Denotes the increase in resources and capabilities of a company	May be inadequate when investigating companies from industries with differing levels of capital intensity
Performance (profits, profitability indicators)	Convincing for entrepreneurs as a sign of well-implemented growth; the expected outcome of growth	Represents the efficiency from growth rather than growth itself
Qualitative indicators/development strategies (internationalization, diversification, product development)	Represent qualitative and more complex changes associated with growth than size indicators only	Denote the ways or modes of accomplishing growth rather than the essence of growth

Source: own work.

To sum up, we propose separating size indicators as measures of growth from performance and qualitative indicators. Performance and qualitative indicators can be used as independent or control variables in the empirical research to reflect better the complexity of the phenomenon studied. As for the size measures, there are different implications of sales and employment from the micro-economic view of entrepreneurs compared to the macro-economic view of policy-makers. The adoption of either of these indicators might be guided by the purposes and decisional problems a specific research project intends to address.

1.3. The methods of identifying high-growers

The delimitation of fast-growing firms is important both for scientific research purposes and for the management practice and public policies that would benefit from this research. Moreover, the behaviors and characteristics of this group of firms may represent benchmarks for the entrepreneurs seeking dynamic growth. The features differentiating gazelles from other companies are treated as determinants or predictors of expansion. This predictive capacity of the attributes of gazelles is relevant both for private investors and providers of financing, and for policy-makers that expect returns on public investment in the form of new jobs and innovations.

Measures and criteria of identification of high-growers are largely empirically driven. They stem from the research that reports the economic impact of a small fraction of rapidly growing firms that predominantly belong to the SME sector (Birch, 1987; Birch & Medoff, 1994; Birch, Haggerty, & Parsons, 1995; Coad, 2009; Stam et al., 2006; Smallbone, Leigh, & North, 1995; Acs, Parsons, & Tracy, 2008; OECD, 2007; 2010). Based on this evidence, the core of high growth is intense size increase in a limited time. To specify this understanding, the expected level and nature of the size increase needs to be determined. This task raises some substantial methodological challenges that should be resolved before choosing the approach relevant for a specific study. First, it needs to be determined whether the threshold is a level of the compound (aggregate) expected outcome or growth dynamics in a specific time span (a "rhythm" of growth), or both. Another critical point is whether the expression of growth outcome and dynamics is in relative or absolute terms. Absolute and relative growth have different implications for entrepreneurs focused on the individual enterprise compared to policy-makers concerned with the macro-economic employment effect.

The threshold aggregate outcome is the compound size increase in a specific period of time expressed as total growth rate or absolute total increase in monetary or employment terms.

Total growth rate is expressed as a formula (Davidsson, Delmar, & Wiklund, 2006, p. 55)

$$g = (S_{t1} - S_{t0})/S_{t0} \qquad (1.1.)$$

In the above mathematical expression, g denotes the compound growth rate during a specific period, while S_{t0} is the size in the beginning of the time considered, and S_{t1} refers to the size at the end of this period.

The approach based on the compound size increase responds to the core of high growth, which is an intense size increase within a limited time span. The most used threshold for the total growth rate is doubling the initial size in terms of employment or/and sales within three to four years (Birch, Haggerty, & Parsons, 1995; Littunen & Tohmo, 2003; Acs, Parsons, & Tracy, 2008; Moreno & Casillas, 2007).

The threshold outcome may, however, be established at a different level, considering the research purpose and sample characteristics. Smallbone, Leigh, and North (1995) adopted an indicator of at least doubling turnover within 10 years, finding a correlation between turnover and employment increases during this period. The lower dynamics they required was justified by examining the established, mature entities rather than young gazelles. Mature firms exhibited lower dynamics over time. However, focusing on this group is justified by the higher absolute growth due to their larger initial size than the young firms (Acs, Parsons, & Tracy, 2008).

While most empirical studies investigate growth based on multi-industry samples, Moreno and Casillas (2007) study high-growers in specific industries. They define rapidly growing firms as those that more than doubled the median sales in their industries over a four-year period. Such an approach is informative for studying the influence of industrial characteristics on growth prospects, as well as understanding the firms' performance in the entire economy. Specifically, high technology and young industries are overrepresented among high growth achievers, leaving the dynamics of other industries unexplained.

The threshold outcome of growth understood as the total growth rate over a specific period is a measure taken at two points in time. It does not take into account the dynamics within this period, i.e., whether the size change was stable, showing a constant rate during intervals within the period, versus a fluctuating rate from one interval to the next, showing rapid growth only within selected intervals. In the long run, it would be more realistic to assume rapid and discontinuous sales or employment increases instead of constant ones. This is true especially for small firms, which grow in a way that is much less planned and more vulnerable to external shocks than large enterprises (Coad, 2007a; 2009).

The approach based on growth rate is biased towards the initial size of the firm and favors SMEs capable of higher growth rates than large firms. Therefore, when determining the threshold outcome of growth, another critical point is differentiating between relative growth, i.e., the growth rate in percentage terms as discussed above, and absolute growth, e.g., an absolute increase in the number of employees or the value of sales (Davidsson, Delmar, & Wiklund, 2006; Shepherd & Wiklund, 2009). Focusing on growth rate and relative growth favors small enterprises, which can more easily accomplish a threshold rate due to their initial smaller size. However, acknowledging this growth rate bias is less relevant from the micro-economic and entrepreneurial perspectives. In the latter case, it rightly reflects the profundity of change that a specific organization experiences relative to its initial scope, size, and extent of operations.

On the other hand, the lower rate of large firms' expansion normally translates into a larger absolute increase in sales or employment and consequently a stronger impact on the growth of the entire economy (Acs, Parsons, & Tracy, 2008). Therefore, absolute growth is more relevant from macro-economic and policy perspectives. Some additional attributes that differentiate high-growers from the remaining population are significant investment expenses, the increased capital needs, and relatively low liquidity and solvency (Moreno & Casillas, 2007). These characteristics demand the attention and active support from policy-makers to protect these firms from failure due to the investment effort and risks they experience.

The threshold outcome of growth in absolute terms (total growth in absolute terms) is a difference in size (as the number of employees or sales value) at the end of a given period, $S_{t1,}$ and at the beginning of it, S_{t0}.

$$g = S_{t1} - S_{t0} \qquad (1.2.)$$

The above rationale for absolute measures underpins Storey's method, based on the requirement of employing at least 50 people after 10 years from the firm's inception (Storey, 1994, p. 114). Therefore, he applied the absolute growth concept in the long-term perspective and only for newly created and not for the established firms. The importance of absolute growth is also recognized in applying methodologies that combine relative growth rates with absolute growth rates. These methodologies acknowledge both the individual achievements of firms (relative size increases) and their input to the economy at large (absolute increases in employment or/and sales) (Birch, 1987; Acs, Parsons, & Tracy, 2008). Acs, Parsons, and Tracy (2008) identified high-impact firms as those that at least doubled sales within the last four years and their employment multiplier, being a relationship between the absolute and relative increase in employment, reached the minimum value of 2.0. Davidsson, Delmar, and Wiklund (2006) criticize this approach for lack of clarity of the result, which neither expresses the number of employees nor sales value.

Growth dynamics or "rhythm" is expressed as the annual growth rate within a given time period, predominantly embracing three to four years. Gibrat's law assumes constant growth rate based on the following formula (Davidsson & Wiklund, 2000; Davidsson, Delmar, & Wiklund, 2006, p. 55):

$$S_{t1} = S_{t0}(1 + g)^{t1-t0} \tag{1.3.}$$

with g denoting annual growth rate. From this viewpoint, growth is equally distributed within a given period, and there are constant relative increases of sales or employment every year. This model is less vulnerable to the initial size of the firm. However, its feasibility can be questioned, specifically in the long run, when the dynamics are discontinuous. Most researchers applying this model assume annual growth rates at either the 25% level within four years (Birch, Haggerty, & Parsons, 1995; Storey, 2001) or the 20% level within three consecutive years (OECD, 2007; 2010). To limit the bias of initial size, it is also recommended that only those firms with at least 10 employees at the outset of the study period be considered (OECD, 2007; 2010). This is, however, controversial, since start-up micro enterprises are excluded and this large group is the most motivated to accomplish an efficient scale of operations (Cieślik, 2014). The dynamism of this group has been reported to demonstrate the impact of entrepreneurial activity and high-growth start-ups on economic growth (Stam et al., 2007; Wong, Ho, & Autio, 2005).

A solution to avoid the biases from assuming relative growth rates is to focus on the annual absolute increase in the amount of employment or sales, according to the following equation (Davidsson, Delmar, & Wiklund, 2006):

$$g = 1/N\sum_{n=1}^{n=N}(S_{tn+1} - S_{tn})/S_{tn} \tag{1.4.}$$

$S_{tn} = S_{t1} + S_{tn}(n-1)/N$, g is the annual growth rate, N is the total number of years considered, and n is a given year; S_{tn} refers to the size in a given year and S_{tN} is the size at the end of the period studied. However, this approach is not commonly used (Davidsson, Delmar, & Wiklund, 2006).

When choosing a methodological approach, one should consider the purpose, theoretical background, and specificity of the objects studied. Table 2 summarizes the discussion on methodological choice regarding the identification of high-growers.

Table 2. Methodological choices regarding the identification of high-growers

Method of identification of high-growers	Advantages	Limitations	Dominant approach
Total growth rate within a given time period	Clear and convincing size increase; well-suited to small firms that experience disruptive and discontinuous expansion	Does not reflect the "rhythm" of growth, namely, how it was being pursued over the period considered; sensitive to the initial size of the firm; not well suited to large firms	At least doubling size within four years
Growth rate in specific time intervals (prevalent annual growth rate)	Less sensitive to the initial size of a firm; informs about the way growth was being pursued; well suited to large firms that expand in a planned and more systematic way	Not well suited to small firms that undergo changes that are less planned and more exposed to external shocks; unrealistic assumption of constant annual size increases in the long run	At least 20% size increases within four years; firms with at least nine employees are considered
Relative growth	Reflects the depth of changes and the level of size increases, depending on the scale of the company; important to understand the pace of growth at an individual firm level; relevant for individual entrepreneurs and policy decision-makers	Less adequate to understand the contribution of high-growers in macroeconomic terms; less relevant for policy-makers	At least doubling size within four years
Absolute growth	Relevant for policy decision-makers as an effect on the entire economy	Does not reflect the depth of changes from an individual firm perspective (relative to a company scale of operations)	Achieving a specific value of sales or number of employees as an aggregate amount or annual amount of sales or jobs
Combined measures of relative and absolute growth	Help to avoid biases from exclusively relative or absolute growth	Interpretation of the final result is unclear	Weighted average of both relative and absolute growth rates

Source: own work.

1.4. Theoretical approaches to firm growth and their relevance for SME expansion

Firm growth is an interdisciplinary research area being developed in entrepreneurship, economics, management, and organization studies. Consequently, it involves a number of theoretical approaches that belong to these academic disciplines and fields and differing ways of understanding this phenomenon. Informative reviews of theoretical approaches to expansion are included in the works of Coad (2007a; 2009), Dobbs and Hamilton (2007), and Wach (2012), among others. Therefore, the present section does not intend to present a review of these widely-known approaches. It rather seeks to identify their relevance to describe and explain the growth of SMEs and to instruct decision-making in this area. To implement this assessment, it is incumbent to explain the unique properties of SME growth compared to large firms. Considering the large population of SMEs, high-growth is a rare behavior of only a small fraction of them. High-growers experience rapid expansion, which means considerable enlargement within a limited time, meaning a huge risk and investment effort (Birch & Medoff, 1994; Moreno & Casillas, 2007). Moreover, due to resource constraints and the liability of smallness (Freeman, Carroll, & Hannan, 1983; Aldrich & Auster, 1986; Daszkiewicz, 2007; Borowiecki & Siuta-Tokarska, 2010), they are less inclined to exploit existing resources and more alert to external opportunities than large firms (Lasagni, 2012; Colombo et al., 2012). However, external collaboration is not only a source of valuable and scarce resources, but it also represents a threat of dependence in relationships with large and dominating partners that externalize costs and specific investment to SMEs (Williamson, 1991; Humphrey & Schmitz, 2002; 2004). Size economies in terms of scale and scope benefits are a strong motivation for SMEs to expand (Garnsey, Stam, & Heffernan, 2006; Storey, 1994). At the same time, size economies are enablers for the expansion of large firms that already enjoy these benefits (Penrose, 1959). Consequently, small companies are driven by opportunity-seeking and size economies, while large firms that already have scale and scope advantages are driven by opportunity and the exploitation of existing resources. This attitude is linked to the planning approach. Due to limited resources, SMEs typically do not systematically plan for growth as do large companies that have adequate resources to implement long-term objectives (Storey, 1994). Because of limited systematic planning and dependence on *ad hoc* external opportunities, the growth of SMEs is featured by discontinuity and chaos rather than a continuous and evolutionary process. They usually do not experience constant growth over time, but may grow intensely one year and not repeat this achievement in the next or following years, demonstrating a low autocorrelation of growth rates (Coad, 2007a). In pursuing expansion, entrepreneurs are often owner-managers, i.e., SMEs normally do not feature a separation of ownership and control (Piasecki, 2001). Therefore, their firms are governance units with well-defined and centralized authority (Penrose, 1959). Finally, the liability of smallness also affects the mode of expansion applied by small firms that are less inclined to choose external, acquisitive modes than their large counterparts (Penrose, 1959; Lockett et al., 2011). Instead, they choose hybrid governance to alleviate high transaction costs and to access complementary resources (Larson, 1992; McKelivie & Wiklund, 2010).

Based on the earlier classifications (e.g., Gibb & Davis, 1990; Dobbs & Hamilton, 2006; Coad, 2007a; 2009; Noga, 2009; Wach, 2012) the following theoretical approaches to firm expansion can be identified:
- stochastic approaches (Gibrat, 1931; Ijiri & Simon, 1977; Sutton, 1997; Botazzi & Secchi, 2003),
- the neoclassical concepts of the optimal and minimum scales of operations (Moore, 1959; Hanoch, 1975; Panzar & Willig, 1977),
- the governance approach to firm boundaries (scope and size issues) based on transaction cost economics (Coase, 1937; Williamson, 1979; 1989; 1991),
- managerial models (Baumol, 1959; Marris, 1963; 1964; Williamson, 1964; Jensen & Meckling, 1976),
- Penrose's theory of firm growth (1959) that developed to the resource-based view of the firm (Wernerfelt, 1984; Barney, 1991; 1999; Peteraf, 1993),
- the views related to the RBV, such as evolutionary economics (Nelson & Winter, 1982; Alchian, 1950; Downie, 1958; Aldrich 1999; Dosi & Grazzi, 2006; Dawid, 2006); and the learning approach (Deakins & Freel, 1998; Dalley & Hamilton, 2000; Macpherson, 2005; Macpherson & Holt, 2007),
- the organizational ecology approach (Hannan & Freeman, 1977; Hannan, 2005; Geroski, 2001).

Gibrat's law (1931) of proportional effects, stating that size increases are stochastic and do not depend on the initial firm size, received some empirical support (Coad, 2009), but it was also questioned by some empirical findings (Moreno & Casillas, 2007). The view on stochastic antecedents and pathways of growth that are underpinned by factors internal and external to the firm reflects the truth of the idiosyncrasy of firm growth. However, some researchers found a negative correlation between firm size and growth, pointing to small firms as enlarging faster than large companies. More recent works develop the stochastic approach by including the influence of abstract shocks and business opportunities on the growth rate distribution (Ijiri & Simon, 1977; Sutton, 1997; Bottazzi & Secchi, 2003).

The assumptions of neoclassical economics about the optimal scale of operations (Moore, 1959; Hanoch, 1975; Panzar & Willig, 1977) were not supported by empirical research and criticized for neglecting the role of firm resources and entrepreneurial capabilities as determinants of expansion (Penrose, 1959). The optimal level of production that maximizes profits at a particular production rate due to economies of scale has been questioned as a rationale and a limit for firms to grow further (Marris, 1999; Coad, 2009). On the other hand, the concept of the minimum efficient scale that minimizes costs with a given production level has been used as a point of reference to differentiate the growth of SMEs and large firms. Namely, increasing size alleviates the cost disadvantage of SMEs compared to firms operating above this scale (Garnsey, Stam, & Heffernan, 2006). Large firms exceeding the minimum efficiency scale may conflict with the goal of profit maximization; their rationale for growth is not economies of scale alone, but economies of growth. These arise from matching a unique combination of a firm's resources and market opportunities, which may or may not pertain to size advantages (Penrose, 1959; Coad, 2009). In the latter instance, average cost savings are attributed to flexibility, innovation, and creativity rather than to size itself.

The neoclassical approach to firm growth is focused on size-related factors and it can be subsumed by the concept of economies of size (Penrose, 1959). These include economies of scale from the increased quantity of an existing good, the increased scale of operations to better utilize administrative infrastructure, and economies of scope from introducing new activities (products, services) (Penrose, 1959). The economies of scope arise from using one indivisible and surplus resource to produce many products and services (Panzar & Willig, 1977; Noteboom, 1993). Economies of size continue to be a strong motivation for small firms to grow. On the other hand, for large firms they act as a driver or a basis for expansion, since these firms already benefit from economies of size.

The governance approach to firm scope and size, i.e., to firm boundaries, is largely based on transaction cost theory (Coase, 1937; Williamson, 1979; 1989; 1991). TCT abandons the firm as a production function in favor of the firm as a nexus of transactions. It corresponds to the neoclassical notion of the optimal scale of operations, stating that the firm's scope and size depend on balancing the costs of internal versus external transactions (1937). However, current developments of this theory and firm boundary studies focus on the transaction cost rationale and *make or buy* decisions rather than on the issue of the optimal scale (Cyfert, 2012). The firm expands due to cost rationale, namely when the costs of market transactions are higher than the costs of internalization. The expansion through diversification into new activities is considered, especially through vertical integration into intermediary products and services (Williamson, 1989; 1991; 2005). This kind of expansion implies a rapid, strong increase in size, often through acquisitions, but it is not limited to this approach. Considering the financial constraints of SMEs, acquisition or high investment in new activities are less accessible for them than for large firms to avoid transaction costs in business relationships (Barney, 1999; Chandler, McKelvie, & Davidsson, 2009). These strategies can be replaced by hybrid forms (such as long-term contracts) (Larson, 1992). The assumption of opportunism of contracting partners reflects the reality of SMEs experiencing the bargaining power of large enterprises (Dewald et al., 2007). On the other hand, the TCT rationale for expanding through employment holds in the resource-constrained contexts typical of young and small firms (Chandler, McKelvie, & Davidsson, 2009). This may indicate that decisions to internalize the entire business activity are less prone to TCT explanations of SME growth than individual decisions about hiring new people.

Managerial models of firm growth (Marris, 1963; 1964; Downie, 1958; Baumol, 1959) assume a separation of ownership and control and conflicting interests of managers and owners (entrepreneurs). Managers derive utility from growth in sales and employment that increase their power and salaries. The ambitions of managers to expand are constrained by the level of profitability required by the owners and by the threat of acquisition. The separation of ownership is not a feature of most high-growers that are predominantly SMEs run by owner-managers. However, the theory is useful in differentiating between growth, as a condition for efficiency, from profit as an outcome proving this efficiency. Owner-managers of small firms need to consider the profit goal as a constraint to their growth ambitions.

Penrose's theory of firm growth is the most powerful and widely adopted approach to the growth of firms, emphasizing a match between the company's resources, especially managerial capabilities, and environmental opportunities (Penrose, 1959). This conceptualization of growth formed a foundation for the RBV (Wernerfelt, 1984; Peteraf, 1993; Barney, 1991; 1999) and learning approaches (Deakins & Freel, 1998; Dalley & Hamilton, 2000; Macpherson, 2005; Macpherson & Holt, 2007). The latter theoretical frameworks offer insights into growth as a process of development and learning, of which the ultimate outcome is value creation. However, they do not sufficiently acknowledge environmental influences on this process. The resource-based view, putting stress on value creation and expanding via the development of the core competence-related resources, is increasingly combined with TCT in determining firm boundaries or it is treated as an alternative to TCT in this regard (Barney, 1999; David & Han, 2004; Carter & Hodgson, 2006). The RBV assumption of the heterogeneity of firm resources is a convincing explanation of the idiosyncrasy of growth paths and factors (Dobbs & Hamilton, 2007). However, both Penrose's approach and the learning and evolutionary approaches are better suited to gradual and slow growth than to the rapid and discontinuous expansion typical of small firms.

The assumption of evolutionary economics on the *growth of the fitter* that best adapts to the environment (Nelson & Winter, 1982; Alchian, 1950; Downie, 1958; Aldrich, 1999; Dosi & Grazzi, 2006; Dawid, 2006) was not supported by empirical findings (Coad, 2009). However, this approach is presently one of the most influential in learning and developing routines, as well as in generating innovations to stimulate expansion (Dosi et al., 1995).

Finally, organizational ecology presents growth as dependent on resources that can be acquired in specific niches (Hannan & Freeman, 1977; Hannan, 2005; Geroski, 2001). Niche strategies were found conducive for the growth of small companies in studies reviewed by Storey (1994). However, in this approach, the population of firms is the unit of analysis rather than individual firms. Therefore, we find an insufficient recognition for the idiosyncrasy of resources, expansion rates, and growth patterns of individual firms shown in other empirical research.

Table 3 presents theoretical approaches to firm growth with a focus on their suitability for research in SME growth.

Table 3. Theoretical approaches to firm growth and their suitability for research in SME growth

Theoretical approach	The focus of an approach	Suitability for research in SME growth	
		Relevant insight	Mismatch
Stochastic models (Gibrat, 1931; Ijiri & Simon, 1977; Sutton, 1997; Botazzi & Secchi, 2003)	Growth as stochastic in terms of antecedents but constant in terms of the rate	Idiosyncrasy of growth factors; growth stimulated by diverse factors	Growth rates of small firms found to be higher than those of large firms; small firms experience irregular and rapid growth
Neoclassical optimal scale of operations and minimum scale of operations (Moore, 1959; Hanoch, 1975; Panzar & Willig, 1977)	Economies of scale and scope; minimal scale of production to ensure lowest costs; optimal scale of operations to maximize profits	Minimal scale of operation as an important target for SMEs	Optimal scale of operations rejected as a limit to expansion
The governance approach to firm boundaries (scope and size) based on transaction cost economics (Coase, 1937; Williamson, 1979; 1989; 1991)	Growth (internalization or hybrid forms) justified by higher costs of market transactions	Determinants of choosing growth modes (specifically expanding through employment); points to transaction costs stemming from asset specificity (idiosyncratic investment) and opportunism experienced by small firms in business transactions	Internalization of business activities less suitable for SMEs as a means of avoiding transaction costs; high capabilities of small innovative firms may be more relevant than asset specificity in determining their decisions on scope and size
Managerial models (Baumol, 1959; Marris, 1963; 1964; Williamson, 1964; Jensen & Meckling, 1976)	Separation of ownership and control, managerial utility different than the owner's utility	Relationships between growth and profitability; profits as conditions for further growth; constraints to unprofitable growth	Predominant unity of control and ownership in SMEs that alleviates discrepancy between the interests of managers and owners
Penrose's theory of firm growth (Penrose, 1959)	Growth as a process of learning and development of which a by-product is an increase in size; expansion based on matching firm capabilities and environmental opportunities	The importance of environmental opportunities and exploiting them based on available resources; the relevance of organic growth rather than acquisitive growth for SMEs	Better suited to large firms that manage a considerable resource base, and for firms that develop in an evolutionary rather than rapid way

Theoretical approach	The focus of an approach	Suitability for research in SME growth	
		Relevant insight	Mismatch
The resource-based view of the firm (Wernerfelt, 1984; Barney, 1991; 1999; Peteraf, 1993)	Firm as a collection of valuable and heterogeneous resources that underpin its competitive advantage and form a basis for growth	Heterogeneity of firms that may justify idiosyncrasy of growth; the importance of value creation and performance as a rationale and a condition for growth	See above
Evolutionary theory (Nelson & Winter, 1982; Alchian, 1950; Downie, 1958; Aldrich 1999; Dosi & Grazzi, 2006; Dawid, 2006)	Growth of the fitter that adapts to the environment best	Learning and developing routines in SMEs; processes of generating innovations to stimulate expansion	Rapid and discontinuous nature of SME growth not recognized
Learning approach (Deakins & Freel, 1998; Dalley & Hamilton, 2000; Macpherson, 2005; Macpherson & Holt, 2007)	Growth as a learning process that ensures value creation; learning as a condition of expansion and its outcome	Stresses the value of competence development for competitive advantage and expansion, an aspect often neglected by the owners of SMEs	The emphasis on evolutionary processes and on development rather than on growth, especially the rapid one
Organizational ecology (Hannan & Freeman, 1977; Hannan, 2005; Geroski, 2001)	Growth dependent on the resources that can be found in specific niches; focus on population of firms and its behaviors	SMEs often operate in niches and grow by exploiting a niche in the international context	Neglected role of an individual entrepreneur; idiosyncrasy of small firm growth that cannot be acknowledged when investigating the population as homogenous

Source: own work.

Each of the theories considered above has merit and sheds light on the nature of firm growth, and can be valid in a specific setting. However, virtually none of them was inspired by the phenomenon of rapid growth and high-growers. Conversely, even if directly addressing size enlargement, they are predominantly better adjusted to slow and continuous growth, like in the case of learning and evolutionary conceptions. Rapid growth may be implied by models that assume introducing a new activity (a product or a service) that becomes a source of the new revenue stream and employment. This would involve Marris's growth through diversification and internalization in transaction cost economics, i.e., vertical integration or diversification through acquisitions or internal growth. Penrose assumes exploitation towards related activities or exploration through the activities unrelated with extant managerial competence (1959). However, this theory presents expansion as continuous and cumulative rather than rapid and discontinuous. According to Penrose, the latter characteristics are valid for large firms expanding through acquisitions towards exploration, i.e., new activities that are unrelated with existing managerial competence, after exploiting opportunities by related activities. The resource-based view modifies this reasoning by pointing to the necessity of concurrent and balanced exploitation and exploration instead of sequentially combining these two mechanisms (Hitt et al., 2011; Sirén, Kohtamäki, & Kuckertz, 2012; Dyduch & Bratnicki, 2010). Moreover, few of the theories explicitly address the growth of small and medium-sized enterprises. Some of the approaches are better adjusted to large firms where control and ownership are separated (e.g., managerial models) and to more established than young firms (Penrose's theory). Therefore, when applying these theories to study the uniqueness of high-growth SMEs, we verify them in a new setting and cannot expect full confirmation of these individual approaches.

1.5. Approaches to systemizing the research on small firm growth

Drawing upon the earlier assessment of the relevance of theoretical approaches to SME growth, in the following subsections, these theories are logically linked with the major research streams that revolved around the field of firm growth. Considering a limited capacity of individual theories and richness of the present empirical research, wider perspectives or research streams were proposed by McKelvie and Wiklund (2010) and by Davidsson, Achtenhagen, and Naldi (2010). These research streams reveal major aspects of the phenomenon and are underpinned by adequate theoretical approaches. They are systemized according to the major research questions about the nature of small firm growth.

McKelvie and Wiklund (2010) summarize the extant research as *growth as an outcome* (asking about predictors and determinants of achieving growth), *growth outcomes* (seeking how to manage the company that accomplished growth), and *growth process* (focusing on how expansion is realized) (McKelvie & Wiklund, 2010). The first two perspectives are established and well-developed approaches, while the third one represents an emerging area of research.

The systemization by Davidsson, Achtenhagen, and Naldi (2010) points to the streams that are both well-developed and recognized as belonging to growth studies, and those that are emerging and refer to growth, but some of them were developed in different research fields and methodologies. These perspectives were systemized according to their focus on *antecedents, effects, amount, modes, and processes of expansion* (Davidsson, Achtenhagen, & Naldi, 2010). *Antecedents* of growth amount are an established and well-developed stream, synonymous with *growth as outcome* studies. The *growth process* as well the *effects of growth* (profitability and firm value as desired effects of growth) are under-researched areas, suffering especially from the scarcity of sound and comprehensive empirical evidence. The *growth mode* perspective refers to the governance of implementing growth. Therefore, it is associated with the growth process perspective and can be treated as part of it. It is a well-developed stream in firm boundary research that encompasses the modes of expansion such as diversification, vertical integration, internal or external growth, and internationalization. Although the boundary studies strongly imply growth, they hardly refer to expansion explicitly, and they are not integrated nor confronted with the main streams of growth research.

Considering the two systemizations of growth streams, they invoke a range of theoretical perspectives and separate some already well-researched streams from new ones, thus recommending further study. The established and new streams are discussed below to point to some theoretical and methodological avenues that can resolve their core research problems. Another important endeavor is to propose how they can mutually enrich one another.

1.6. The established streams of research in firm growth

The stream called *the outcomes of growth* (McKelvie & Wiklund, 2010) or *descriptive models* (Dobbs & Hamilton, 2006) builds upon the life cycle concept and deals with how to manage a company that has achieved substantial growth. As life cycle models assume stage development, some authors point to their contribution to the growth process stream (Davidsson, Achtenhagen, & Naldi, 2010). However, the process approach to growth addresses a different question, namely, why and how growth is implemented (Garnsey, Stam, & Heffernan, 2006). Therefore, it will be discussed separately as a positive (descriptive) approach relative to normative (prescriptive) stage models.

The abundant models of stage growth, such as those by Greiner (1972), Scott and Bruce (1987), Churchill and Lewis (1983), generally have strong linear and deterministic assumptions of development phases. Small firms occupy predominantly very early development stages and few of them attains more advanced phases of life cycle models (McKelvie & Wiklund, 2010). These approaches do not reflect the reality of the irregular and idiosyncratic patterns of firm expansion. Moreover, the critiques of these approaches point to the lack of theoretical background and empirical support that would validate the life cycle pattern of organizational development. Nevertheless, some of these conceptions were targeted at SMEs to capture the specificity of their development stages (Churchill & Lewis, 1983; Scott & Bruce, 1987). The stage models do not capture the process of growth, because expansion embraces only one or two individual phases among the life cycle stages considered. The remaining phases involve structural changes that may or may not include size enlargement and depict firm development rather than firm growth. However, if freed from the assumption of linearity and predetermined sequence of phases, stage models offer insights on some plausible scenarios and business models that represent a company, as well as provide insight on how to manage a firm at a specific development stage (Levie & Lichtenstein, 2010; Dobbs & Hamilton, 2007). Levie and Lichtenstein (2010) conducted an extensive review of growth stage models and proposed their reconceptualization into a *dynamic states approach*, assuming the heterogeneity of firms as well as the non-linearity of their development patterns. More open and situational adaptation of the life cycle framework can provide the revitalization of stage models. According to Levie and Lichtenstein (2010), accomplishing new development stages might be explained by a nexus of three factors, namely, opportunity recognition, business model, and value increase. Notwithstanding, life cycle models are not intended to treat expansion as the desired target and to explain how to accomplish it by specific actions and competences. They are rather focused on how growth challenges management systems, demanding continuous transformation and adaptation. The focus on evolution and adaptation links them with the RBV as well as learning and evolutionary conceptions.

Growth as a desired outcome (McKelvie & Wiklund, 2010) and its *antecedents* (Davidsson, Achtenhagen, & Naldi, 2010) became a focus of the second stream of studies, which is also called *deterministic* (Dobbs & Hamilton, 2006). This focus is driven by the importance of firm expansion for the creation of employment and the definition of innovation policies. Therefore, learning about the antecedents that may be regarded as determinants or predictors of a company's rapid expansion facilitates adequate support policy and management methods. One of the main contributions of this group of studies lies in the identification of factors correlated with firm expansion, characterizing the entrepreneur, the firm, and its strategy, that proved to be significant in most of the cases (Barringer, Jones, & Neubaum, 2005; Coad, 2009; Moreno & Casillas, 2007; Gilbert, McDougall, & Audretsch, 2006; Macpherson & Holt, 2007; Storey, 1994). The studies in this stream are predominantly empirically-driven and less theory-driven. However, their methodological underpinnings refer to the resource-based factors of characteristics of the entrepreneur and the firm. They also denote some industrial and environmental factors stemming from industrial economics and the organizational ecology approach. Moreover, their predominant empirical focus resonates with stochastic approaches that assume growth depends on a plethora of organizational and environmental factors. The important difference is that the rationale of these studies is deterministic, i.e., they aim at the identification of universal factors of growth. Notwithstanding considerable achievements based on numerous empirical studies, uncertainty remains about the real mechanisms of growth and the cause-effect relationships that may arise during this process. In other words, it is not clear which factors are growth determinants and which are only associated with or stimulated by growth (Dobbs & Hamilton, 2006; Wright & Stigliani, 2013). Moreover, the meaning and importance of some of these determinants are not consistent (Achtenhagen, Naldi, & Melin, 2010; Dobbs & Hamilton, 2006; Garnsey, Stam, & Heffernan, 2006). The observed ambiguity is attributed to differing methodologies and measures of expansion adopted in these typically quantitative studies (McKelvie & Wiklund, 2010; Shepherd & Wiklund, 2009; Weinzimmer, Nystrom, & Freeman, 1998). The current status of this stream can be treated as a deadlock situation, where a plethora of investigations and results provide little explanation of growth antecedents (McKelvie & Wiklund, 2010; Shepherd & Wiklund, 2009; Weinzimmer, Nystrom, & Freeman, 1998). The present achievements are also regarded as a mature stage of the stream that does not require more empirical investigations (Davidsson, Achtenhagen, & Naldi, 2010). Nevertheless, the proponents of these alternative views call for new focus and methodologies in the research on expansion (Dobbs & Hamilton, 2007; Davidsson, Achtenhagen, & Naldi, 2010; McKelvie & Wiklund, 2010; Hansen & Hamilton, 2011). This new focus is motivated by the need to explain the inconsistencies of extant empirical findings and advance the knowledge of growth.

1.7. The emerging streams of research in firm growth

The new areas proposed in the literature are the *effects, process, and modes of growth* (Davidsson, Achtenhagen, & Naldi, 2010). The important question arises: how to tackle these research topics in terms of the theoretical background that might be adopted in future investigations.

The effects of firm growth are well-researched in relation to the entire economy, since it was a major reason for the policy-makers interest in high-growers. Probably this macro-economic effect influenced the regard for growth as a desired outcome rather than a way to accomplish or increase efficiency. The reason for this approach also stems from the importance of expansion for the survival of start-ups and young, small enterprises. Another justification for neglecting the effects of growth might be the ambiguity in understanding and measuring growth. Namely, treating both size and efficiency indicators as measures of expansion conflates growth and its results. Whereas, as noted earlier, growth measured by size increase is a way of accomplishing efficiency in terms of profitability and the firm's value (Zbierowski, 2012).

The enterprise-level effects of growth on efficiency are less substantiated and positive outcomes are assumed rather than tested. Few studies that undertake tests of growth effects find strong positive influence of past profitability on future sustainable and high growth (Davidsson, Steffens, & Fitzsimmons, 2009; Steffens, Davidsson, & Fitzsimmons, 2009; Zbierowski, 2012). These studies adopt the resource-based perspective and this perspective, putting stress on value from growth, represents an adequate theoretical background for the research on growth effects (Davidsson, Steffens, & Fitzsimmons, 2009; Steffens, Davidsson, & Fitzsimmons, 2009). Other relevant approaches to study effects in terms of profitability include managerial theories of growth, such as by Marris (1963; 1964) and Baumol's (1959) models that explain relationships between growth and profit.

Another emerging pathway of research complements and broadens the earlier studies by focusing on the growth process (Davidsson, Delmar, & Wiklund, 2006; Leitch, Hill, & Neergaard, 2010; McKelvie & Wiklund, 2010; Stam, 2010; Dobbs & Hamilton, 2011; Wright & Stigliani, 2013; Koryak et al., 2015). It intends to explore why and how growth is implemented through the lenses of entrepreneurs' perceptions and decision-making (Wiklund & Shepherd, 2003; Wiklund, Davidsson, & Delmar, 2003; Garnsey, Stam, & Heffernan, 2006; Hansen & Hamilton, 2011; Wright

& Stigliani, 2013). Unlike the life cycle perspective, it seeks to explain proactive decisions and activities for stimulating growth, not just adaptive and reactive strategies. On the other hand, alternatively to the deterministic stream, it intends to unveil mechanisms and cause-effect relationships among the factors leading to growth, not only individual success factors. During periods of intense growth, there may be differences in the modes, rationales, motives, and mechanisms of company behavior, stemming from the characteristics of its capabilities and the environment in which it operates. These changes might potentially explain differing assumptions of theoretical frameworks and some discrepancies in the extant empirical findings on growth determinants. Such a research focus requires in-depth, explorative studies, investigating the phenomenon in specific contexts and possibly in a real-time perspective to unveil entrepreneurs' perceptions, decisional rules, and actions. These complex issues imply qualitative empirical approaches to be the first wave of investigations forming new theoretical approximations, based on the analytical generalization (Dobbs & Hamilton, 2007; Hansen & Hamilton, 2011; Wright & Stigliani, 2013). The next wave of investigations would require quantitative studies resulting in statistical generalizations about why and how growth is accomplished. The theoretical background for studying the process of firm growth can be derived from Penrose's (1959) growth theory that cultivated the resource-based view of the firm and the theories related to it, such as the learning and evolutionary approaches.

The growth mode is an issue overlapping the growth process (Davidsson, Achtenhagen, & Naldi, 2010) and even treated as a leading theme of this perspective (McKelvie & Wiklund, 2010). This is because the growth mode is also a characteristic of how expansion has been accomplished by adopting various governance structures. Namely, it can be implemented through organic (internal) or acquisitive (external) modes. Moreover, it can adopt other related structures such as internalization (vertical integration), diversification, and hybrids, including long-term relational contracts, or formal contracting arrangements, such as outsourcing, licensing, or franchising. These topics open the research on the growth process to broader issues of governance modes and firm boundaries (size and scope) discussed in economics, industrial organization, and strategic management. Up until now, these topics have been hardly discussed in the entrepreneurship literature on firm growth. Nor has the boundary literature directly addressed the high growth phenomenon, especially in small companies. A notable exception in entrepreneurship literature is a study by Chandler, McKelvie, and Davidsson (2009), who adopted transaction cost economics to explore relationships between sales growth and employment growth. Davidsson, Delmar, and Wiklund (2006, p. 47) assert that the process perspective portrays the firm as a governance structure delimited by control and administrative boundaries. The governance structure represents a unit of analysis focused on decision-making and entrepreneurial problem-solving during the process of expansion. Such a unit of analysis concentrated on choices and actions is consistent with the essence of studies on the growth processes, which treat entrepreneurial perceptions and decisions as a central point of investigations. Life-cycle models partially address this process; however, they describe developmental stages among which expansion is only one stage. Therefore, they do not focus on the growth process, but rather on the development process. The latter involves qualitative structural changes; however, it does not necessarily encompass the increase in firm size.

The contemporary governance literature is dominated by the RBV and TCT approaches, which seem to conflict, but are increasingly perceived as complementary views on the firm's boundary decisions.

Due to the complexity and idiosyncrasy of growth determinants and pathways revealed in empirical findings (Storey, 1994; Garnsey, Stam, & Heffernan, 2006; Coad, 2007b), individual theories have limited capacity to describe this phenomenon. Moreover, extant empirical research has explained only a limited variance in firms' growth with the use of the theoretical assumptions discussed above (Weinzimmer, Nystrom, & Freeman, 1998; Storey, 1994). This raises a skepticism regarding the explanatory and predictive capacity of these individual approaches to inform public policy and management of rapidly growing companies.

The theoretical frameworks for the research streams on firm growth are summarized in Table 4. These broad research streams pose fundamental questions about the nature of growth. Considering the limitations of individual theories discussed in the preceding section, the integration of two or more approaches may be a promising solution to develop a theoretical framework for tackling such questions. The approaches linked to a particular stream can possibly be combined to provide a more comprehensive explanation of the issues studied in each perspective.

Table 4. The research streams in firm growth – the major research questions and the relevant theoretical background

Research stream on firm growth	Established streams		Emerging streams	
	Studies on growth determinants and predictors	Studies on firms' internal adaptation after achieving growth (stage models)	Studies on growth effects	Studies on the growth process
Research questions	What are determinants and predictors of growth?	How to manage a firm that has accomplished growth?	What are effects of growth?	Why and how is growth accomplished?
Relevant theoretical background	Penrose's theory and the resource-based view (*growth determinants that stem from the characteristics of managerial and firm capabilities as well as from environmental opportunities*)	Dynamic states approach (*stages of life cycle models as plausible scenarios appropriate to various firms; they emerge as an outcome of opportunity recognition, value-creating efforts*)	Penrose's theory and the resource-based view (*growth effects measured by profitability and value increase*)	Penrose's theory and the resource-based view (*growth as a cumulative process of learning; value increase as a rationale for growth; resource exploitation and exploration as mechanisms of growth*)
	Evolutionary economics (*the role of innovation in fostering expansion; the role of routines and adaptive capacity, i.e., fitting with environmental conditions*)	Penrose's theory and the resource-based view (*each business model or the firm's development stage based on a different combination of firm capabilities that require different managerial skills*)	Managerial models (*the relationships between the firm's growth and profits*)	Transaction cost theory (*transaction cost reduction as a rationale for growth; decisional criteria to select the most efficient growth mode*)
	Learning approach (*routines, processes and tacit knowledge as drivers of expansion*)	The learning approach (*development stages of life cycle models as the outcomes of the learning process*)		Learning and evolutionary approaches (*growth as a cumulative process of learning and innovation development; growth as adaptive process*)
	Organizational ecology (*the identification of the market niche as a growth determinant*)	Evolutionary economics (*each development stage as a set of the firm's new routines; the life cycle framework as a combination of innovations and routines*)		Organizational ecology (*growth as a process of niche exploration*)
	Stochastic approaches (*pointing to a plethora of internal and external growth factors*)			

Source: own work based on Davidsson, Delmar, & Wiklund, 2006, pp. 45–48; Dobbs & Hamilton, 2006; McKelvie & Wiklund, 2010; Davidsson, Achtgenhagen, & Naldi, 2010; Gancarczyk & Iturriagagoitia, 2015.

One of the most critical differences among research streams and theoretical perspectives relates to the role of size increases as a property of growth. Namely, this quantitative aspect can be considered only as a by-product of growth, while the core of expansion is development. The latter qualitative aspect involves learning and development as well as advancements in a number of organizational areas. From other perspectives, size increase, especially a considerable and rapid one, is a critical measure and a property of the phenomenon that enables its delimitation due to the uniqueness in the population of firms. Notwithstanding, these perspectives recognize expansion as a qualitative development either as an outcome or driver of size increase or both. Despite this considerable difference in the emphasis they put on size issues, these two perspectives acknowledge a multidimensional and idiosyncratic nature of expansion embracing all elements of an organization, as well as a plethora of factors affecting its emergence, process, and outcomes.

This book belongs to the latter perspective that treats size increase as a starting point to the delimitation of this phenomenon and further intends to reveal the complexity of the process of achieving it. Such an approach is motivated by the insights from the empirical research that revealed the uniqueness of growth in quantitative terms, understood as high-growth. Acknowledging the importance of size does not mean the emphasis on the optimal scale of operations that has been questioned as a rational barrier to further size increase. What is stressed here is the importance of size increase without ambition to establish an optimal point as a limitation to further expansion. Delimitation of growth and high-growers as the objects of investigations is instrumental to designing research that would appropriately explore this phenomenon.

1.8. A cross-fertilization among the established and emerging research streams in firm growth

The research streams in firm growth focus on different research questions and contribute with adequate insights and achievements. However, they seem to develop quite independently, with little mutual sourcing from findings and results. This limited cross-fertilization might thwart the development of ideas and the resolution of some substantial methodological problems they still face. Nevertheless, there are opportunities for these streams to mutually enrich and reinforce one another, thus supporting knowledge

Table 5. Research streams in firm growth and their prospective cross-fertilizations

Research stream on firm growth	Established streams		Emerging streams	
	Studies on growth determinants and predictors	Studies on firms' internal adaptation after achieving growth (stage models)	Studies on growth effects	Studies on the growth process
Achievements	Characteristics of the entrepreneur, the firm, its strategy and environment, correlated with growth and treated as determinants and/or predictors of firm expansion	Firm routines, process, and structures that require adjustments after growth took place; identification of business models that might be adopted based on opportunity recognition and with the aim of value creation	The outcomes of growth in terms of the firm's value and profitability	The explanation of why and how growth is pursued in terms of the entrepreneur's decisions and actions; the mechanisms that organize the process of growth studied in the context of the firm's capabilities and external environment
Under-researched issues or limitations	Ambiguity of the meaning and impact of some factors studied; overload of factors identified; the mechanisms of expansion (causalities among determinants) under-researched	Reactive and adaptive attitudes proposed but proactive strategies of accomplishing growth neglected; unrealistic determinism of development stages	Ambiguity of effects and determinants as a potential limitation, since feedback relationships might occur among these factors	Idiosyncrasy of the findings and the difficulty to generalize based on the research that adopts context-dependent and situational approach
Cross-fertilizations among the research streams in firm growth	Growth process studies can check the causalities among determinants of expansion identified in this research perspective. The stream on the growth process can explain the growth process can explain the present inconsistencies in the understanding of growth determinants by tracking their changes when expansion is being pursued. Studies on growth effects might check the impact of growth determinants on specific growth effects	The studies on the growth process can benefit from and contribute to stage models by learning how business models should be transformed and adapted to changing internal and external conditions when pursuing growth. The studies on growth effects can benefit from and contribute to stage models by identifying business models and capabilities that lead to specific effects	The studies on growth effects can benefit from and contribute to the studies on growth determinants by separating the effects and outcomes of growth and by determining when expansion is desirable. The studies on growth effects can contribute to the studies on growth processes and stage models by pointing to the effects of specific processes, firm capabilities, business models	The studies on growth process can benefit from and contribute to the studies on growth determinants by pointing to conditions when specific determinants are valid. These studies can also contribute to stage models and to the research in growth effects by exploring how specific capabilities and business models (stages) are created to accomplish expansion and desired effects

Source: own work based on Davidsson, Delmar, & Wiklund, 2006, pp. 45–48; Dobbs & Hamilton, 2006; McKelvie & Wiklund, 2010; Davidsson, Achtgenhagen, & Naldi, 2010; Gancarczyk & Iturriagagoitia, 2015.

accumulation in the entire field. This task of building on and drawing from other areas of inquiry is a special challenge for new and emerging perspectives relative to the existing stock of knowledge. Table 5 proposes the prospective input from the new perspectives to the earlier approaches and how they can benefit from more established research streams.

The studies on the growth process can benefit from and contribute to the studies on growth determinants by pointing to conditions when specific determinants are valid. These conditions, i.e., contextual issues, are at the core of investigating expansion. Growth process studies can explain the present inconsistencies in the meaning and influence of some factors and predictors of expansion by tracking their changes during the time of expansion. Moreover, these studies can unveil cause-effect relationships among expansion determinants, and these causalities will potentially provide additional highlights about the meaning and impact of individual factors. Studying the firm growth process can also contribute to stage models and to the research in growth effects by exploring how specific capabilities and business models (development stages) are created to implement expansion and generate desired effects. Additionally, stage models provide input to researching expansion processes by explaining how business models should be transformed and adapted to changing internal and external conditions when pursuing growth.

The emerging studies on growth effects can benefit from and contribute to the studies on growth determinants by separating the effects and outcomes of growth and by determining when expansion is desirable. Investigating the growth effects might reveal the impact of growth determinants on specific growth outcomes and might explain the antecedents of given growth results. Similarly, the studies on growth effects can contribute to the studies on growth processes and stage models by pointing to the outcomes of specific processes, capabilities, and business models.

1.9. The core of the firm growth process

The extant knowledge on entrepreneurial growth revolved around measures and determinants of this phenomenon and around challenges the firm faces after enlarging its size as reflected in life cycle models (Davidsson, Delmar, & Wiklund, 2006; Dobbs & Hamilton, 2007; McKelvie & Wiklund, 2010). However, little is known about the process of why and how growth is achieved (Garnsey, Stam, & Heffernan, 2006). The research in the firm growth process aims to explain why and how growth is implemented and to identify entrepreneur's decisional rules within a timespan of intense size increases (Davidsson, Delmar, & Wiklund, 2006; Garnsey, Stam, & Heffernan, 2006; Dobbs & Hamilton, 2007; Leitch, Hill, & Neergaard, 2010; McKelvie & Wiklund, 2010; Stam, 2010; Hansen & Hamilton, 2011; Wright & Stigliani, 2013).

The development of research in the SME growth process will contribute to the entrepreneurial process perspectives (Van de Ven & Engleman, 2004; Steyaert, 2007; Venkataraman et al., 2012; Gaweł, 2013; Glinka & Gudkova, 2011). These perspectives emphasize the interconnected causes of changes and attempt to link causal relations among drivers of change with timing and sequence (Garnsey, Stam, & Heffernan, 2006; McKelvey, 2004; Van de Ven & Poole, 1995; Gaweł, 2013; Glinka & Gudkova, 2011). Within entrepreneurial process perspectives, the entrepreneurial journey as a flow of events (the entrepreneur's decisions and actions) is proposed to be a primary unit of analysis (Selden & Fletcher, 2015). Consequently, the growth process can be treated as a pathway that encompasses the timing and sequence of events interconnected by causal relationships. The outcomes of this pathway are accomplishing the enlargement of the firm's size and competence development. Such an understanding of the expansion phenomenon would imply an established sequence of events or growth phases that might be considered as one pathway or pattern of the firm growth process. However, the empirical findings show the nature of growth as irregular, disruptive, and discontinuous, as well as caused by clusters of varied and, to some extent, ambiguous determinants.

Therefore, it is doubtful that only one pattern of the growth process exists, since the determinants identified in extant research can explain only a limited variance in firms' growth (Weinzimmer, Nystrom, & Freeman, 1998; Shepherd & Wiklund, 2009; Davidsson, Achtenhagen, & Naldi, 2010). The deterministic assumptions would probably lead to theoretical constructs similar to the stage or life cycle models of company expansion. Instead, it is better to argue that there are a variety of growth patterns (pathways) (Levie & Lichtenstein, 2010). Consequently, *the firm growth process could be described as discrete patterns encompassing the flows of events and timing governed by some causal mechanisms.*

Following the above considerations, *a key question emerges, how these flows of events are organized and how they should be conceptualized.* Without such rules, we would probably deal either with arbitrary and overly deterministic proposals of one model or pattern of growth or with a multitude of growth processes described as pathways identified in particular research settings. The entrepreneurial process perspectives propose some mechanisms to identify the defining rule of how the timing and events are organized in the conditions of uncertainty (Selden & Fletcher, 2015; Sarason, Dean, & Dillard, 2006; Gaweł, 2013; Glinka & Gudkova, 2011).

The mechanisms of the entrepreneurial process are described as effectuation and causation (Sarasvathy, 2001; 2009; Venkataraman et al., 2012), bricolage (Baker & Nelson, 2005; Garud & Karnøe, 2003), or reflective interpretation (Sarason, Dean, & Dillard, 2006). The effectuation and causation mechanism focuses on how decisions are made in terms of calculative and planned or intuitive and emergent choices (Sarasvathy, 2001; 2009). Bricolage, in turn, assumes the entrepreneurial process as a constructivist approach to resource environments that consists of combining available resources to address new problems and opportunities (Baker & Nelson, 2005). Reflective interpretation or self-reflexive capacity enables entrepreneurs to analyze and evaluate the current state of affairs relative to past assumptions and expectations and to decide whether to pursue or modify the course of actions (Sarason, Dean, & Dillard, 2006). These contributions treat the entrepreneur's perceptions and cognition as a focal point and define the entrepreneur's logic of making decisions and pursuing actions that create the entrepreneurial journey (Selden & Fletcher, 2015; Muñoz & Dimov, 2015). Moreover, they are consistent and complementary in seeing the entrepreneur as an agent combining the ideas, resources, and expectations from past experience to deal with an uncertain future. This is a constructivist approach that assumes opportunities are not discovered as existing objectively, but subjectively created by entrepreneurial individuals through the recombination of objectively existing resources (Sarason, Dean, & Dillard, 2006; Selden & Fletcher, 2015; Muñoz & Dimov, 2015).

An alternative, but complementary, way of theorizing on the entrepreneurial process is to a lesser extent directed at describing the mechanisms of making decisions or the general logic of entrepreneurial choices and actions. It is rather intended *to reveal micro-causalities that lead to a given sequence of events.* This is achieved by proposing some *structural elements, i.e., the elements that structure this process, such as markers, artifacts, or enabling constraints* (Selden & Fletcher, 2015; Muñoz & Dimov, 2015; McMullen & Dimov, 2013; Sarason, Dean, & Dillard, 2006). The concept of enabling constraints was originally developed in philosophical studies by Juarrero (2001), who used it to explain intentional behavior and causes of human action. Selden and Fletcher propose that the structural elements of the entrepreneurial process are path-dependent artifacts that emerge from previous events and affect the future ones. *The artifacts constrain and enable new events, i.e., the entrepreneur's decisions and actions. They are enablers, since they act as facilitators of entrepreneurial decisions and actions, but they also constrain by shaping and limiting future states* (Juarrero, 2000; Selden & Fletcher, 2015). The examples of artifacts as enabling constraints include a business idea (plan) and organizational design, the products and technologies adopted, etc.

As such, the concept of enabling constraints invokes path-dependent thinking. The artifacts, once established, limit the accessible range of options for entrepreneurial decisions and actions. At the same time, they enable future choices since they structure decisional options and thus provide the ability to select alternatives and act. Therefore, the enabling constraints approach modifies the path dependence view focused on myopia and inertia. Namely, it points to the value of constraints as enablers. *Enabling constraints are not purely objective determinants since they are context-specific, i.e., they depend on external conditions that may act as moderators of their influence.*

The concept of enabling constraints can be extended beyond the artifacts as the outcomes of past events that shape the future ones. Namely, its content is essentially close to the meaning of institutions or decisional rules explaining human behavior and actions (Sarason, Dean, & Dillard, 2006). Such an approach is relevant to growth process research that places entrepreneurs' perceptions and decisional rules at the core. In this research, the entrepreneurial cognition and perceptions as to "why" and "how" problems occur when the expansion is being realized are at the core (Wiklund & Shepherd, 2003; Wiklund, Davidsson, & Delmar, 2003).

Consequently, we need to consider what influences these choices and what determines particular artifacts as the outcomes. This would extend the events caused by artifacts "upstream" towards the origins of the artifacts that are embedded in perceptions, convictions, and approaches to problem-solving, i.e., to self-reflexive evaluation. *The extended causal framework would start from the entrepreneur's self-reflexive evaluation regarding the reality of the firm and its environment to decisions and actions (events) leading to the emergence of the artifacts that concurrently constrain and enable future events.* This framework needs to acknowledge the feedback loops among two groups of enabling constraints, namely, the perceptional ones (the entrepreneur's perceptions, values, and convictions) and the artifactual ones (the results of decisions and actions leading to the development of capabilities an enterprise). Moreover, the perceptional enabling constraints are embedded in and emerge from an entrepreneur's individual experience and assessment of the resources and environment, i.e., the context. These contextual issues affect the entrepreneur's attitudes, which are, in this sense, path-dependent.

Considering the above discussion, *the growth process of firms can be described not only as a flow of events, but also as a structuration process in which enabling constraints (entrepreneurial self-reflexive evaluation and artifacts) determine the flow of decisions and actions (events).* The growth process has distinctive characteristics with regard to the entrepreneurial process in general. Therefore, it deserves the research that would identify the enabling constraints specific to high-growth firms.

One of the special features of the growth process relative to the overall entrepreneurial process is that the former does not start from the creation of a company, since expansion refers to the existing firm with its capabilities and business model (OECD, 2007). Davidsson, Delmar and Wiklund (2006, p. 47) assert that in the growth process perspective, the firm is treated as a governance structure, a decision-making unit within which entrepreneurial decisions and actions take place. These decisions and actions affect an individual firm's boundaries (Jacobides & Winter, 2007).

Moreover, the extant research about the process of expansion provides some initial foundations to explore the perceptual enabling constraints, such as a dynamic process (Penrose, 1959; Garnsey, Stam, & Heffernan, 2006) or dynamic state (Levie & Lichtenstein, 2010) approaches. In the latter case, the opportunity recognition and value increase that lead to specific business models (Levie & Lichtenstein, 2010) can be treated as structural elements or enabling constraints in the growth process. Their nature is perceptual, since they refer to motivations as drivers of action.

Following the guiding role of enabling constraints, a general framework of the growth process is shown in Figure 2.

According to the proposed framework, *the growth process of a firm encompasses a sequence of events structured by entrepreneurial self-reflexive evaluation and the artifacts that lead to the enlargement of the firm's size and scope associated with competence development. This structuration results in different patterns of the growth process due to the contextual influences of the firm's capabilities and environment.*

The growth process has a dual nature. On one side, it is a flow of observable events (the entrepreneur's decisions and actions). On the other side, it is a structuration process, determined by the entrepreneur's self-reflexive evaluation and artifacts as enabling constraints. The entrepreneur's self-reflexive evaluation is based on the perceptions, values, and convictions

Structuration of patterns
of the growth process through   The flow of events (observable
enabling constraints: entrepreneurial   decisions and actions) and actions)
self-reflexive evaluation and artifacts

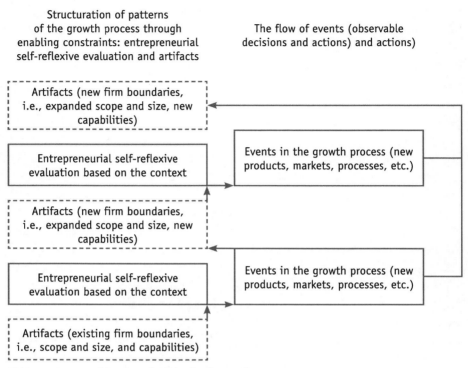

Figure 2. A general framework of the firm's growth process

Source: own work.

of the entrepreneur shaped by the context of individual experience and the environmental resources at hand. The entrepreneur's sense-making is also enabled and constrained by artifacts, i.e., the existing firm boundaries (size and scope) and capabilities. These two types of enabling constraints (entrepreneurial self-evaluation and artifacts) affect the flow of observable events. The crucial *challenge is to explain the nature of the entrepreneur's self-reflexive evaluation, that is, his or her perceptions, convictions, and decisional rules that lead to the emergence of events and artifacts.* Different characteristics and configurations of these perceptual enabling constraints may provide for different patterns of the growth process. This would extend the framework by Selden and Fletcher (2015), who explored how artifacts emerge from past events and how they impact future events. The extended framework points to another type of enabling constraints that are generic for artifacts. In this sense, it goes back (upstream) in the causal relations of the growth process by proposing how artifacts (new firm boundaries, i.e., expanded scope and size and new capabilities) emerge.

2. THE RESOURCE-BASED VIEW (RBV) AND TRANSACTION COST THEORY (TCT) AS ALTERNATIVE APPROACHES TO THE GROWTH PROCESS OF FIRMS

2.1. The rationale for adopting the RBV and TCT to explain the growth process of SMEs

As noted earlier, the growth process involves this phase of the entrepreneurial process when there exists an established venture with given size and scope (boundaries) and capabilities. The core of entrepreneurial decisions at this stage is close to those of the agents in industrial economics and strategic management that undertake actions and choices within the context of the existing firm capabilities (artifacts), past experience, and environmental influences. Therefore, in order to explain how entrepreneurs perform a self-reflexive evaluation that leads to expanding firm boundaries, we need to recognize their interpretative rules (Selden & Fletcher, 2015; Sarason, Dean, & Dillard, 2006).

Such rules reveal how the entrepreneurs identify and interpret opportunities for new products, markets, and processes (Shane & Venkataraman, 2000) that finally turn into the expanded scope and size of the firm. This calls for an adequate theoretical background. However, the scarcity of research on the growth process is associated with a limited range of theories to explain this phenomenon (Dobbs & Hamilton, 2007; McKelvie & Wiklund, 2010). The major theoretical foundations of firm growth were laid by Penrose (1959) and they were further developed into the resource-based view of the firm (the RBV) (Garnsey, Stam, & Heffernan, 2006). However, recent studies suggest generating new concepts to capture the heterogeneity of expansion that was earlier identified in the large-scale quantitative studies on growth determinants (Dobbs & Hamilton, 2007; McKelvie & Wiklund, 2010; Wright & Stigliani).

Theories of the growth process can be either inductive and empirical-ly-driven or adopt and test relevant existing approaches. The first method would acknowledge an explorative nature of this new perspective. However, its disadvantage would be an idiosyncrasy of methodologies and findings. This would hamper knowledge accumulation, which is a limitation recognized in the present research on growth determinants and predictors (i.e., on the antecedents of growth as an outcome). Applying and testing extant theoretical approaches ensures consistency in understanding the assumptions and variables and facilitates the comparability and generalizability of the methodologies and findings. A possible drawback of this approach is the inadequacy of these existing theories to explain the new phenomena. Namely, the findings from empirical research based on an extant theory may be biased towards this theory rather than reveal the real nature of the phenomenon studied. However, by combining the most relevant extant theories that complement one another, we can avoid this bias and accomplish the required conceptual and external validity of the research. Moreover, adopting and testing extant theories is an initial step of theory building in a given field before novel concepts emerge based on verifying these theories. Such new highlights can be expected if more of these theories are confronted in a new context, namely in the context of high-growth firms being predominantly small and medium-sized enterprises.

A theoretical agenda that comprehensively addresses the issue of expanding firm boundaries has been developing in industrial economics, organization science, and strategic management as an integration of the resource-based view (the RBV) of the firm and transaction cost theory (TCT) (Argyres & Zenger, 2012; David & Han, 2004; Carter & Hodgson, 2006; Mayer & Salomon, 2006; Tsang, 2000; 2006; Williamson, 1999; Foss, 1993; Combs & Ketchen, 1999; Foss & Foss, 2004; Freiling, Gersch, & Goeke, 2008). In particular, research findings in firm boundaries provide the evidence about the validity of these approaches (c.f. Newbert, 2007; Arend, 2006; Arend & Levesque, 2010; Combs et al., 2011; Lafontaine & Slade, 2007; David & Han, 2004; Carter & Hodgson, 2006; Macher & Richman, 2008; Rindfleisch et al., 2010). Combs et al. (2011) suggest that the RBV and TCT may be complementary and integrated with the adoption of adequate mediators and moderators in specific contexts of internal capability and the external environment. This would enable the accumulation of knowledge through one comprehensive approach regarding the firm's size and scope (Combs et al., 2011; Leavitt, Mitchell, & Peterson, 2010).

These two theoretical approaches have been increasingly adopted in the entrepreneurship literature as well, to highlight opportunity recognition (Foss & Foss, 2008), rent creation and appropriation (Alvarez, 2007), innovation (Michael, 2007), and growth issues (Davidsson, Steffens, & Fitzsimmons, 2009; Garnsey, Stam, & Heffernan, 2006; Chandler, McKelvie, & Davidsson, 2009; Verwaal et al., 2010). Individual studies investigated growth performance and measures from the perspective of the RBV (Davidsson, Steffens, & Fitzsimmons, 2009; Garnsey, Stam, & Heffernan, 2006), growth modes from the perspective of TCT (Chandler, McKelvie, & Davidsson, 2009) or hybrid expansion from the angle of both RBV and TCT variables (Verwaal et al., 2010). These initial findings point to the need to jointly consider transaction cost and capability issues when investigating decisions and actions related to expansion (Chandler, McKelvie, & Davidsson, 2009; Davidsson, Steffens, & Fitzsimmons, 2009; McKelvie & Davidsson, 2010; Verwaal et al., 2010).

Consequently, in this book, the method of applying the RBV and TCT to explore and describe the process of the growth of small and medium-sized enterprises is proposed. Adopting the integrated RBV-TCT approach to explain the growth process of these enterprises is justified by their relevance for entrepreneurial decision-making in this process, as per the arguments below.

At the growth stage of the entrepreneurial process, the entrepreneur's decisions are essentially boundary decisions (Davidsson, Delmar, & Wiklund, 2006, p. 47; Davidsson, Achtenhagen, & Naldi, 2010, p. 179). Entrepreneurial high growth is founded on increasing the scope of the firm through new products, services, processes, and markets. It is not merely an incidental increase in sales as a response to *ad hoc* market changes. Specifically, when growth in employment is considered, there needs to be a solid basis for significant and sustainable size enlargement. Both theories refer to growth as expanding the size and scope of the firm. As an extension and advancement of Penrose's theory of growth, the RBV represents a leading theoretical perspective in this research area. However, recent developments point to the explanatory power of the RBV for the broader theme of firm boundaries, as well. Here, the RBV is complementary to TCT, which is considered to be a leading perspective on boundary choices (Argyres & Zenger, 2012; Leiblein, 2003; Leiblein & Miller, 2003). On the other hand, TCT has been increasingly adopted to explain growth modes and measures (Chandler, McKelvie, & Davidsson, 2009; Verwaal et al., 2010; McKelvie & Wiklund, 2010). TCT deals with growth by examining the issues of vertical integration or diversification at large, as well as hybrid modes of expansion (Ray et al.,

2013). The advancement of both theories leads to their converging foci and calls for their joint application in the area of firm boundaries and growth (Chandler, McKelvie, & Davidsson, 2009; McKelvie & Wiklund, 2010).

Both TCT and RBV address the issues of why and how to expand firm boundaries, the questions that are fundamental to explain the process nature of growth (Garnsey, Stam, & Heffernan, 2006; Wright & Stigliani, 2013). These approaches provide insights about why (in terms of motives and rationale) and how (in terms of mechanisms and modes) to expand the existing boundaries of the firm (Gancarczyk, 2015a; 2015c; 2016b).

These two perspectives demonstrate conflicting views on some aspects of firm boundaries (Tsang, 2000). However, they are increasingly perceived as complementary and to be applied jointly in studying boundary, performance, and growth issues (Combs et al., 2011; Ray, Xue, & Barney, 2013; Chandler, McKelvie, & Davidsson, 2009; McKelvie & Wiklund, 2010; Williamson, 1999). Empirical evidence and theoretical achievements in these areas are still developing, and in the research on growth, they are at the inception stage. Therefore, integrating and testing these theories in the context of high-growth SMEs will contribute to both boundary studies and growth studies.

In boundary studies, this will broaden the research in the new context of high-growth SMEs. This context is largely unexplored in boundary studies of vertical integration, diversification, and hybrid modes (Davidsson, Achtenhagen, & Naldi, 2010; McKelvie & Wiklund, 2010). If introduced to boundary literature, it will add the entrepreneurial perspective to extant research focused primarily on the managerial perspective. In entrepreneurial studies, it will address the research gap in developing the theoretical background for the growth process of SMEs.

Despite being young and developing theoretical approaches, RBV and TCT provide alternative, yet coherent, sets of notions and assumptions about firm growth understood to be increasing scope and size (Argyres & Zenger, 2012). Applying these approaches together will help to avoid the problem of the idiosyncrasy of methodologies and the ambiguity of findings that prevent knowledge accumulation, which are typical shortcomings of inductive and empirically-based approaches to theory building (Leavitt, Mitchell, & Peterson, 2010; Bitektine, 2008). The deductive approach that adopts extant theories supports methodological replicability and compatibility, thus providing for better-founded generalizations (Bitektine, 2008).

The possible bias of findings from the research based on influential theories is reduced in this instance by combining two alternative but complementary views instead of sticking to only one theory.

Considering the arguments, we will explore how SME entrepreneurs make decisions and act during launching and implementing expansion when they adopt the RBV-TCT perspectives. Following the general framework of the firm growth process (Section 1.9.), we approach this process through the lens of structuration theory (Sarason, Dean, & Dillard, 2006). We intend to identify some structural elements that explain the entrepreneur's self-reflexive evaluation leading to particular decisions and actions that result in artifacts, such as the new scope and size of the venture (Sarason, Dean, & Dillard, 2006; Selden & Fletcher, 2015). In this sense, structural elements will demonstrate the properties of enabling constraints that organize the flow of events within the "journey" of entrepreneurial growth (Juarrero, 2000; Selden & Fletcher, 2015). These structural elements will be extracted from the resource-based and transaction cost approaches to firm growth.

2.2. The structural elements of the growth process

The process perspective focuses on the research questions of why and how specific phenomena take place and on identifying the entrepreneur's decisional rules within a timespan of intense size increases (Sarason, Dean, & Dillard, 2006; Wiklund & Shepherd, 2003; Wiklund, Davidsson, & Delmar, 2003). The structuration of this process is based on the entrepreneur's cognition and actions. The perceptions as to why and how entrepreneurs pursue growth became a focus of attention and a major point of reference (Wiklund & Shepherd, 2003; Wiklund, Davidsson, & Delmar, 2003). Addressing and explaining these issues would disentangle the structuration in which entrepreneurs identify and evaluate opportunities to generate the flow of events (decisions and actions) (Sarason, Dean, & Dillard, 2006; Selden & Fletcher, 2015). Consequently, it is assumed that the structuration depends upon the entrepreneurial cognition and perceptions, and that specific growth decisions emerge from these individual perceptions (Garnsey, Stam, & Heffernan, 2006; Wright & Stigliani, 2013).

To explore the structuration in a systematic way, we need to identify constituent (structural) elements of the entrepreneur's self-reflexive evaluation regarding the "why" and "how" dimensions of expansion. These elements as foundations of decision-making are offered by TCT and the RBV to describe scope and size choices (c.f., Tsang, 2000; Jacobides & Winter, 2007). In the following sections, based on a stylized interpretation of the RBV and TCT assumptions, we propose that structural elements of the growth process are motives, rationale, mechanisms, and modes. The nature of these elements is consistent with major problems raised in extant pioneering conceptualizations of the growth process. The problem of why entrepreneurs launch growth can be described as motives and rationale that direct their decisions and actions. The motives refer to behavioral assumptions on the attitudes of entrepreneurs and other economic agents in making decisions (Wright & Stigliani, 2013). The growth rationale consists of economic reasons and goals for enlarging the company's size. The growth mechanisms involve interdependencies among factors (cause-effect relationships) that lead to the choice of a specific governance mode. The growth modes denote different governance structures for implementing growth in terms of hierarchy (internal or external expansion), market, and hybrid structures (McKelvie & Wiklund, 2010). Internal growth means the expansion of the organizational hierarchy independently, based on the firm's own resources. External growth, through mergers and acquisitions, involves combining resources with other firms to acquire complementary capabilities. Internal and external modes assume the expansion of current boundaries of the organizational hierarchy. However, current research on growth points to another mode, namely the hybrid mode implemented through joint ventures and cooperation such as outsourcing and subcontracting, licensing, franchising, etc. (Larson, 1992; Coad, 2009; 2010; Magala, 2010; McKelvie & Wiklund, 2010). Technological advancements decrease the importance of scale, scope, and experience economies, and stimulate the emergence of expansion modes different from traditional organic or acquisitive growth (McKelvie & Wiklund, 2010; Coad, 2009; 2010). The hybrid mode goes beyond the organizational hierarchy towards a governance structure that combines the complementary resources of independent firms to ensure their individual growth in employment, sales, and asset value (Larson, 1992; Ireland, Hitt, & Vaidyanath, 2002; Murphy et al., 2012). Specialization and the resulting inter-organizational linkages draw specific attention to this governance mode to capture the heterogeneity of expansion from the traditional hierarchy delimited by employment and ownership boundaries (Williamson, 1989; Grossman & Hart, 1986).

Below, the growth process is interpreted through the lens of the two approaches and its structural elements of each theory are discussed separately. This acknowledges their alternative and, to some extent, conflicting views. However, it is also a prelude to combining the theories and treating them as complementary explanations of the phenomenon under study (Leavitt, Mitchell, & Peterson, 2010).

2.3. The structural elements of the growth process according to the RBV

The resource-based view (the RBV) was initiated as a theory of firm growth by Penrose (1959) and it can be treated as a contemporary extension of this theory towards a general theory of firm size and scope (Conner & Prahalad, 1996; Tsang, 2000; Holcomb & Hitt, 2007; Leiblein, 2003; Argyres, 2012). In this research area, the RBV is currently employed either as a competitive or complementary view to the more established transaction cost economics (TCT) (Gautam, Barney, & Muhanna, 2004; Mayer & Salomon, 2006). We focus on the RBV assumptions about growth and firm boundaries. However, this perspective is also adopted to explain the nature of the firm (Pitelis & Teece, 2009; Hodgson, 2004; Pitelis & Pseiridis, 1999) and predominantly to strategic management of performance and competitive advantage (Gautam, Barney, & Muhanna, 2004; Kraaijenbrink, Spender, & Groen, 2010). When discussing the growth phenomenon via this perspective, we will draw from Penrose's view as the backbone of the RBV approach to growth. However, we also enrich this view with relevant contemporaneous advancements of the RBV stream of research (Garnsey, Stam, & Heffernan, 2006).

According to the RBV, the nature of the firm is associated with capabilities and performance (Amit & Schoemaker, 1993; Barney, 1991; Hamel & Prahalad, 1990; Kogut & Zander, 1992; Peteraf, 1993; Wernerfelt, 1984). Namely, the firm is a unique bundle of capabilities or resources, and thus companies are heterogeneous and differ in competitive positions (Bratnicki, 2000; Zakrzewska-Bielawska, 2011). Resources and capabilities, the core RBV concepts, are intuitively clear notions. However, they have not been strictly defined and sometimes are used interchangeably (Barney, 1991; Gautam, Barney, & Muhanna, 2004), while in other instances capabilities are deemed to include resources, competencies, and activities (Amit & Schoemaker, 1993). Capabilities that are valuable, rare, inimitable, immobile and non-substitutable (Barney, 1991) underpin the competitive advantage. Such capabilities are also considered firm-specific, interdependent, and forming the firm's core competencies (Hamel & Prahalad, 1990). Such properties of capabilities ensure the competitive advantage and the improved performance, i.e., the creation of value and Ricardian rent. Consequently, the *rationale for growth* is value creation from new combinations of existing resources and from economies of growth, scale, and scope (Penrose, 1959; Chandler, 1992; Nooteboom, 1992; Romanows-ka, 2001). Economies of scope result from better utilization of indivisible surplus resources, such as managerial and employee competence, brand, or R&D facilities.

According to Penrose (1959), growth is a dynamic and cumulative pro-cess of organizational learning, accompanied by size increases as a side ef-fect. This learning process depends on absorptive capacity (Cohen & Lev-inthal, 1990) and dynamic capabilities (Teece, Pisano, & Shuen, 1997; Teece, 2007; Krzakiewicz & Cyfert, 2016; Najda-Janioszka, 2016), which are critical to absorbing and transforming knowledge and to generating innovations (Un & Montoro-Sanchez, 2010). The success of expansion is determined by the match between the firm's resources and market oppor-tunities (Penrose, 1959; Peteraf, 1993; Wernerfelt, 1984).

The mechanisms of growth are closely associated with the modes of growth as their results. The *major mechanism of growth* is the exploitation of existing indivisible resources to utilize them better. Resource exploita-tion is pursued by novel uses of the existing assets, and is successful when new products and services are consistent (core-related) with the firm's core competencies (Hamel & Prahalad, 1990). This growth mechanism leads a company portfolio towards related diversification. The mechanism of resource exploitation is predominantly associated with an organic (inter-nal) mode of growth that is based on the company's own independently developed capabilities.

The entrepreneurial and managerial competencies constrain growth based on indivisible resource exploitation. The condition of bounded ra-tionality leads a manager-entrepreneur to the path-dependent exploitation of the extant knowledge base into relevant activities (Penrose, 1959; Lock-ett & Thompson, 2001). In this process, the current knowledge, including practices and routines, plays a major role. Bounded rationality, meaning that economic agents intend to make rational choices but are limited in the ability to do this, is free from opportunism (Conner & Prahalad, 1996; Lockett, Thompson, & Morgenstern, 2009). The presumed *motives* of contracting parties are trust and mutuality rather than self-interest seeking with guile (Barney, 1991; Tsang, 2000; Williamson, 1999).

The current knowledge base poses limits to the firm's boundaries and to organic growth based on the resource exploitation. However, this would mean that a firm employs incremental and less risky undertakings, avoid-ing a more radical innovation that is needed to establish a competitive advantage. To sustain and upgrade the competitive position, it is necessary to explore and commercialize uncertain breakthrough knowledge. This invokes *another mechanism of growth* – exploration. Resource exploration removes the earlier limits to growth and expands the firm's boundaries into the areas that are not related to the existing core competencies. Consequently, the firm's portfolio may develop into unrelated diversification (Penrose, 1959; Sirén, Kohtamäki, & Kuckertz, 2012; Gancarczyk, 2015). The implied mode of growth is external, through mergers and acquisitions that would enable sourcing knowledge and material infrastructure from other entities (Penrose, 1959). Another possibility is internal growth supported by the acquisition of talent with knowledge unavailable in the company.

Penrose's original view focused on the two modes of growth discussed earlier, namely, internal (organic) and external (acquisitive), depending on the relationship with the extant core competencies. Further development of the RBV highlights the rationale and benefits of hybrid modes and holds that they are appropriate when the company seeks complementary capabilities in the conditions of environmental uncertainty and the scarcity of its own resources to independently invest in a new activity (Ireland, Hitt, & Vaidyanath, 2002).

The RBV theory is criticized for its fragmentation and, except for the classical Penrosian framework, lack of coherent, systemized delivery (Tsang, 2000). Recent theoretical advancements respond to this limitation (Acedo, Barroso, & Galan, 2006; Newbert, 2007; Gautam, Barney, & Muhanna, 2004; Nandialath, Dotson, & Durrand, 2014). However, they are predominantly inductive and do not fully mitigate some problems, such as ambiguity of concepts and basic notions, often leading to tautologies, as well as leaving some issues unresolved (Czakon, 2010). The RBV underlines value creation as a rationale for firm existence and growth (Gautam, Barney, & Muhanna, 2004; Nandialath, Dotson, & Durrand, 2014; Newbert, 2007), but it undervalues the cost side of these phenomena (Williamson, 1999; Tsang, 2000; Arend, 2006). Moreover, it does not provide a systematic procedure for selecting between market exchange or hierarchy and hybrid modes that would differentiate its assumptions from those of TCT (Argyres & Zenger, 2012). For instance, TCT assumes different levels of uncertainty that can either imply internalization of an activity within the organizational hierarchy (high level) or implementing it in hybrid structures (medium level). Without a more detailed examination of these levels leading to different governance modes, there is ambiguity about the consistency or discrepancy between the views of the RBV and TCT in this regard.

Table 6. The structural elements of the firm growth process according to the RBV approach and its critiques

The structural elements of the growth process	The RBV approach to the growth process structural elements	The critiques of the RBV approach
Motives of economic agents	Motives free of opportunism; trust and mutuality dominate	The unrealistic assumption of the lack of opportunism may be harmful for businesses; trust should not be unconditional and blind
Rationale	Value increase	The costs rationale for growth are neglected; the unclear causal relationship between resources and value (tautology)
Mechanisms	Resource exploitation (new activities related to and built upon the existing core competencies); resource exploration (new activities unrelated to the existing core competencies); matching the firm's competencies with external opportunities	Ambiguity of the key concepts of resources, capabilities and the core competencies
Modes	Organic (internal), external or hybrid growth (mergers and acquisitions) are dependent on the consistency with a firm's core competencies	No systematic procedure or clearly defined criteria for choosing among growth modes; limited normative value (usefulness for managerial choices)

Source: own work.

Kraaijenbrink, Spender, and Groen (2010) synthesize the critiques of the RBV and optimistically maintain that most drawbacks can be addressed by the current achievements or by more elaborate future research in this perspective. However, three critical points remain a challenge for the research agenda (Kraaijenbrink, Spender, & Groen, 2010). These include clarifying and delimiting the fundamental concepts of resource, value, and competitive advantage. The RBV is heavily criticized for tautology in explaining the essence of key concepts, such as resources, capabilities, and core competencies (Williamson, 1999; Arend, 2006), as well as the critical relationship between capabilities and performance, i.e., value creation and competitive advantage (Kraaijenbrink, Spender, & Groen, 2010; Obłój, 2007).

Table 6 summarizes the characteristics of the structural elements of the firm growth process according to the RBV assumptions, as well as the critiques questioning these assumptions.

The polemics with the RBV explanations of the growth process can logically be derived from TCT's assumptions and reflect its alternative view of the structural components of motives, rationale, mechanisms, and modes.

The opportunistic motivations of economic agents that should not be neglected or replaced by the practically artificial assumption of trust, the cost rationale for determining firm scope and size, as well as the ambiguity of major constructs and tautologies in defining them were early identified by Williamson (1999). Similarly, deficiency of systematic and theoretically workable hypothesis with practical relevance for entrepreneurial and managerial choices resonates with the views of TCT proponents (Arendt, 2006; Arend & Lévesque, 2010).

2.4. The structural elements of the growth process according to TCT

Transaction cost theory emerged as a theory of the firm, explaining its nature and emergence, and as a theory of firm boundaries specifically focused on vertical integration (Hardt, 2009). TCT considers the firm as one of the governance structures or modes, that is, regulatory mechanisms for conducting an economic exchange, directed at economizing transaction costs (Coase, 1937; Williamson, 1991; Gorynia, 1999; Ząbkowicz, 2003, 2015; Boehlke, 2010, pp. 214–251). Transaction costs are the comparative cost of implementing transactions under alternative governance structures, including market, organization, and hybrids that fall between the latter generic structures (Williamson, 1989, p. 142). These costs are incurred *ex-ante*, before signing the contract (the costs of drafting, negotiating, and safeguarding an agreement), and *ex-post*, after signing it (the costs of maladaptation and adjustment) (Williamson, 1993). The governance modes, including the market, the firm, and hybrids, are selected based on the comparative analysis of transaction costs they generate. Each human or business activity can be interpreted as a transaction, a sort of exchange when a good or service is transferred across a technologically separable interface (Williamson, 1989, p. 142; Ratajczak, 2011). Williamson (1999), emphasizes Common's (1932) triple of properties of the transaction as a unit of economic analysis. Since the nature of transactions is defined by conflict, mutuality, and order, governance provides order to mitigate conflicts that would otherwise prevent parties from mutual gains (Williamson, 1999).

The *rationale* for firm emergence and growth is economizing transaction costs when operating in the market is too expensive (Williamson, 1975; 1991; 1998; 2002; 2005). Both Coase (1937) and Williamson (1975) acknowledge the costs of exchange in the market and in the firm.

Williamson (1975; 1991) described the properties of these modes and differentiated another type, hybrids being long-term exchange relationships that demonstrate the properties of both market transactions (spot, price-based) and transactions within the firm (organizational hierarchy).

The determinants of transaction costs stem from the attributes of the transaction and the environment of a specific exchange. These attributes include asset specificity, transaction frequency, and uncertainty. Asset specificity denotes idiosyncratic investments that cannot be redeployed to alternative uses without losing productive value (Williamson, 1993). The examples of asset specificity include human, physical, site, timing, and other dedicated resources. Idiosyncratic investment results in the bilateral dependency of contracting parties, which makes exchange relations complex. Namely, the contract requires the drafting of terms and conditions, which, due to bounded rationality, can never be fully specified. These unspecified gaps provoke opportunistic behavior to exploit them and to generate quasi-rents (Klein, Crawford, & Alchian, 1978). Transaction frequency means the number of exchanges conducted in a period of time. Finally, uncertainty embraces opportunism and unpredictability of the environment (Williamson, 1975). Opportunism represents a behavioral uncertainty, i.e., self-interest seeking with guile, and unpredictability of the environment (Williamson, 1975). Highly specific assets increase the complexity and frequency of transactions with a particular partner. Idiosyncratic investments that are uneven, i.e., disproportionally higher on the part of one entity, expose it to an excessive dependence, opportunism, and quasi-rent seeking (Klein, Crawford, & Alchian, 1978). High level of asset specificity leads to the increased frequency and uncertainty (opportunism), and eventually to increased transaction costs in the market. The consequence is a decision to integrate the transaction within the firm, i.e., to expand (grow).

Opportunism is assumed to be a *motive* of economic agents, due to bounded rationality, information asymmetry, and unavoidably incomplete contracts (Wojtyna, 2004). Opportunism in TCT needs to be distinguished from traditional egoistic or selfish behavior, which features purposeful actions to mislead, deceive, and confuse the partner. Williamson considers the opportunistic behavioral motivations as workably realistic, unlike motivations free of opportunism that are analytically convenient but artificial (1993).

The *mechanism of growth* is explained by the alignment hypothesis, which states that transactions differing in their attributes are aligned with governance structures that differ in their costs and benefits to economize transaction costs (Williamson, 1991; 2005). The choice of an appropriate governance structure is based on the comparative analysis of these solutions. The firm grows when the comparative transaction costs of implementing a particular transaction in the market are higher than pursuing this transaction internally or in hybrid structures. Since the alignment between transactions and governance modes is based on the comparative analysis of various governance solutions, it involves an experimental, situational approach. The mechanism of expansion consists of experimenting with governance structures to match their properties with the properties of transactions. It implies fluid and constantly changing firm boundaries to find an efficient way of implementing each transaction. It can be argued that this is a dynamic approach, but without the assumptions of path dependence – history, continuity, and learning (Williamson, 1999). Instead, it is based on singular choices, in which the earlier experience does not matter (Langlois, 1992; Hodgson, 1998).

The lack of a historical, iterative, and learning context for entrepreneurial and managerial decisions became one of the major critiques of TCT for being a static perspective, compared to the dynamic resource-based view (Langlois, 1992; Hodgson, 1998). Focused on an individual transaction (a particular exchange with a given entity), it overlooks the benefits (and not only costs) that a specific investment may bring by broadening the scope of cooperation in the long-run and by external effects (Kang, Mahoney, & Tan, 2008). Although TCT involves a micro-analytical and ahistorical approach, it acknowledges the value of continuity in transacting business through the adaptation and private ordering of on-going contractual relations (Williamson, 2002; 2005; Klimczak, 2004).

Another critique of TCT stems from its exclusive emphasis on the cost rationale for company growth while ignoring value creation as a justification (Pitelis & Teece, 2009; Pitelis & Pseiridis, 1999; Zajac & Olsen, 1993; Hardt, 2009). Moreover, its emphasis on opportunism as a motive of economic agents raises controversies and even resistance to such a pessimistic explanation of transaction costs and human behavior at large (Conner & Prahalad, 1996; Hodgson, 2004). Empirical studies provided opposing evidence, depending on the context of transacting, such as the case of Japanese corporations where trust and cooperative attitude were found to be the major motives (Holmström & Roberts, 1998). The assumption of opportunism implies lack of trust, which may cause the loss of potential benefits and increase the costs of safeguards.

TCT overemphasizes the risks and uncertainties raised by an individual exchange, suggesting *ad hoc* and hard incentives. However, it underrates the potential benefits of iterative inter-firm exchanges in the long run to decrease transaction costs. It is worth noting that TCT provides a solution for developing trust in the long-term perspective. This solution consists of acknowledging opportunism and developing safeguards as a starting point and a basis for credible commitments. Trust should not be blind and unconditional, and it is built during the process of cooperation (Gancarczyk, 2010a). Despite the reported psychological distance or even reluctance to accept the notion of opportunism, the concept of transaction costs as burdens to economic exchange enjoys wide facial validity among entrepreneurs and practitioners (Love & Roper, 2005).

Additionally, TCT provides important insights about growth modes with regard to hierarchy expansion and hybrid expansion, the latter specifically relevant in the contemporary economy and for small and medium-sized businesses (Larson, 1992; Coad, 2009; Magala, 2010; McKelvie & Wiklund, 2010; Ratajczak-Mrozek, 2010; Gancarczyk & Gancarczyk, 2017). Although it proposes the nature and criteria of choosing hybrid governance, it does not differentiate between organic and acquisitive growth in hierarchy expansion, nor does it provide a method for choosing between these two modes. Such insights are offered by the resource-based theory.

The proposed impact of asset specificity and opportunism on the level of transaction costs and on the decision about the internalization of a given activity was also questioned. Sampson (2004) reported that high asset specificity and opportunism raised the costs of external transacting higher than the costs of a misaligned internal organization. These determinants might be less relevant in the context of scarce resources or low competence preventing vertical integration (Argyres, 1996; Carter & Hodgson, 2006). Moreover, the opportunism of one party may be controlled by the high competence of the other party, even in the presence of idiosyncratic investment (Barney, 1999; Mayer & Salomon, 2006). TCT raised a strong skepticism regarding the underrated role of firm capabilities and core competencies.

Finally, neglecting the role of individual goals and the proactive attitudes of managers and entrepreneurs, and attributing them with merely adaptive choices to avoid transaction costs, is often considered to be an unrealistic view. To address this limitation, TCT is often combined with resource-dependence theory (Pfeffer & Salancik, 1978), which assumes that managers and entrepreneurs proactively act to subordinate suppliers and buyers and to maintain their own independence (Fink et al., 2006; Gales & Blackburn, 1990).

The above critiques of TCT challenge the explanation of the growth process given by this perspective. Much of the polemics stems from confronting TCT with the resource-based theory as an alternative view on the issues of firm scope and size (Table 7).

Table 7. The structural elements of the firm growth process according to the TCT approach and its critiques

The structural elements of the growth process	TCT approach to the growth process structural elements	The critiques of the TCT approach
Motives of economic agents	Opportunism as self-interest seeking with guile	Opportunism is not the only motivation for human action, as mutuality and trust also regulate social relationships
Rationale	Reduction of transaction costs out of organization	A passive approach that neglects entrepreneurs' individual goals and proactive strategies, focusing only on cost reduction
Mechanisms	Discriminating alignment hypothesis – aligning characteristics of a particular transaction (activity) with the governance mode in order to optimize transaction costs	The characteristics of the transaction are not the only and most powerful determinants of vertical integration and other governance forms; capabilities and the core competencies are neglected
Modes	Hierarchy (internalization) or hybrid growth dependent on the level of asset specificity, transaction frequency, and uncertainty	TCT does not discriminate between internal and external growth and does not provide criteria to choose between them

Source: own work.

Like the polemics with the RBV explanations of the growth process, we need to acknowledge the influence of the RBV perspective when identifying the drawbacks of TCT. The skepticism for opportunistic explanations of human behavior and the passive approach to individual goals of entrepreneurs instead of proactive attitudes, as well as the emphasis on capabilities and core competencies as determinants of governance mechanisms and modes, are strongly underpinned by the capability perspective (Conner & Prahaled, 1996).

2.5. The RBV and TCT as alternative views on the structural elements of company growth

Based on the earlier analysis, it can be stated that the RBV and TCT are comparable, i.e., they propose alternative assumptions about the structural elements of the growth process. Confronting these alternative approaches results in research problems that need a resolution (Table 8), since each perspective experiences skepticism regarding its major assumptions. These polemics are mutual, since the critiques of the RBV are founded on the assumptions of TCT and vice versa.

As discussed earlier, the RBV and TCT differently explain the major structural elements of the expansion process. The way they describe these elements reflects their overall approach to decision-making. Namely, the RBV represents the evolutionary and long-term perspective in which path dependence and learning play crucial roles, and in which history matters as a decisional context. This approach is descriptive and positive in explaining how decisions and actions should be pursued.

TCT is a structural and micro-analytical approach that uses the comparative analysis of governance modes to economize transaction costs (Langlois, 1992). The decisional context in this instance is formed by alternative governance modes and the criteria of their selection. This approach is prescriptive and normative in recommending how choices and actions should be implemented.

The different views demonstrated here raise important research problems that are relevant for theory and practice, not only because they are contradictory in explaining the behaviors of economic actors, including entrepreneurs. The structural elements perceived by entrepreneurs are by nature enabling constraints that generate decisions and actions in the entrepreneurial process. Therefore, they translate into a flow of observable events forming a history of the expansion process.

Confronting the assumptions of the theories about the motivations of economic agents raises an important problem of what drives the behaviors of high-growth entrepreneurs – trust or opportunism. From the point of view of TCT, the implications might be the costs of safeguards against possible opportunism and transaction costs stemming from the unfair behavior of contracting parties. The assumption of opportunism may predict a quite different contracting behavior compared to the context free of opportunism or regulated by trustful behavior. The proactive and value-oriented

Table 8. The RBV and TCT alternative approaches to the structural elements of the growth process and the resulting research problems

Elements of growth process	The resource-based view	Transaction cost theory	Research problems
Motives of economic agents	Motives free of opportunism; trust and mutuality dominate	Opportunism as self-interest seeking with guile	What drives behaviors of high-growth entrepreneurs – trust or opportunism?
Rationale	Value increase	Reduction of transaction costs out of organization	What is the rationale for pursuing growth – value or reduction of transaction costs?
Mechanisms	Resource exploitation (new activities related to and built upon the existing core competence); resource exploration (new activities unrelated to the existing core competence); matching the firm's competence with external opportunities	Discriminating alignment hypothesis – aligning characteristics of a particular transaction (activity) with the governance mode in order to optimize transaction costs	What is a mechanism of growth – is it aligning a new activity with the existing capabilities (especially the core competence) or aligning a new activity with the governance mode?
Modes (governance structures)	Organic (internal), external or hybrid growth (mergers and acquisitions) dependent on the consistency with a firm's core competence	Hierarchy (internalization) or hybrid growth dependent on the level of asset specificity, transaction frequency, and uncertainty	What are determinants of the growth mode (relatedness with the core competence or characteristics of the transaction)?
Decision-making perspective	The evolutionary and long-term perspective that involves both path dependence and learning; history forms a decisional context	A structural and micro-analytical approach based on the comparative analysis of governance modes; alternative governance modes and criteria of their selection form a decisional context	Is there a compatibility or discrepancy between evolutionary perspective and structural perspective on decision-making in the process of growth?

Source: own work.

rationale for growth may bring alternative investment choices and portfolio development rather than an adaptive rationale that merely aims at reducing transaction costs in the market exchanges. The entrepreneur's perception of the mechanism of growth may align a new activity with capabilities (the existing capabilities, especially the core competencies, or quite novel capabilities). Another option might align a new activity with the requirements of the business partner. The choice between the two attitudes is to focus on capabilities versus the requirements of a given transaction.

A further consequence is the governance mode for the growth pursuit. The adjustment to transaction characteristics provides either organizational hierarchy (internalization) or hybrids, depending on the level of asset specificity, the uncertainty, and the frequency of transacting with a given partner. The adjustment to capabilities results in the internalization or hybrids, depending on environment uncertainty as well as the availability of one's own resources and partners with complementary assets. Moreover, capability-driven modes of growth will include organic or acquisitive expansion, depending on relatedness with the core competence.

2.6. Empirical tests, theoretical advancements, and the convergence of the foci of the RBV and TCT

The alternative or even conflicting views of the RBV and TCT stimulated empirical research to test these perspectives. The first wave of empirical verifications was focused on checking the validity of each of these theories separately.

The empirical tests of TCT provided evidence of the impact of asset specificity and uncertainty, predominantly understood as opportunism, on managerial decisions about the firm's scope and size (Lafontaine & Slade, 2007; Klein, 2005; Shelanski & Klein, 1995; Lafontaine & Slade, 1997; 2001; Masten & Saussier, 2000; Rindfleisch & Heide, 1997; Shelanski, 1991). The early seminal research focused on the causes of increasing firm scope by vertical integration and confirmed the shortcomings of contracts and opportunism as determinants of backward integration (Klein, Crawford, & Alchian, 1978; Monteverde & Teece, 1982). The TCT explanations of supply chain management were initiated by Anderson and Schmittlein (1984), who proved the relevance of asset specificity, uncertainty, and opportunism in the choice of forward integration to marketing and distribution.

Other studies, such as Masten, Meehan, and Snyder (1991), focused on the costs of governance modes, including those misaligned with transaction characteristics (Sampson, 2004). Asset specificity was found to strongly affect the drafting and the costs of executing long-term contracts (Joskow, 1987; Lyons, 1994). Excessive complexity of the transaction results in adopting informal contracts rather than formal agreements (Joskow, 1987). Moreover, faced by incomplete contracts, the parties choose contract terms allowing for private ordering and dispute resolution as well as adaptation to changes instead of judicial resolutions (Goldberg & Ericsson, 1987).

The validity of asset specificity, contract complexity, and uncertainty was generally confirmed in the review by Lafontaine and Slade (2007). Similarly, Macher and Richman (2008) found support for asset specificity and opportunism as determinants of firm boundaries, while Rindfleisch et al. (2010) identified the relationship between opportunism and governance modes.

Still, there are reviews arguing that the findings about the validity of asset specificity and uncertainty are not fully convincing (David & Han, 2004). It is argued that company capabilities may moderate TCT variables and that the RBV approach needs to be adopted as complementary to transaction cost analysis (Williamson, 1999; Argyres & Zenger, 2012) or even replace it (Carter & Hodgson, 2006). When the capability and environmental conditions are unfavorable, the companies generally consider the threat of opportunism and the partner's bargaining power. This is specifically relevant to small and medium-sized companies that experience market pressure from large buyers and are vulnerable to external changes (Vervaal et al., 2010; Díez-Vial, 2010; Chandler, McKelvie, & Davidsson, 2009). There is also evidence that companies demonstrating well-developed capabilities are less vulnerable to the environment, including potential opportunism from suppliers and buyers (Shervani, Frazer, & Challagalla, 2007; Mayer & Salomon, 2006; Chandler, McKelvie, & Davidsson, 2009). Well-developed capabilities decrease the influence of asset specificity and opportunism on company decisions to integrate activities (to grow) or to outsource and cooperate (Barney, 1999). Those findings confirm the need to integrate the RBV and TCT in the studies on growth.

Finally, a more recent meta-analytical review by Combs et al. (2011) acknowledges strong support for the validity of both TCT and the RBV. At the same time, they explain the varying conclusions in the earlier studies by their methodological approach, namely vote counting instead of statistical meta-analysis.

The major critique about extant empirical studies referring to the RBV and TCT is that they do not sufficiently utilize the conceptual frameworks of these approaches (Tsang, 2006; Arend, 2006). The methodology adopted in the research studies is largely selective – focused on isolated factors and omitting, for instance, major behavioral assumptions and the investigation of their relationships as stated in the theory (Tsang, 2006).

The RBV approach enjoys wide recognition for its face validity and assumptions intuitively convincing to researchers and practitioners. The absence of limiting behavioral assumptions, such as opportunism in TCT, does
not raise controversies or resistance. These are probably reasons for limited
testing the RBV's validity compared to the research checking the validity of
transaction cost economics (Combs et al., 2011). Theoretical and empirical
achievements of this perspective were reviewed by Acedo, Barroso, and
Galan (2006), Arend (2006), Armstrong and Shimizu (2007), Arend and
Levésque (2010), Lockett, Thompson, and Morgenstern (2009), Newbert
(2007), and Combs et al. (2011). Most of these reviews focus on identifying major assumptions, developments, and trends within the RBV, such as
dynamic capabilities (Teece, Pisano, & Shuen, 1997; Teece 2007), absorptive
capacity (Cohen & Levinthal, 1990), relationship (Dyer & Singh, 1998; Lavie, 2006), and knowledge (Grant, 1996) approaches. They are less inclined
to question, test, or confirm the validity of this approach. Moreover, due
to the continued scarcity of deductive and systemized delivery of this theory,
the reviews are inductively oriented to accumulate the advancements in this
perspective (Acedo, Barroso, & Galan, 2006; Armstrong & Shimizu, 2007;
Lockett, Thompson, & Morgenstern, 2009).

Much rarer are critical reviews, such as Foss, Klein, Kor, and Mahoney
(2008), Kraaijenbrink, Spender, and Groen (2010), and Arend (2006). Even
fewer studies perform a systematic review to gather empirical tests of the validity of this approach or to evaluate the methodologies applied in these tests.
The research by Arend (2006), Newbert (2007), and Combs et al. (2011)
takes this scarcer approach and demonstrates an important evolution in synthesizing and making inferences from empirical tests of the RBV. Arend
(2006) questions the methodologies of the empirical support for the RBV,
pointing out that they do not properly reflect the underlying theoretical assumptions, but only invoke this theory as a context for their investigations.
Newbert (2007), in turn, finds limited empirical support for both the RBV
and TCT when comparing the percentage of studies supporting and not
supporting these theories with the use of significance tests.

Finally, taking a more refined, meta-analytical methodological approach,
Combs et al. (2011) propose that empirical support for the RBV and TCT
is strong, despite their alternative assumptions. The empirical support for
both competing theories suggests that they may be complementary under different conditions of firm capabilities and environmental influences.
Therefore, the current state of testing the validity of these theories does not
call for finding whether they hold, but under what conditions they hold. This

would require further research to identify adequate mediators and moderators of the RBV and TCT influence that represent these conditions to finally combine the perspectives into one consistent framework and develop a new theory (Combs et al., 2011; Leavitt, Mitchell, & Peterson, 2010).

The efforts to check the validity of both theories can be perceived as an evolution from testing the RBV and TCT individually to reviewing studies accumulating knowledge from individual tests, to studies that confront empirical evidence for both perspectives and call for further theoretical and empirical research to combine these theories. The present stage of the research aimed at integrating them explains the conditions under which they are valid rather than whether they are valid. Figure 3 reflects the evolution of the research testing the validity of the RBV and TCT, and it points to the outcomes generated by this research.

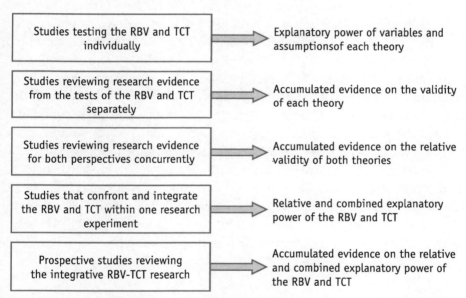

Figure 3. The evolution of the research testing the validity of the RBV and TCT and its results
Source: own work.

Methodologies that confront and integrate the RBV and TCT within one research experiment are increasingly adopted; still they represent a novel methodological approach. Studies reviewing the integrative RBV-TCT research are in the early stages. Probably due to the young and developing stream of research that integrates the RBV and TCT, there are no systematic reviews of such approaches published yet. Initial efforts in this area are delivered in conceptual papers based on narrative reviews and stylized approaches that accumulate knowledge from various achievements in this area, including both individual and integrative empirical tests, as well as review papers of various foci. Therefore, there is a research gap of integrative studies that would synthesize the relative and combined explanatory power of the RBV and TCT. However, a more evident research gap exists in the systematic review and synthesis of extant findings from the studies that integrate both approaches to explain firm size and scope, including growth.

The reported polemics about the theoretical and practical validity of the theories show that they are still in the process of developing and establishing consistency among their major constructs. Both theories have undergone an evolution of their focus and explanatory ambitions towards expanding their scope and power of generalizing. The evolution of the scope of the RBV explanatory ambitions from the theory of firm growth (Penrose, 1959), towards the theory of competitive advantage and performance (Hamel & Prahalad, 1990; Barney 1991; Amit & Schoemaker, 1993; Gautam, Barney, & Muhanna, 2004), to the theory of firm boundaries (Barney 1999; Ray, Xue, & Barney, 2013), and firm nature (Foss, 1993; Jacobides & Winter, 2007; Pitelis & Teece, 2009) means expanding its scope and power of generalizing. This development is driven by confronting the assumptions of the RBV with the more established transaction cost theory. TCT evolved in the opposite direction, from the theory of the firm (its nature and emergence) (Coase, 1937; Foss, 1993) and the theory of firm boundaries (scope and size) (Williamson, 1975; 1991; 1993; 2005; Klein, Crawford, & Alchian, 1978; Grossman & Hart, 1986), to the theory of performance and competitive advantage (Foss & Foss, 2008; Alvarez, 2007), and more recently towards the theory explaining growth (Chandler,

The expansion of the RBV's focus

1950s and 60s	Early 1990s	Late 1990s and early 2000s	2000 and later

→

Firm growth	Firm competitive advantage and performance	Firm boundaries (scope and size)	Firm nature

←

2000 and later	Early 2000s	1960s–1990s	1930s

Figure 4. The expansion and convergence of the theoretical foci of the RBV and TCT

Source: own work.

McKelvie, & Davidsson, 2009; Verwaal et al., 2010). Figure 4 presents the expansion and convergence of theoretical foci of the RBV and TCT where time spans indicate the launch of a particular focus.

Considering the evolution of the theoretical foci of the RBV and TCT presented in Figure 4, we observe a convergence of their scopes. They are currently adapted to the range of topics related to the theory of the firm, namely, its nature, competitive advantage and performance, boundaries (scope and size), and growth. The observed convergence of the research foci increases the capacity of these theories to comprehensively tackle the growth process phenomenon, which involves the increase of size and scope, i.e., expanding boundaries, and is motivated by performance (efficiency rationale) and competitive advantage.

3. THE INTEGRATIVE RBV-TCT APPROACH TO THE SME GROWTH PROCESS

3.1. Methodology for developing an integrative RBV-TCT framework of the growth process of SMEs

The justification for explaining the SME growth process through the lens of the integrative resource-based and transaction cost approaches was discussed in Section 2.1. However, the methodological question emerges about how to perform this integration. Considering the state of establishing the empirical validity of the both theories, the most suitable approach is a methodology of theory pruning (Leavitt, Mitchell, & Peterson, 2010; Shareff, 2007; Davis, 2006; Gancarczyk, 2015a; 2016). Theory pruning consists of reducing extant theories by confronting their assumptions and then combining them if they prove to be valid or rejecting them if they are not valid. This methodological concept and the related procedure resonate with the state of the art in the empirical studies synthesized by Combs et al. (2011). As reported above, they found both theories confirmed by empirical evidence and called for new research that would integrate them by using the contingencies under which they hold, as well as causal mechanisms that explain the predictions of these theories (Combs et al., 2011). Theory pruning involves two stages of analysis that include establishing the comparability of the theories and checking their validity to either reject inadequate approaches or to integrate them into one theoretical framework.

The first stage of the procedure aims to find whether the theories are comparable, i.e., they can be treated as alternative views of a particular phenomenon according to a set of criteria (Leavitt, Mitchell, & Peterson, 2010). This first stage has already been completed and positively verified in Sections 2.4, 2.5, and 2.6. Moreover, in Section 2.6 we found converging theoretical foci of these theories that support their comparability both in firm growth and in the broader themes of firm boundaries, competitive advantage, and performance. All these issues pertain to the growth process phenomenon, which involves size and scope increase, i.e., expanding boundaries, and is motivated by performance (efficiency rationale) and competitive advantage. The first stage of theory pruning emphasizes a similar focus of the theories, but examines their alternative views about the structural elements of the growth process.

The second stage of the procedure aims at assessing the compatibility of the two approaches towards company expansion in order to either reject one of them or to integrate them. Despite the views on the confirmed validity of both theories (c.f. Combs et al., 2011; Leiblein, 2003; Ray, Xue, & Barney, 2013), there are studies that assign them different explanatory power depending on some conditions of the firm's resources and the environment (Williamson, 1999; Mayer & Salomon, 2006; Chandler, McKelvie, & Davidsson, 2009; Ray, Xue, & Barney, 2013). This varying explanatory power can be delineated with the use of adequate moderators and mediators. The latter constructs denote the contingencies that affect which theory holds under what conditions and whether they are complementary. Moderator variables offer new control variables, such as the level of technology advancement, the quality of the institutional environment, and the access to scarce resources that might change the relationships among the major determinants by either affecting their strength or direction of influence. Moderators point to the conditions under which major theoretical variables hold, but they do not eliminate theories and their variables. Mediators, however, might eliminate theories or reduce some of their predictors (determinants and moderators). By nature, they mediate causal relationships by introducing a construct that explains why or how a specific dependence exists.

The compatibility of the theories has been recently established with the use of a qualitative meta-analytical approach or meta-synthesis by Gancarczyk (2015a; 2016b), resulting in a set of propositions regarding entrepreneurial decision-making in the growth process. Here we will report on this analysis and adopt its results for developing an integrative RBV-TCT theoretical framework of the SME growth process. This framework, in turn, will be verified in new empirical research.

The meta-analysis (Hoon, 2013; Sandelowski, Docherty, & Emden, 1997; Paterson et al., 2001; Weed, 2005) was conducted to synthesize the theoretical and empirical studies of the SME growth process and to test the RBV and TCT assumptions. The meta-analysis conducted by

Gancarczyk (2016b) referred not only to generalizing the research findings, but also to the methodologies used to operationalize the major variables of the TCT and RBV assumptions. This synthesis was not based on quantitative meta-analysis directed at aggregating effect size. Instead it aimed at an interpretive explanation based on aggregating primary evidence of both qualitative and quantitative studies (Hoon, 2013). The outcome of such a meta-synthesis is the identification of logics that emerge across the studies, together with the inclusion of the context (Yin, 2009). The contextualization in the studies considered was represented by moderators and mediators that affect the major variables and the assumptions of both theories.

The synthesis was based on a systematic and novel literature review in the area of firm boundaries that links the RBV and TCT. As noted in Section 2.6., the extant literature reviews predominantly only one of the approaches. The current stage of empirical advancements in testing the predictive value of the RBV and TCT proves that such studies are less relevant than confronting and integrating these approaches into one framework to develop a new theory (Combs et al., 2011; Leiblein, 2003; Ray, Xue, & Barney, 2013; Chandler, McKelvie, & Davidsson, 2009). Therefore, the synthesis from the systematic literature review did not aim to assess the individual validity of the theories but to check their compatibility. In particular, we were interested in the research that integrates the RBV and TCT into one methodological framework and in the possibilities to apply these findings to the explanation of the growth process.

The systematic review of the integrative RBV-TCT studies was focused on the boundary literature. Within this literature, growth is reflected in hierarchy development strategies such as vertical integration, diversification, market penetration, and development, or in hybrid modes such as franchising, joint ventures, licensing, and alliances. Recently, we observed successful attempts to apply the RBV (Davidsson, Steffens, & Fitzimmons, 2009; Garnsey, Stam, & Heffernan, 2010), and TCT (Chandler, McKelvie, & Davidsson, 2009) or both (Verwaal et al., 2010) to explain performance, processes, and modes of hierarchy and hybrid expansion. Therefore, we treat growth as a phenomenon that belongs to broader research on company boundaries; and we attempt to explain it by integrating the two theories, thus adopting a deductive approach to theory building. The boundary decisions refer to growth as well (Argyres & Zenger, 2012; Combs & Ketchen, 1999; Jacobides & Winter, 2007). Vertical integration and diversification often overlap in entrepreneurial decisions (Ray, Xue,

& Barney, 2013). Moreover, increasing the company's scope by product or service innovations is treated as a generic method of growth, valued even higher than expanding sales within the existing portfolio (Davidsson, Delmar, & Wiklund, 2006).

The qualitative meta-analysis was based on a systematic review of 29 empirical and 24 theoretical papers to get an overview of the methodologies, the constructs applied, and the findings. The detailed selection procedure was based on a replication of the methodology earlier elaborated by David and Han (2004), who assessed the empirical support for TCT, and Newbert (2007), who performed a similar review of the RBV. The search was performed in the largest accessible database, namely ABI Inform Complete. Due to the early endeavors to integrate the RBV and TCT for growth purposes, the reviewed literature relates predominantly to the wider issue of boundaries rather than growth exclusively. To control for the potential bias of relying on the search engine, the leading entrepreneurship and small business journals were searched manually for the evidence from the high-growth context. These periodicals included, among others, *Entrepreneurship Theory and Practice*, *Entrepreneurship and Regional Development*, *International Small Business Journal*, *Journal of Business Venturing*, *Journal of Small Business Management*, *Small Business Economics*, and *Strategic Entrepreneurship Journal*. The results were limited in numbers but considerable in the successful application of the Penrosian and RBV approaches (Garnsey, Stam, & Heffernan, 2006; Davidsson, Steffens, & Fitzsimmons, 2009), and of TCT with recommendations to combine this theory with the capability perspective (Chandler, McKelvie, & Davidsson, 2009). Finally, the integration of the RBV and TCT to explain hybrid expansion was performed by Verwaal et al. (2010).

Rigorous screening of the studies aimed at selecting only those that explicitly and systematically adopted both theories by testing their major variables and assumptions. The resulting collection of 29 empirical studies with differing methodologies enabled the qualitative (non-statistical) meta-analytical approach. This approach was based on extracting major themes and approaches and on the stylized synthesis of results. The stylized approach allowed for expanding the final sample of articles with 24 theoretical papers that integrated the RBV and TCT by using the same search procedure as employed for the empirical studies. The final sample of 53 papers represents the early stage of research in this area. However, it is sizable enough to provide a systematic qualitative analysis for future research directions (c.f. Hodgson & Carter, 2006 with 27 empirical studies for TCT).

Figure 5 presents a methodological procedure to develop a theoretical framework of the growth process of SMEs based on the integration of the RBV and TCT. The procedure is based on the theory pruning procedure combined with a systematic literature review. Its foundation is the results of the meta-synthesis performed earlier by Gancarczyk (2015a; 2015c; 2016).

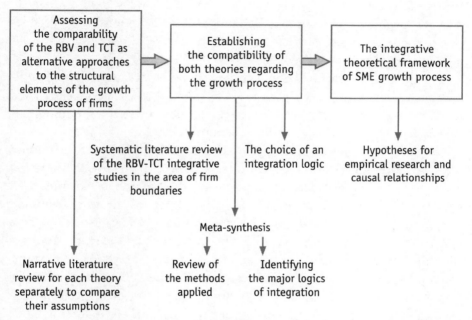

Figure 5. A methodological procedure to develop a theoretical framework of the growth process of SMEs based on the integration of the RBV and TCT

Source: own work.

The procedure starts with assessing the comparability of the RBV and TCT as alternative approaches to the structural elements of the growth process, already explained in Chapter 2. The establishment of compatibility of the RBV and TCT involves a systematic review of integrative RBV-TCT studies of firm boundaries; the qualitative meta-analysis that synthesizes the methodologies and results, and extracts the major logics for integrating the theories. The next step will include the choice of an integration logic to develop a theoretical framework to be verified by new empirical research. The resulting theoretical framework will encompass theory development and research hypotheses. The stage of establishing the compatibility of the two approaches will follow in the next sections.

3.2. The overview of the methodologies and results of the integrative RBV-TCT studies

In the first step of the meta-synthesis of the RBV-TCT literature, we focused on methodological considerations and the results of the studies reviewed (Gancarczyk, 2015a). *Within empirical studies in boundary decisions that explicitly integrate the RBV and TCT*, we sought to identify research problems, the major RBV and TCT assumptions and variables tested, moderators and mediators of their influence, and findings in terms of relative explanatory power (Table 9).

The general conclusions about the methodologies adopted in the empirical studies reviewed are like those of Tsang (2006) when he elucidated the empirical tests of transaction cost economics. There is a methodological variety of studies that challenges a comparative analysis. The studies do not adopt comprehensive sets of variables from both theories, but rather select the elements relevant to the problems investigated. The combination of theories is often imbalanced. The studies adopt one theory comprehensively and select some constructs from the other; at the start assuming the primacy of one of the approaches and testing moderating or catalyzing effects from the other. Another difficulty in comparing the study results is the differing operationalization of variables and assumptions. An example can be proxies for transaction costs, which are approached indirectly either as transaction characteristics without regard for the institutional environment or with explicit inclusion of this environment (Fabrizio, 2012; Brahm & Tarziján, 2014). Another major construct of TCT, asset specificity, appears as an individual variable (Leiblein & Miller, 2003) or as part of another crucial construct, e.g., uncertainty (Mayer & Salomon, 2006). The selective and varying adoption of theories is often caused by the restricted access to primary or secondary data to form proxies for the major variables.

This methodological variety impedes a quantitative analysis, but it is still sufficient to identify the evidence for variables and assumptions of the RBV and TCT with relatively high explanatory power as well as the relationships between the constructs of these perspectives.

Table 9. The empirical studies that integrate the RBV and TCT in exploring firm boundary decisions

Article	Research problem	Dependent variable(s)	Independent variable(s) RBV	Independent variable(s) TCT	Moderators /mediators	Main findings
Argyres & Silverman (2004)	Centralized or decentralized organization of an internal R&D structure	Type of innovation (performance measure)	Capability characteristics (firm-level factors such as diversification) – a significant control variable	Governance type (hierarchical or hybrid governance)	N/A	Centralized R&D governance generates a larger and broader impact on the technological development than decentralized governance, due to reduction of transaction costs of coordination. Capability-broadening search increases the range of technologies underpinning the innovations generated
Brahm & Tarziján (2014)	How the transaction cost and capabilities theories interact to explain 'make or buy' decisions	Vertical integration	Capabilities	Contractual hazards (temporal specificity, quality measurement, changes in law)	Contractor's productive capabilities	High transaction costs and high capabilities interact negatively in the explanation of vertical integration
Brewer, Ashenbaum, & Carter (2014)	Procurement outsourcing decisions	Scope of procurement outsourcing, performance of procurement outsourcing	Resource position	Opportunism potential	N/A	TCT through fear of opportunism as the primary driver of the extent of outsourcing. The RBV appears to be the primary determinant of the performance results of the outsourcing decision
Ceccagnoli et al. (2010)	The demand-side of technology outsourcing by integrating TCT with the analysis of internal R&D capabilities	Technology outsourcing	Internal R&D productivity	Co-specialized assets (asset specificity), transaction costs	N/A	Firms with relatively more co-specialized complementary assets or relatively strong internal R&D productivity have a lower propensity to source a technology

Article	Research problem	Dependent variable(s)	Independent variable(s) RBV	Independent variable(s) TCT	Moderators /mediators	Main findings
Chen & Chen (2002)	The choice of governance for international strategic alliances	Type of alliance governance	Resource dependency, resource complementarity	Asset specificity, technological and behavioral uncertainty	N/A	TCT explains the choice of alliances different from those explained by the RBV
Díez-Vial (2007)	Vertical boundaries of firms	The degree of vertical integration between two stages in the production process	Similarity between stages	Specific assets, measurement problems, demand uncertainty, technological uncertainty	N/A	Firms undertake vertical integration to reduce transaction costs between complementary and specific stages and to share internal capacities and knowledge among similar phases of the value chain. Transactional attributes are more relevant than capabilities in explaining firms' boundaries
Fabrizio (2012)	How firms' capabilities and institutional environments influence governance decisions	Vertical integration or external sourcing	Productive capabilities, prior contracting experience	Institutional safeguards	Capabilities, transaction costs	The impact of firm capabilities on governance varies with the level of transaction costs, which is itself a function of the institutional environment
Forlani, Parthasarathy, & Keaveney (2008)	How ownership control and firm capability interact to affect the amount of risk associated with international entry-modes	The risk associated with governance modes		Governance type	Firm capability	Managers associate different risks with different governance modes depending on the level of firm capabilities. The decisions about international entry risk and governance are jointly influenced by transaction cost and resource-based factors

Article	Research problem	Dependent variable(s)	Independent variable(s) RBV	Independent variable(s) TCT	Moderators /mediators	Main findings
Glaister (2004)	The rationale to form international equity joint ventures	International equity joint ventures	Capability factors	Transaction cost factors	N/A	Both transaction cost and resource-based views influence decisions on joint ventures; the theories are complementary rather than substitute for each other
Gulati, Lawrence, & Puranam (2005)	Adaptation in vertical relationships	Procurement mode Performance of procurement mode	Differentiation, reciprocal task interdependence	Transaction instability	N/A	Performance differences of procurement modes depend on the fit between adaptive capacity and adaptation requirements and not only on the match between governance and transaction hazards
Jacobides & Hitt (2005)	How productive capability differences shape vertical scope	Vertical integration	Productive capabilities	Transaction costs	Transaction costs	Transactional logic may partly explain the boundary decisions, but capability considerations dominate
Kumar (2010)	What factors influence differential wealth gains and private benefits from joint ventures	Wealth gains, private benefits from joint ventures (performance measures)	Value of resources, scope of joint venture, joint venture capabilities	Appropriability regime, bargaining power	Firm's ability to extract private benefits	Both resource-based and transaction cost factors are relevant for extracting benefits from joint ventures
Lai & Chang (2010)	The relationship between corporate motivation and governance structure and the performance of R&D alliances of SMEs	Performance R&D alliances	Intangible resource, complementary resource	Uncertainty, specificity of transaction objective	Types of governance structure, corporate capabilities are non-significant	Positive and significant relationships between corporate motivation derived both from the RBV and TCT on the performance of R&D alliances in SMEs

Article	Research problem	Dependent variable(s)	Independent variable(s) RBV	TCT	Moderators /mediators	Main findings
Leiblein & Miller (2003)	Firm boundaries in high-technology industries	Vertical integration	Experience in the production process or experience in outsourcing, the scope of the portfolio	Asset specificity, demand uncertainty	N/A	Governance of production decisions is strongly influenced by both transaction and firm-level effects
Lo, Frias, & Ghosh (2012)	Governance in interfirm relationships	Type of governance, conditions of contracting (price negotiation)	Realized differentiation, brand strength	Interface complexity, technological uncertainty, vendor's specific investments	N/A	Parties create value through the partner-specific investment and coordination activities and through the employment of heterogeneous, firm-specific resources. Governance structures reflect a discriminating alignment with these two forms of value-creating capabilities
Mayer & Salomon (2006)	The impact of technological capabilities and contractual hazards on governance	Internal governance, market governance	Technological capabilities (governance capabilities)	Contractual hazards (hold-up from asset specificity, appropriability, and observability problems)	N/A	TCT and the RBV variables have independent and joint effects on governance decisions. Strong technological capabilities lower transaction costs and enable choosing the market instead of internalization
Majocchi, Mayrhofer, & Camps (2013)	Factors affecting the choice between joint ventures and non-equity alliances in foreign market entry	Alliance mode choice	Firm-specific characteristics	Host country institutional characteristics (legal protection and appropriability hazards)	N/A	Firm size (potential) and institutional and political factors confirmed as significant determinants of alliance mode choice in SMEs

Article	Research problem	Dependent variable(s)	Independent variable(s) RBV	Independent variable(s) TCT	Moderators /mediators	Main findings
Murphy et al. (2012)	How entrepreneurial firms can better procure and benefit from outsourcing arrangements.	Outsourcing mode and benefits	Resources (valuable, rare, imperfectly imitable, non-substitutable)	Asset specificity, uncertainty, infrequency	N/A	Both the RBV, TCT, and the resource-dependence theory highlight the choice of modes for and benefits from outsourcing in SMEs
Mutinelli & Piscitello (1998)	The influence of firm-specific assets and transaction cost factors on the firm's international entry mode	Foreign entry mode	Firm-specific assets (size, international experience, product differentiation)	Uncertainty (legal barriers, country risk, information costs, information asymmetry)	N/A	Both capability-based and transaction cost factors justify the use of joint ventures as a favorable entry mode
Ordanini & Silvestri (2008)	Determinants of outsourcing decisions on recruitment and selection	The intensity of HR recruitment and selection activities	Competitive motivations	Efficiency drivers	Types of processes outsourced	TCT predictors more important for outsourcing standard (administrative) HR activities; the RBV predictors more important for strategic HR activities
Poppo & Zenger (1995)	To test competing theoretical explanations for make-or-buy decisions in the computer companies	Performance of governance types, likelihood of governance types	Magnitude of skill set	Asset specificity, ease of performance measurement	N/A	Strong support for TCT assumptions about asset specificity and opportunism in the governance decisions. The RBV assumptions partially supported by the importance of extensive skill set for outsourcing
Ray, Xue, & Barney (2013)	How IT capital moderates dependence between asset type and vertical integration and diversification	Vertical integration, Diversification	Narrowly and broadly valuable assets	Transaction cost (indirectly invoked)	IT capital	For resources with a narrow application, IT capital decreases the company scope (support for TCT), for resources with a broad application, IT capital increases the firm scope (support for the RBV)

Article	Research problem	Dependent variable(s)	Independent variable(s)		Moderators /mediators	Main findings
			RBV	TCT		
Ryoo (2012)	Conditions of the governance choice for technology sourcing in high-tech SMEs	The internal or external governance for technology sourcing	Technological capability, entrepreneurial strategic orientation	Specialized asset investment, technological uncertainty, environmental uncertainty		The RBV predictions valid for the choices of governance in small high-tech firms. TCT predictions were not confirmed in this setting (integration was adopted contrary to its assumptions on the influence of uncertainty and asset specificity
Silverman (1999)	Technological resource as a determinant of the direction of diversification	Type of industries to which the company diversifies	Existing technological resources	Contractual hazards	N/A	TCT and the RBV demonstrate strong complementarities. Firms diversify based on the relative applicability of the existing resources to new businesses (related diversification)
Steensma & Corley (2001)	Firm boundaries for technology sourcing (licensing and acquisition).	Licensing or acquisition in technology sourcing	Opportunity for sustainable advantage	Threat of opportunism	Management stockholdings, firm risk perception, slack resources	TCT better holds when management stockholdings are low and slack resource is high. The RBV plays a larger role when a slack resource is low and firm is risk-oriented
Safizadeh et al. (2008)	Vertical integration or outsourcing related to the back-office operations	Vertical integration	Competency in the process, tacit-knowledge-based and interdependent tasks	Uncertainty from asset specificity, opportunism	N/A	Predictions from both theories supported
Schilling & Steensma (2002)	What factors influence technology sourcing decisions	Acquisition, licensing	Potential for competitive advantage affected by technology attributes	Opportunism as influenced by technology attributes	N/A	The RBV explains why a firm pursues particular resources rather than others, but TCT explains the governance mode undertaken for accessing these resources

Article	Research problem	Dependent variable(s)	Independent variable(s) RBV	Independent variable(s) TCT	Moderators /mediators	Main findings
Tseng & Chen (2013)	The influence of transaction cost factors and the moderating influence of firm capability on the extent of outsourcing	Domestic outsourcing	International experience, subsidiary scale	Environmental dynamism, technology level	Firm capabilities	Technology level and subsidiary scale negatively related with outsourcing. The capability factors can reduce transaction costs and increase outsourcing
Verwaal et al. (2010)	The relationship between firm size and hybrid governance in venture capital firms	Syndication frequency (adoption of alliances)	Capabilities	Adaptive coordination efficiency	Resource access needs, resource access capabilities	Small firms have higher access needs and higher capability advantage in efficient coordination of hybrid governance. Large firms demonstrate higher resource access capabilities and experience higher transaction costs of coordinating alliances

Source: own work.

The main dependent variables refer to the firm scope and size and are mostly vertical integration (acquisition or internal development) or outsourcing and diversification. There are also studies that investigate hybrid forms of governance regarding alliances (alliance type and performance as focal points) (Chen & Chen, 2002; Lo, Frias, & Ghosh, 2012). The main TCT determinant is uncertainty as an aggregate construct that comprises technological and environmental uncertainty, closely linked to contractual hazards (covering asset specificity, measurement, and appropriability problems) and opportunism. Another major independent variable of TCT is asset specificity, either researched independently or as a part of contractual hazards. Opportunism and transaction costs are less likely to be directly measured variables; however, they are present as reference categories in all the articles. Overall, uncertainty appears to be the broadest concept that involves ambiguity from contractual hazards and environmental dynamism, including partner opportunism, and that eventually results in transaction costs.

The main independent variables representing the RBV are capabilities and competitive advantage. Capabilities is the main, general category encompassing resources, competencies, and activities; they cover a wide variety of components and thus they are either broadly or narrowly defined. Their specific kind is represented by governance capabilities that control transactions (Mayer & Salomon, 2006). As for individual components of capabilities, we observe different characteristics of resources (resource dependency, resource complementarity, access to resources, subsidiary scale, technology uniqueness and inimitability, the scope of the existing portfolio, technological resources, and resource value). Furthermore, competencies and activities involve proficiency in a particular resource, reciprocal task interdependence, tacit-knowledge-based and interdependent tasks, and experience in production or outsourcing. Value and opportunity for competitive advantage are the major reference categories, i.e., they hardly exist as measured variables, but they are present indirectly in the theory and final interpretations. Value is either not reflected in the variables or reflected indirectly as performance. Competitive advantage remains a reference category in most of the articles, but it is not likely to be specified as an independent variable. Instead, there are the concepts of opportunity for sustainable advantage, differentiation, and resource position.

There are also interdependencies or convergences among TCT and the RBV notions and variables, such as firm specificity (firm-specific, complementary, and interdependent core-related assets) and transaction specificity (transaction specific assets), which are often, and at least to some extent, understood as synonymous and having similar impact on the company scope (Poppo & Zenger, 1995). The evidence of this convergence is combining the categories of firm-specific and transaction-specific factors into one set of variables (technology uniqueness and barriers to its imitation) in order to test both TCT and RBV predictions (Schilling & Steensma, 2002).

All the studies report findings that demonstrate complementarities between the theories and their compatibility. A majority of them attribute the similar predictive power to the RBV and to TCT factors or their individual explanatory roles, while some research points to one of the approaches as more powerful (Poppo & Zenger, 1995; Jacobides & Hitt, 2005; Jacobides & Winter, 2005; Díez-Vial, 2007). The latter results may, however, be also affected by the study design, in which one of the theories is treated as the focal framework, and the other one is added to act as a moderator. We observe that either the RBV capabilities act as moderators of the impact of the TCT determinants (Jacobides & Winter, 2005; Tseng & Chen, 2013) or that TCT determinants act as moderators of the impact of the RBV variables (Jacobides & Hitt, 2005; Jacobides & Winter, 2005; Fabrizio, 2012). Other moderators that affect the strength of the assumptions tested include IT capital (Ray, Xue, & Barney, 2013), management stockholdings, firm risk perception, and slack resource availability (Steensma & Corley, 2001). We can also identify moderators as contexts in which the predictive power of the two theories differ. In the case of operational processes, TCT assumptions on size and scope hold, while in the case of strategic processes, the RBV demonstrates stronger validity (Ordanini & Silvestri, 2008). The low level of slack resources and risk-orientation form a context in which the RBV proves valid, while for low level of management stockholdings and high slack resources, TCT prevails (Steensma & Corley, 2001). We can state that the contexts mentioned denote the firm's capabilities and these are widely used as moderators of governance determinants. As a mediator of relationships between the theories, the one proposed is productive capabilities (Brahm & Tarziján, 2014). Overall, the capabilities play a special role in the study designs, acting as determinants, moderators, and mediators.

The complementarity of RBV and TCT is evidenced by both independent and joint effects of variables and assumptions. The interesting results are yielded by the investigation of joint effects, when one of the predictors moderates the influence of another, such as strong technological capabilities lowering transaction costs and enabling managers to choose the market instead of internalization (Mayer & Salomon, 2006). This interaction between capabilities, transaction costs, and value creation, earlier theorized by Foss and Foss (2005), is also explored in other articles. The dynamic feedback relationship between transaction costs and capabilities can be found in Fabrizio (2012). Namely, lower transaction costs allow for productive capabilities to act as a determinant; higher transaction costs will limit the influence of productive capabilities on transaction costs. According to Tseng and Chen (2013), capability factors can reduce transaction costs, thus increasing the possibility of outsourcing. Brahm and Tarziján (2014) state that high transaction costs and high capabilities interact negatively in the explanation of vertical integration.

When analyzing the theoretical papers, we focused on the arguments in favor of combining the theories and on the ways they are combined to form a ground for a new theory. The theoretical studies in the sample researched (Table 10) are all narrative reviews, and none of them was found by the use of a systematic literature search.

Table 10. The theoretical studies that integrate the RBV and TCT in exploring firm boundary decisions

Article	Research problem	Main findings
Argyres & Zenger (2012)	A strategic theory of firm boundary choices that relies on both the RBV and TCT	Both perspectives are intertwined and separating them is misleading. Boundary decisions are determined by unique complementarity among assets and activities
Combs & Ketchen (1999)	Interfirm cooperation and its performance implications	Resource-abundant firms used cooperation only when it was helpful to minimize governance costs. Low resource firms cooperated regardless of their exchange conditions; resources took primacy over exchange conditions
Conner & Prahalad (1996)	A resource-based – knowledge-based theory of the firm	Knowledge-based considerations can prevail over opportunism in establishing the governance
Foss & Foss (2005)	Relationships between transaction costs and value creation and appropriation	The ability to create, appropriate, and sustain value depends on the property rights and the transaction costs of executing property rights
Holcomb & Hitt (2007)	Conditions leading to strategic outsourcing	A model of strategic outsourcing that adopts transaction- and capability-based factors
Ireland, Hitt, & Vaidyanath (2002)	Management of strategic alliances	Alliance management presented as a source of competitive advantage with the use of TCT, social network theory, and the RBV
Jacobides & Winter (2005)	Boundary decisions (vertical scope) in the industry	Theoretical framework explaining co-evolution of capabilities with transaction costs in determining vertical scope in the industry
Jacobides (2008)	Vertical scope determinants	The model suggesting how capabilities and transaction costs affect the scope of firms

Article	Research problem	Main findings
Kim & Mahoney (2006)	The influence of IT technology on the governance of vertically integrated firms	Relation-specific IT system determines inter-firm governance due to sunk costs and leads to less vertical integration and a smaller number of suppliers
Kulkarni & Ramamoorthy (2005)	The firm's choice of employment contracts	A typology of employment contracts by distinguishing two types of human asset specificity (both theories applied)
Langlois (1992)	The theory of firm boundaries with the inclusion of time	Dynamic transaction costs as an explanation of vertical integration
Leiblein (2003)	How the choice of governance affects the creation and appropriation of value	A set of propositions about the integration of the RBV, TCT, and real options theory with the use of value creation and appropriation
Lepak & Snell (1999)	The choice of employment modes	The proposition of employment modes and their determinants
Madhok & Tallman (1998)	The explanation of the failure of collaborative relations and to manage them	The proposal of the process of governance instead of governance mode; understanding of transaction-specific and relationship-specific expenditures as an investment in future value rather than cost
Madhok (1997)	Foreign entry modes	Vale as a primary determinant of the foreign entry mode over transaction cost explanations
Madhok (2002)	Institutional structure of production (vertical scope)	A triangular alignment proposed between the governance structure, transaction, and resource attributes in setting up the vertical scope and the role of firm identity and strategy in this alignment emphasized
Mahoney (2001)	A theory of sustainable rents	The resource-based theory of the firm should not ignore the assumption of opportunism
McIvor (2009)	The evaluation of outsourcing decision	Variables of both theories are applicable in decisions on outsourcing; however, firms can also make outsourcing decisions based on only one of the approaches
Meyer, Wright, & Pruthi (2009)	Knowledge management in foreign entry strategies	The RBV approach complement TCT in explaining knowledge management in foreign entry strategies; value as a primary driver of entry
Pitelis & Pseiridis (1999)	The RBV and TCT are alternative approaches to the theory of the firm	The integrative framework proposed that includes resource value perspective dynamic transaction costs
Pitelis & Teece (2009)	The nature and essence of the firm	Transaction cost and property right theories integrated into a more general, capability-based theory
Tsang (2000)	The formation of joint ventures	Both perspectives synthesized to recognize both transaction costs and benefits (value) in the explanation of joint ventures
Williamson (1999)	Determinants business strategy	The combination of both theories proposed; the RBV can complement TCT by pointing to the context of firm capabilities
Zajac & Olsen (1993)	The explanation of inter-organizational strategies	The proposal of a transactional value instead of transaction costs

Source: own work.

The analysis of the argumentation yields the logics that resonate with the conclusions from the overview of empirical papers. Namely, the integration adopts the following logics: the additive and converging logic (balancing the theories as equivalent and complementary, sometimes with reduction, replacement, or convergence of major constructs and assumptions); the logic of structural problem-solving (integration through assigning them a predictive power for separate structural elements of the growth process with the use of moderators), and the evolutionary logic (by dynamic integration with the use of evolution as a mediator) (Gancarczyk, 2015c).

3.3. The logics of integrating the RBV and TCT and the choice of the logic relevant for explaining the SME growth process

Three logics of integrating the RBV and TCT were recently identified by Gancarczyk (2015c). Here a discussion of these approaches is provided to form a ground and a justification for the selection of the integration logic to be applied in the theoretical model of the SME growth process and subsequent empirical research. The identification of the logic was based on a systematic review of the empirical and theoretical literature which was later processed with the use of a qualitative meta-analysis, i.e., meta-synthesis or meta-interpretation (Hoon, 2013; Sandelowski, Docherty, & Emden, 1997; Paterson et al., 2001; Weed, 2005). The synthesis was based on identifying the major themes and findings about the joint and individual explanatory power of both theories, grouping studies consistent with these views, and structuring the research evidence they provided (Hoon, 2013). According to the methodology of integrating theories (Leavitt, 2010), adequate mediators and moderators serve as constructs in combining existing theories and generating a new one. Theoretical studies predominantly introduce some mediating and moderating constructs to perform integration, even when they do not indicate this operation explicitly. Empirical studies directly declare the introduction of these kinds of variables and subsume their explanatory power.

The additive and converging logic consists of combining the main variables of the two theories into one research scheme and the replacement or convergence of some concepts and notions. The justification for this method is a need for a comprehensive framework to inform decision-making in firm boundaries, including growth (Conner & Prahalad, 1996; Kulkarni & Ramamoorthy, 2005; McIvor, 2009; Holcomb & Hitt, 2007). In the theoretical studies on firm boundaries, the RBV and TCT are considered different but complementary views that offer a more inclusive set of variables to be matched within one decision context. Combining the main variables of the two theories into one research scheme assumes their equal importance, and it is deemed necessary to avoid improper choices, since both transaction costs and value creation should be considered (Kulkarni & Ramamoorthy, 2005; Holcomb & Hitt, 2007). Therefore, capabilities and their role in creating value are jointly considered with the uncertainty that results in transaction costs (Conner & Prahalad, 1996; Tsang, 2000; Holcomb & Hitt, 2007). The operation of combining the variables of both theories is probably best reflected in decision matrices that serve governance choices (Lepak & Snell, 1999; Kulkarni & Ramamoorthy, 2005; McIvor, 2009; Holcomb & Hitt, 2007). Entrepreneurs growing their businesses need to consider both approaches, since they offer insights for both strategic and operational issues (Foss & Foss, 2005; 2008; Pitelis & Teece, 2009; Pitelis & Pseiridis, 1999). The RBV gives a ground for strategic and creative decisions about new products and markets to create value in the long run (Conner & Prahalad, 1996; Pitelis & Teece, 2009; Pitelis & Pseiridis, 1999; Mahoney, 2001). TCT offers guidance as to operational and ongoing choices directed at efficiency attainment with existing alternatives in the form of accessible resources and markets (Mahoney, 2001; Pitelis & Teece, 2009). Value development, exploitation, and protection are conditioned by the effective management of uncertainty and the resulting transaction costs (Argyres & Zenger, 2012; Foss & Foss, 2008).

The methodologies of the empirical studies reflect the logic of combining the major constructs of the RBV and TCT. These studies underline the validity of both theories in resolving specific problems of firm scope and size (Silvermann, 1999; Leiblein & Miller, 2003; Meyer & Salomon, 2006; Ray, Xue, & Barney, 2013; Safizadeh et al., 2008). A differing focus of the RBV and TCT regarding strategic and operational decisions is reflected in Ordanini and Silvestri (2008), who investigated strategic and operational outsourcing. There are also findings pointing to the superiority of one approach, such as Díez-Vial (2007), Poppo and Zenger (1995), as well as Brewer, Ashenbaum, & Carter (2014) for TCT in determining governance choices. In this research evidence, the capabilities serve as a complementary factor that explains the performance and results of governance structures. On the other hand, some researchers (Jacobides & Hitt, 2005;

Mutinelli & Piscitello, 1998) find the capability perspective to be more relevant for determining firm boundaries. As indicated in these differing results, a dominance of one approach does not completely preclude the influence of the other that proposes a different focus in the process of making entrepreneurial and managerial choices.

Besides the above additive approach that gathers the major constructs from both theories, tests them, and develops a new, more comprehensive theory, there are also convergences of the alternative constructs. This often leads to reducing or replacing some variables of one of the approaches. As an example, transaction costs are acknowledged to be valid, but are determined by tacit knowledge instead of opportunism (Conner & Prahalad, 1996; Madhok, 1997; Mahoney, 2001). It can be posited that the latter view uses knowledge creation and flow as a mediator to combine the theories and explain their joint influence on boundary decisions. Zajac & Olsen (1993) proposed transactional value instead of transaction costs to highlight the nature of inter-organizational relationships. The alignment hypothesis was modified to acknowledge capabilities as independent variables, replacing transaction characteristics in governance choices (Kulkarni & Ramamoorthy, 2005; Meyer, Wright, & Pruthi, 2009).

The convergence among the alternative constructs is reflected in the notions of firm specificity (firm-specific, complementary, and interdependent core-related assets) instead of transaction specificity (transaction-specific assets) or in treating these constructs interchangeably (Poppo & Zenger, 1995; Schilling & Steensma, 2002).

Overall, the logic of adding, matching, and converging the RBV and TCT variables results in the following conclusions:

Decisions on scope and size are jointly determined by both approaches. The entrepreneurs and managers pursuing growth consider concurrently both groups of determinants. Namely, their choices are based on the assessment of the firm's capabilities relative to the environmental uncertainty, and the value from growth relative to the transaction costs associated with a specific boundary problem (Gancarczyk, 2015c; 2016).

The logic of structural problem-solving establishes a division of roles between the RBV and TCT in responding to specific problems of firm boundaries (Williamson, 1999). As per several theoretical studies, the RBV is best suited to address why a specific strategy is established (Conner & Prahalad, 1996; Leiblein, 2003; Ireland, Hitt, & Vaidyanath, 2002). It does so by providing the rationale of value and by highlighting the motives that direct behaviors of business partners as trust and mutuality rather than opportunism.

TCT addresses how the strategy is pursued by proposing mechanisms and modes. Namely, it points to the mechanism of discriminating the alignment hypothesis linking transaction characteristics with discrete governance modes to economize transaction costs. Moreover, it provides the determinants of asset specificity and uncertainty to choose the governance mode (Leiblein, 2003; Pitelis & Teece, 2009; Argyres & Zenger, 2012).

A perspective that dominates the context of why or how problems is still moderated by the variables of the alternative view. The strategic rationale of value is moderated by transaction cost and uncertainty considerations (Conner & Prahalad, 1996; Madhok, 1997; Foss & Foss, 2005; Pitelis & Teece, 2009; Meyer, Wright, & Pruthi, 2009). Governance capabilities act as moderators of the transaction cost impact on the boundary decisions (Mayer & Salomon, 2006; Tseng & Chen, 2013; Ray, Xue, & Barney, 2013; Steensma & Corley, 2001; Kumar, 2010; Verwaal et al., 2010). The alignment hypothesis provides a method of determining whether to adopt hierarchy or hybrid modes. The choice between organic and acquisitive growth needs to be performed based on the alignment with core-competence, a concept provided by the RBV (Kim & Mahoney, 2006; Conner & Prahalad, 1996; Madhok, 1997; Foss & Foss, 2005; Pitelis & Teece, 2009; Meyer, Wright, & Pruthi, 2009). Organic (internal) growth results from developing core-related activities, i.e., from their alignment with core competence, based on the exploitation approach. Acquisitive (external) growth is an outcome of exploring new activities, unrelated with the present core competence.

In the empirical studies, the RBV was found relevant for explaining why particular allocative decisions take place, while the TCT approach proved to be useful in explaining how the governance mode was chosen to develop particular assets (Schilling & Steensma, 2002). The studies that highlight the "why" dimension underline the dominance of the RBV's rationales, such as value, performance, and competitive advantage (Table 9, c.f. Brewer, Ashenbaum, & Carter, 2014; Ceccagnoli, 2010; Gulati, Lawrence, & Puranam, 2005; Jacobides & Hitt, 2005; Lo, Frias, & Ghosh, 2012; Poppo & Zenger, 1995; Silverman, 1999; Schilling & Steensma, 2002). As TCT constructs, asset specificity as well as behavioral and environmental uncertainty appropriately predict how the governance mode is established (Table 9, c.f. Brahm & Tarzíjan, 2014; Brewer, Ashenbaum, & Carter, 2014; Lai & Chang 2010; Ceccagnoli & Salamon, 2006; Chen & Chen, 2002; Díez-Vial, 2007; Fabrizio, 2012; Gulati, Lawrence, & Puranam, 2005). At the same time, the theory dominating in a specific decisional domain is found to be moderated by the factors of the alternative approach.

Consequently, capabilities versus transaction costs and uncertainty mutually moderate each other (Table 9, c.f. Tseng & Chen, 2013; Ray, Xue, & Barney, 2013; Steensma & Corley, 2001; Kumar, 2010; Verwaal et al., 2010; Mutinelli & Piscitello, 1998; Fabrizio, 2012; Jacobides & Hitt, 2005).

Considering the reasoning about the foci of the RBV and TCT, these theories address core problems of the process approach, namely, why and how specific decisions take place. The "why" dimension, in which the RBV dominates, incorporates motives and rationale. The "how" dimension refers to mechanisms and modes applied in boundary decisions. This division of explanatory roles does not mean a separation of the theories. They can be integrated by using the process mediator that embraces these "why" and "how" dimensions. The process dimensions act as mediators to explain the theoretical and practical validity of the RBV and TCT in specific decisional contexts.

The logic of division of roles and differing explanatory power between the theories considered provides the following conclusions (Gancarczyk, 2015c; 2016):

The RBV explains entrepreneurial and managerial decisions on "why" issues related to firm boundaries, with the moderating impact of TCT. Namely, trust-mutuality relations and value increase represent the dominant motive and rationale in making governance choices moderated by uncertainty and transaction cost considerations.

TCT explains entrepreneurial and managerial decisions about "how" to establish firm boundaries, but the moderating effects from the RBV should also be acknowledged. Namely, the growth mechanism follows the alignment of the governance mode with transaction characteristics and capability characteristics.

In particular, the choice between the hierarchy and hybrid modes is determined by asset specificity, uncertainty, and transaction frequency with moderating effects from the firm's capabilities. The choice between organic and acquisitive governance depends on the relatedness of a given transaction (business activity) with the core competencies of a firm.

The evolutionary logic proposes a dynamic integration that takes co-evolution as a mediator of the joint explanatory power of the RBV and TCT. During the evolution of the life cycle of the firm, capabilities and transaction costs interact and mutually stimulate each other (Jacobides & Winter, 2005; Pitelis & Teece, 2009). Determining firm boundaries and pursuing its growth is an evolutionary and learning process. The following causal relationships can be inferred. Transaction costs affect the choice of governance mode, which may be a market, hierarchy, or hybrid structure. The governance arrangements, specifically knowledge governance associated with a specific mode, influence the development of capabilities (Madhok & Tallman, 1998; Madhok, 2002). For example, there can be hierarchical or hybrid structures of R&D functions that impact the breadth of innovation (Argyres & Silverman, 2004). Transaction costs are treated as semi-exogenous, being dependent on transaction characteristics, but also depend on firm capabilities (Pitelis & Pseiridis, 1999; Zajac & Olsen, 1993). Governance capabilities (Dyer & Singh, 1998; Argyres & Liebeskind, 1999; Madhok, 2002), contribute to relational capital or transactional value (Madhok & Tallman, 1998; Zajac & Olsen, 1993). However, governance capabilities also affect transaction costs, and when there is high asset specificity, they enable hybrid governance instead of internalization. The feedback relationships between capabilities and transaction costs culminate in dynamic transaction costs (Nooteboom, 1992; Langlois, 1992). These acknowledge historical experience and learning, which is opposite to the original static and micro-analytic stance of TCT (Langlois, 1992; Pitelis & Pseiridis, 1999; Zajac & Olsen, 1993). To sum up, firm capabilities and transaction costs interact in the process of firm development and growth, provide for heterogeneity among companies, and jointly affect value creation and competitive advantage (Foss & Foss, 2005).

The evidence from empirical studies verifies the feedback loops between capabilities, transaction costs, and learning effects that impact firm growth and its eventual boundaries. The type of foreign entry governance implies the possibility of knowledge development with moderating effects from transaction costs raised by information asymmetry and partner opportunism. Due to the superior capabilities that decrease transaction costs, market or hybrid governance can be an accessible alternative to hierarchy governance (Mayer & Salomon, 2006; Tseng & Chen, 2013). Minor transaction costs enable the capabilities to become a determining factor of governance choice, while significant transaction costs prevent the capabilities from affecting this choice (Jacobides & Hitt, 2005; Fabrizio, 2012). Brahm and Tarziján (2014) posit that high transaction costs and high capabilities substitute for each other and interact negatively in the explanation of vertical integration.

The above synthesis enables the following conclusions (Gancarczyk, 2015c; 2016):

In the long-term and evolutionary perspective, an interaction can be observed between the firm's capabilities and transaction costs in shaping firm boundaries. Namely, transaction costs moderated by the capabilities influence the choice of governance mode. The governance mode impacts the learning processes and how capabilities develop to further affect the level of transaction costs. Therefore, the attainment of value creation is a joint effect of the capabilities and transaction costs as determinants of firm boundaries and growth.

The three logics of integrating the RBV and TCT in the literature on firm boundaries are summarized in Table 11.

The additive and converging logic adopts the RBV and TCT variables as main decisional criteria based on matching them within one experiment. In this regard, it tests the explanatory power of these theories in a specific setting. Another possibility employed in this approach is to converge some alternative notions by treating them as equivalents (such as firm specific assets and transaction specific assets; adopting alignment logic for both theories) as well as substituting alternative variables (tacit knowledge instead of opportunism as a determinant of governance modes). In these cases, there are interesting new theoretical concepts. However, some of the original, empirically confirmed predictors of the RBV and TCT are lost in the decision-making process. Therefore, in its additive format, this logic is comprehensive in compiling the major alternative variables. However, it is directed at testing the theories rather than exploring specific boundary problems. In its converging and reducing or/and replacing format, this logic explores some new theoretical propositions but loses its comprehensiveness.

The evolutionary logic covers a long-term approach to entrepreneurial decision-making that acknowledges feedback relationships among transaction costs, governance, capabilities, and value from growth. It offers an adequate metaphorical reflection of the dynamics of the process approach to setting boundaries and pursuing the growth of firms. Moreover, it is comprehensive and nuanced enough, since it embraces the major theoretical constructs of both theories, their causal relations, and feedback effects among these constructs. On the other hand, this approach to integration is difficult to operationalize and explore in-depth in empirical research. It operates at high levels of abstraction and metaphorical description, thus losing a clear decision-making orientation. This abstraction is partially caused by the exclusive focus on impersonal processes and interdependencies and not on an individual agent's (entrepreneur's) perceptions and decisions in these processes. As a result, the normative value and practical implications of this approach remain unclear.

Table 11. Three logics of integrating the RBV and TCT in the boundary literature

Type of integrative logics	Syntheses of the logics	Mediator for integrating the theories	Assessment of the relevance for the firm's growth process
The additive and converging logic combines the main variables of the two theories into one research scheme, replaces and/or converges some concepts and notions. Types of decisions are proposed as mediators of the RBV and TCT influence	Decisions on scope and size are jointly determined by both approaches. The entrepreneurs and managers pursuing growth consider both groups of determinants concurrently. Namely, their choices are based on the assessment of firm capabilities relative to environmental uncertainty, and value from growth relative to transaction costs associated with a specific boundary problem	Type of decision-making (strategic or operational decisions)	Pros: decision-oriented and comprehensive in its additive format; establishes a new theory in its converging format. Cons: in its converging format excessively reduces the theories; in its additive format useful for matching and testing the theories rather than integrating them into a new theory
The evolutionary logic proposes a dynamic integration that takes co-evolution as a mediator of the joint explanatory power of the RBV and TCT	In the long-term and evolutionary perspective, there can be observed an interaction between firm capabilities and transaction costs in shaping firm boundaries. Namely, transaction costs moderated by capabilities influence the choice of governance mode. The governance mode impacts learning processes and how capabilities develop to further affect the level of transaction costs. Therefore, the attainment of value creation is a joint effect of capabilities and transaction costs as determinants of firm boundaries and growth	The concept of evolution of firms and industries	Pros: adequate metaphorical reflection of the dynamics of the process approach to setting boundaries and pursuing growth of firms and industries; comprehensive and nuanced in embracing the major theoretical constructs of both theories and causal relations, including feedback effects Cons: difficult to operationalize and explore in-depth in empirical research; too abstract and metaphorical and thus losing a clear decision-making orientation; the focus on processes and dynamics and not on an individual agent's (entrepreneur's) perceptions and decisions; unclear normative and practical implications

Type of integrative logics	Syntheses of the logics	Mediator for integrating the theories	Assessment of the relevance for the firm's growth process
The logic of structural problem-solving establishes a division of roles between the RBV and TCT in responding to specific problems of firm boundaries. It adopts the "why" and "how" problems as mediators highlighting the influence of the RBV and TCT factors	The RBV explains entrepreneurial and managerial decisions on "why" issues relating to firm boundaries, however, with moderating impact of TCT. Namely, trust-mutuality relation and value increase represent the dominant motive and rationale in making governance choices moderated by uncertainty and transaction cost considerations. TCT proves valid for entrepreneurial and managerial decisions about "how" to establish firm boundaries, but the moderating effects from the RBV should also be acknowledged. Namely, growth mechanism follows the alignment of the governance mode with transaction characteristics and capability characteristics. Particularly, the choice between hierarchy and hybrid modes is determined by asset specificity, uncertainty, and frequency of a transaction with moderating effects from the firm's capabilities. The choice between organic and acquisitive governance depends on the relatedness of a given transaction (business activity) with the core competence of a firm	The problems of "why" and "how" in shaping firm boundaries including growth	Pros: enables strong decisional orientation, tackling the major processual issues of "why" and "how"; explains the structuration of the growth process by decomposing it into constituent elements; enables both testing the theories (comprehensive enough since includes their core constructs); allows also to propose a new theory by distinguishing different problems for which the RBV and TCT are suitable, and by nuancing dominant theories with moderators; opens a possibility to investigate micro-causalities between the entrepreneur's perceptions and decisions and actions; opens avenues for normative thinking and practical implications Cons: structural view needs to be investigated in the context of time and environment to acknowledge dynamic nature of process

The logic of structural problem-solving retains the richness and comprehensiveness of joining two theories and involves the core of the growth process described earlier in Section 1.9. It is clearly focused on the major problems of "why" and "how" in the process approach. Furthermore, it decomposes boundary and growth decisions into structural, constituent elements. In a given theory, the dominant approach is moderated by some variables from the alternative theory. This logic has a strong decision-oriented profile and ensures a comprehensive tackling of problems by employing all the key variables and enhancing them with moderators. In doing this, it enables both testing the theories and advancing the inferences into a more in-depth description of particular elements, such as motives, rationale, mechanism, and modes, without ignoring the impact of well-confirmed variables.

The logic of structural problem-solving is also prospective in revealing the micro-causalities between the characteristics of the structural components and the resulting decisions and actions. As indicated in Section 2.5, motives, rationale, mechanisms, and modes are expected to impact the choices about the way that contractual relationships are governed (the motives of trust or opportunism), the types of new activities that are either opportunity-driven or necessitated by contractual hazards (the rationale of value or transaction cost avoidance), the sources or drivers of new activities (the firm's own capabilities or the requirements of transacting with a given business partner), and the modes in which growth is pursued (hierarchy or hybrids, internal or external governance).

The opportunities for investigating in-depth causal relationships resonate with the core of the growth process presented in Section 1.9. As proposed in this general framework, the process of growth has a dual nature embracing the structuration of the patterns of expansion (the entrepreneurs' perceptions and extant artifacts as enabling constraints) and the flow of events that involves the decisions and actions stimulated by the enabling constraints. This logic of integrating the RBV and TCT explains the entrepreneur's decisional rules that enable and constrain the subsequent flow of events. First, it gives the opportunity to explore the structural elements of the entrepreneur's perceptions of motives, rationale, mechanisms, and modes. Second, it stimulates the investigation of micro-causalities that explain how the enabling constraints (the entrepreneur's perceptions and artifacts) affect specific decisions and actions in setting up the firm's boundaries, including growth issues. To sum up, this logic enables testing the theories by including their major constructs and it offers a new integrative theory. Moreover, due to its clarity, the logic of structural problem-solving opens avenues for normative reasoning and practical implications. Its limitation may be the structural way of decomposing reality rather than providing a dynamic and contextual view. This limitation needs to be addressed by acknowledging the context of time, prior experience, and environmental issues. Considering the above assessment of the integrative logics, the structural approach has been chosen for further theory development, the formulation of hypotheses, and subsequent theoretical models of the SME growth process based on the integration of the RBV and TCT.

We have assessed the three logics of integrating the RBV and TCT in the studies of firm scope and size and identified the most suitable one for developing a theoretical framework of the SME growth process. The next step for developing this framework, as indicated in Section 3.1, is to use the selected logic to develop the research hypotheses and specify the causal relationships to be operationalized in subsequent empirical investigations. The integrative logic was selected based on the literature on firm boundaries, which includes the issue of growth in the broader context of firm scope and size. Moreover, the studies were not exclusively conducted in the context of SMEs, but covered a variety of firms that included them. Thus, in order to capture SME specificity, we developed hypotheses about the structural elements of the growth process by comparing the outcomes of the review of the RBV-TCT literature with the literature of SME growth. Moreover, following the descriptive model of the growth process in Section 1.9, we pointed out the importance of the structural elements of the growth process (motives, rationale, mechanisms, and modes) as enabling constraints that facilitate the flow of events (entrepreneurial decisions and actions).

3.4. The "why" dimension of the SME growth process: behavioral motives and rationale

Behavioral motives

The assumptions about the motives of partners in an economic exchange are important enabling constraints that affect the level of perceived behavioral uncertainty and the associated governance of exchange relationships (Lado, Dant, & Tekleab, 2008; Rindfleisch et al., 2010; Cordes et al., 2011). The RBV claims that trust and mutuality rather than opportunism drive the choice of exchange partners, and the former are a basis for performance and competitive advantage (Tsang, 2000; Barney, 1991; Barney & Hansen, 1994). TCT posits that opportunism is a relevant motive in business relationships affecting transaction costs (Williamson, 1975; 1989; Rindfleisch & Heide, 1997; Rindfleisch et al., 2010; Wathne & Heide, 2000). Trust is a willingness to rely on the actions of another party and to abandon control over the actions performed by the trustee (Mayer, Davis, & Shoorman, 1995). It means the acceptance of uncertainty and expectations instead of safeguards and incentives, and it is a conviction about the reliability (trustworthiness) and goodwill of the trustee (Mayer, Davis, & Shoorman, 1995; Ring & Van de Ven, 1994; Lewicki & Bunker, 1996). In TCT, opportunism represents behavioral uncertainty and it denotes self-interest seeking with guile, directed at short-term maximization of quasi-rents at the cost of the partner (Williamson, 1975). Opportunism should be controlled by adequate safeguards, such as contract terms. However, contracts are unavoidably incomplete, leading to opportunistic behaviors after they are signed (Jap & Anderson, 2003; Wathne & Heide, 2000; Williamson, 1975; 1989; 1991; 1998; 1999). The perceived danger of opportunism raises the costs of safeguards or may discourage undertakings and ventures, which bring excessive behavioral uncertainty.

Small entrepreneurial ventures are heavily exposed to dealing with the tension of trust versus opportunism, both in internal and external relations. Trust is conducive for business transacting and cooperation, especially in the hybrid governance structures (Larson, 1992; Weaver & Dickson, 1998; Ireland, Hitt, & Vaidyanath, 2002). However, since most relations are not regulated by formal agreements, trust needs to be supported with relational contracts and informal institutions, where mutuality and the expectation of future business affect behaviors (Dewald et al., 2007; Freiling & Laudien, 2012). On the other hand, SMEs face the opportunism of larger buyers and suppliers (Besser & Miller, 2010; Everaert, Sarens, & Rommel, 2010). In such contexts, mitigating opportunism through specific formal contracting and market signaling are conditions for growth and innovation (Michael, 2007; Chowdhury, 2011). According to TCT, excessive opportunism in external relations can be a justification to grow through internalization. However, this theory undervalues the role of resource constraints and the perceived threat of complexity, loss of direct control, and opportunism from employees that might discourage SME entrepreneurs from enlarging their businesses (Chandler, McKelvie, & Davidsson, 2009; Cordes et al., 2011). It can be argued that small firms assume trust in business relations and tolerate a certain level of opportunism to pursue growth (Barney, 1999; Chandler, McKelvie, & Davidsson, 2009). Such an approach is consistent with the evidence in the literature on firm boundaries, which emphasizes a paradoxical tension of trust as the major motive and some influence of opportunistic behavior (Gancarczyk, 2016; Lado, Dant, & Tekleab, 2008; Leiblein, 2003; Ireland, Hitt, & Vaidyanath, 2002).

Based on the above discussion, we formulate the following hypothesis regarding motives in business exchange as perceived by entrepreneurs pursuing growth process.

Hypothesis 1. *In the process of growth, entrepreneurs perceive trust to be the major motive of exchange partners limited by the perceived opportunism.*

Motives, as structural elements, act as enabling constraints, therefore, their importance lies in affecting entrepreneurial decisions and actions (the flow of events). Therefore, it can be expected that the types of motives perceived by high-growth entrepreneurs will be associated with adequate governance tools in business relationships. These are going to be incentives, contracts, and other safeguards employed in business relationships in the case of hybrid growth or the integration within hierarchy governance.

Growth rationale

Consistent with differing behavioral assumptions about the motives of partners in economic exchange, the RBV and TCT offer alternative rationales for firm growth.

According to the RBV, the rationales for growth are economies from indivisible excess resources and, eventually, value creation from new combinations of existing resources or from new resources (Tsang, 2000; Barney, 1991; 1999; Hamel & Prahalad, 1990; Kogut & Zander, 1992; Penrose, 1959; Peteraf, 1993; Wernerfelt, 1984). Since there is a strong identification of an entrepreneur with his or her venture, creating value is considered at both the personal and business levels (Steyaert, 2007). Personal value achievement is exemplified in opportunity exploitation, income enhancement, and self-fulfillment (Alvarez, 2007; Sarason, Dean, & Dillard, 2006; Storey, 1994). The value of business denotes capability development, successful performance, and competitive advantage (Argyres & Zenger, 2012; Alvarez & Barney, 2007; Zott & Amit, 2007).

In TCT, the rationale for expanding is the reduction of transaction costs, i.e., comparative costs of exchange in different governance structures, including the market, the firm, or hybrids (Coase, 1937; Williamson, 1989, p. 142, 1989; 1991; 1998; 1999; 2002; 2005). Williamson's methodology of the transaction cost reasoning is called the reduced form model, since it does not provide the direct measurement of transaction costs, but treats them as a reference category that governs managerial choices (Masten, Meehan, & Snyder, 1991). Due to difficulties in separating transaction costs from production costs, the total cost of exchange is investigated, including both production and transaction costs (Benham & Benham, 2000).

The research that integrates the RBV and TCT in explaining firm scope and size emphasizes the importance or even primacy of the RBV in explaining the rationale as value and competitive advantage (Leiblein, 2003; Ireland, Hitt & Vaidyarath, 2002; Gulati, Lawrence & Puranam, 2005; Jacobides & Hitt, 2005; Lo, Frias, & Ghosh, 2012; Schilling & Steensma, 2002). However, it is also postulated that factors of the alternative TCT approach should be considered as a complementary constraint on the value rationale (Conner & Prahalad, 1996; Madhok, 1997; Foss & Foss, 2005; Meyer, Wright, & Pruthi, 2009). Namely, the level of transaction costs affects the level of value that is possible to achieve (Foss & Foss, 2005; 2008).

Entrepreneurship research on growth determinants focuses primarily on positive, value-driven stimuli, such as personal satisfaction, growth aspirations, or willingness to expand (Storey, 1994; Wiklund, 1999; Wiklund & Shepherd, 2003; Barringer, Jones, & Neubaum, 2005; Gilbert, McDougall, & Audretsch, 2006; Dobbs & Hamilton, 2007; Delmar & Wiklund, 2008). The RBV perspective is reflected in the entrepreneurship studies on growth determinants that identify the drivers of growth among the characteristics of the entrepreneur, the firm, and its strategy (Storey, 1994; Barringer, Jones, & Neubaum, 2005; Gilbert, McDougall, & Audretsch, 2006; Dobbs & Hamilton, 2007; Wasilczuk, 2000; 2005). Thus, the resource-based factors in these areas were largely empirically confirmed, forming a profile of high-growers (Storey, 1994; Barringer, Jones, & Neubaum, 2005; Gilbert, McDougall, & Audretsch, 2006; Dobbs & Hamilton, 2007; Coad, 2007b; 2009; Macpherson & Holt, 2007; Rodríguez-Gutiérrez, Moreno, & Tejada, 2015). However, the entrepreneurship and SME research on growth predictors does not employ core theoretical constructs of the RBV, but it only explores internal characteristics of high-growers and their access to external resources.

Environmental impediments to expansion, such as uncertainty and transaction costs, are under-researched relative to positive determinants and drivers of growth stemming from the internal characteristics of high-growers (Wiklund & Shepherd, 2003; Lensink, Van Steen, & Sterken, 2005). However, the rarity of expansion might suggest the obstacles and barriers to expanding SMEs, including excessive transaction costs of internal management and effective control by the entrepreneur (Chandler, McKelvie, & Davidsson, 2009), as well as dysfunctional institutions (Dominiak, Wasilczuk, & Starnawska, 2016). Transaction costs are supported as a rationale by empirical evidence that relates to vertical integration and diversification leading to SME upgrading in value chains (Díez-Vial, 2007; 2010; Everaert, Sarens, & Rommel, 2010). SMEs seek to improve their bargaining position and capability exploitation by introducing new but related activities and are more inclined to expand than large firms, due to lower transaction costs of internal organization (Díez-Vial, 2007; 2010). On the other hand, when internalizing and developing hierarchical governance, they encounter the opportunity cost of losing flexibility in market transactions (Díez-Vial, 2010). Compared to large firms, SME growth meets more obstacles in hybrid structures as well, since they experience higher transaction costs of alliance coordination and formation (Vervaal et al., 2010).

These findings show that the growth pursuit, besides value as a major positive rationale, also involves considerable exchange costs and uncertainty that constrain exploiting opportunities.

Following the above discussion about relationships between value and transaction costs as rationales for growth, we formulate Hypothesis 2.

Hypothesis 2. In the process of growth, entrepreneurs perceive value as the major rationale for growth, supplemented by transaction cost considerations.

The growth rationale, as one of the major structural elements of the growth process, acts as an enabling constraint. The importance of this rationale lies in its influence on the kind of growth activity to be undertaken. Value and performance rationales stimulate the seeking of opportunities to exploit the existing capabilities or to explore new ones, thus resulting in a portfolio diversified around capabilities and opportunities (Penrose, 1959; Hamel & Prahalad, 1990; Davidsson, Delmar, & Wiklund, 2006; Hitt et al., 2011; Sirén, Kohtamäki, & Kuckertz, 2012). If transaction costs are not assumed to be a reason for growth, one does not consider constraints in choosing how to expand scope and size. However, when transaction costs act as a constraint, an entrepreneur intends to improve his or her bargaining position by internalizing the activity featured by the excessive costs of exchange and demanded by the customers/suppliers. This raises the probability of a portfolio built around the requirements of specific business partners, based on vertical integration (Williamson, 1991; 1999; Díez-Vial, 2007; 2010).

Consistent with the value or transaction cost rationale, the entrepreneurship literature on growth adopts either the RBV or TCT approaches to developing the business portfolio through innovations. However, the studies in this area do not combine these theories but utilize them as individual theoretical foundations. The RBV literature on generating innovations focuses on the role of learning and knowledge development in this process (Garnsey, Stam, & Heffernan, 2006; Coad, 2009; Macpherson & Holt, 2007). The TCT-backed studies consider lowering transaction costs as a necessary condition to recognize and exploit opportunities (Foss & Foss, 2008), and ultimately generate innovations (Michael, 2007). In the conditions of uncertainty and risk associated with innovation development, venture creation and growth represent safeguards of property rights to creating and appropriating rents from new products and services (Alvarez, 2007). There is still the need to jointly consider capabilities and transaction costs as predictors of developing a portfolio through innovations.

3.5. The "how" dimension of growth: mechanisms and modes

The mechanisms and modes of growth explain how growth is implemented. The mechanisms involve interdependencies among factors (cause-effect relationships) leading to increasing the firm's size and choosing a specific mode of growth. Growth modes denote different governance structures of either hierarchy expansion (internal/organic or external/acquisitive modes) or hybrid expansion (joint venture, franchising, or licensing) (McKelvie & Wiklund, 2010). According to the RBV, the major mechanism of growth is exploitation, i.e., novel uses of the existing resources that are matched with market opportunity by entrepreneurial vision (Penrose, 1959). The manager-entrepreneur makes choices in the conditions of bounded rationality that leads to path-dependent exploitation of the current stock of knowledge into related activities (Freiling, Wassermann, & Laudien, 2012; Ray, Xue, & Barney, 2013). Thus, the organic (internal) mode of growth emerges by developing products and services consistent with the firm's core competencies (Hamel & Prahalad, 1990).

The limits to organic growth, as set up by extant routines, practices, and path-dependent knowledge, can be overcome by another mechanism of growth: exploration, i.e., launching the areas of activity that are not related to the existing core competencies (Penrose, 1959; Hitt et al., 2011; Sirén, Kohtamäki, & Kuckertz, 2012). Exploration is often conducted through the acquisitive or external mode of growth (take-overs and mergers) as a mode alternative to the organic one, or it is performed organically, based on the firm's own resources.

In TCT, the mechanism of growth emerges from Williamson's discriminating alignment hypothesis, which states that transaction costs can be optimized by aligning an individual transaction with the most appropriate governance structure – the market, the firm, or a hybrid, based on the comparative transaction cost analysis (Williamson, 1999; 1991; 2005). Consequently, the firm expands when the comparative transaction costs associated with implementing a specific transaction internally or in hybrid structures are lower than the costs of implementing it in the market. TCT differentiates between internalization within the hierarchy and possible hybrids, contingent on asset specificity, transaction frequency, and uncertainty (Williamson, 1975). However, it does not provide the criteria to discriminate between internal and external growth, which is a major merit of the RBV.

Despite the alternative approaches to growth mechanisms and modes, both theories follow to some extent the alignment logic that originated from TCT. The difference rests in the basis for identifying a new activity and the mode of its implementation. TCT asserts that the mechanism of growth is transaction-specific, i.e., based on aligning a new activity and its mode with transaction characteristics or requirements of transactions with specific suppliers and buyers. Thus, its focus is environmental/external. The RBV assumes the alignment with firm-specific and internal resources in choosing the new activity and its mode as predominant due to path dependence. However, the RBV also might break the alignment rule through exploration.

The "how" issues of mechanisms and modes of expansion are under-explored in the entrepreneurship and small business literature compared with the "why" problems (McKelvie & Wiklund, 2010; Chandler, McKelvie, & Davidsson, 2009; Davidsson, Achtenhagen, & Naldi, 2010). In particular, the causes of choice and the relative performance of expansion modes for small businesses require more research (Davidsson, Achtenhagen, & Naldi, 2010). Moreover, extant entrepreneurship studies on governance modes focus primarily on the rationale and drivers of hybrids, such as alliances, joint ventures, and different forms of networks. This emphasizes the importance of hybrid structures for small and young entrepreneurial ventures as alternatives to organic or acquisitive growth (Watson, 2007; Rindova et al., 2012; Iacobucci & Rosa, 2010).

A vast number of theoretical and empirical studies on firm boundaries acknowledge the role of TCT in explaining how the governance mode is established, since it provides a systematic way and adequate criteria for addressing this issue (Leiblein, 2003; Argyres & Zenger, 2012; Brahm & Tarzíjan, 2014; Brewer, Ashenbaum, & Carter, 2014; Díez-Vial, 2007; Fabrizio, 2012; Gulati, Lawrence, & Puranam, 2005; Jacobides & Hitt, 2005; Mayer & Salomon, 2006). On the other hand, there is also the evidence of firms following the alignment of new activity and its mode with capabilities (Love & Roper, 2005; Kim & Mahoney, 2006; Conner & Prahalad, 1996; Meyer, Wright, & Pruthi, 2009; Ray, Xue, & Barney, 2013). The seminal findings from the entrepreneurship and small business literature reveal the moderating effect of the access to resources on governance choice driven by the major determinants of asset specificity, frequency, and uncertainty (opportunism) (Chandler, McKelvie, & Davidsson, 2009; Verwaal et al., 2010). Thus, we hypothesize that firms combine these two mechanisms of growth by applying the alignment of the new activity's transaction (customer or supplier) requirements with the existing capability base.

Hypothesis 3. *In the process of growth, entrepreneurs perceive the mechanism of growth to be based on aligning the new activity and its mode (hierarchy or hybrid, organic or acquisitive) with the transaction characteristics and with the firm's capabilities. Namely, the choice between hierarchy and hybrid modes depends on the transaction characteristics, while the choice between organic and acquisitive modes depends on the relatedness with the firm's core competencies.*

The mechanisms and modes of growth are structural elements of the growth process and act as enabling constraints as well. Namely, the pursuit of the growth mechanism will affect the sources of growth. Growth can be stimulated by the needs of business partners, which reflects a TCT approach of adaptation or adjustment to the transaction characteristics. An alternative possibility is the growth driven by the adjustment to the firm's own capabilities or going beyond them toward other opportunities, as suggested in the RBV. The boundary and entrepreneurship research reviewed above provides the evidence of the entrepreneurial flexibility and acknowledges both sources of growth in entrepreneurial decisions, as we hypothesize above. The adjustment type is associated with specific kinds of governance modes, as per the theoretical studies in the RBV and TCT.

3.6. Contextual influences and moderators of the RBV and TCT variables on the process of growth

The integrative RBV-TCT research is supported by the observation that both theories, despite their alternative assumptions, proved to be valid in the empirical studies on firm scope and size and on the firm's high growth (Combs et al., 2011; Davidsson, Steffens, & Fitzsimmons, 2009; Garnsey, Stam, & Heffernan, 2006; Chandler, McKelvie, & Davidsson, 2009; Verwaal et al., 2010). Therefore, each of them can be a relevant explanation of the phenomena embedded in different contexts of the company's capability and the business environment (Mayer & Salomon, 2006; Ray, Xue, & Barney, 2013). This assertion resonates with the perceived motives, rationale, mechanisms, and modes of growth process as context-specific enabling constraints in the entrepreneurial decisions and actions (Selden & Fletcher, 2015).

Regarding the motives in business exchange, asset specificity, i.e., the adjustment to a particular transaction or to transacting with an individual customer or supplier, increases the firm's dependence and potential opportunism (Barney, 1999; Chandler, McKelvie, & Davidsson, 2009; Majocchi, Mayrhofer, & Camps, 2013; Brouthers, 2002). Superior resources make a company offering more valuable than that of competitors and raise the dependence of cooperators, thus lowering the plausibility of their opportunism (Barney, 1999; Majocchi, Mayrhofer, & Camps, 2013).

Similarly, the perceived rationale of growth may be affected by the resource and business exchange conditions. High capabilities improve the bargaining power and enable effective governance of collaboration (Dyer, 1996; Argyres & Liebeskind, 1999; Madhok & Tallman, 1998; Madhok, 2002; Brahm & Tarziján, 2013; Ray, Xue, & Barney, 2013). As a result, the perceived importance of transaction cost rationale is diminished, thus favoring value as a primary justification for growth. High asset specificity, in turn, raises dependence, behavioral uncertainty, and consequently the importance of transaction costs as a rationale (Díez-Vial, 2007; 2010; Brahm & Tarziján, 2013; Ray, Xue, & Barney, 2013). Small entrepreneurial ventures are vulnerable to asset specificity and dependence problems, e.g., often being suppliers to a limited number of larger customers (Nooteboom, 1993; Brouthers & Nakos, 2004; Everaert, Sarens, & Rommel, 2010). However, the SMEs demonstrating capability advantages establish a stronger bargaining position and are able to alleviate the problems of dependence raised by specific assets (Barney, 1999).

The moderating role of the firm's resources and asset specificity is also suggested in choosing the mechanism of setting-up the firm's scope and size. The prevalence of the alignment of the new activity (new product, service, market) to the core competence or to transaction characteristics is moderated by the level of the existing firm capabilities and the level of adjustments to transactions with customers and suppliers. Advantageous governance capabilities enable more effective handling of external contracts to provide an alternative to internalizing them within the organization, even in the face of high asset specificity (Kim & Mahoney, 2006; Conner & Prahalad, 1996; Madhok, 1997; Foss & Foss, 2005; Meyer, Wright, & Pruthi, 2009). Similarly, TCT determinants, specifically asset specificity, act as moderators of the impact of the RBV variables (Fabrizio, 2012; Jacobides & Hitt, 2005). High asset specificity increases the probability of aligning a new activity to transaction requirements imposed by customers or suppliers.

Consequently, the motives, rationale, mechanisms, and modes of growth can be affected by the initial levels of a firm's resources (capability) and the asset specificity required in transactions with key buyers and suppliers. These two moderators, being the key variables of the RBV and TCT, represent the context of internal resources and external contracting. Moreover, their differing characteristics impact the variety of motives, rationale, mechanisms, and modes in the process of SME growth. Therefore, we formulate the following hypotheses:

Hypothesis 4. *The characteristics of motives, rationale, mechanisms, and modes of growth are affected by moderators during the growth process. Namely, the levels of resource advantage over competitors and transaction asset specificity have moderating effects on how entrepreneurs perceive motives in business exchange, rationales for growth, and the mechanisms and modes of growth.*

Hypothesis 5. *The explanatory power of the RBV and TCT towards SME growth process depends on the contextual characteristics of SMEs' capabilities and transactional environment.*

Hypothesis 5.1. *In the conditions of limited company potential (low resource advantage) and unfavorable transactional environment (high asset specificity), entrepreneurs conform to the principles of TCT.*

Hypothesis 5.2. *In the conditions of favorable company potential (high resource advantage) and transactional environment (low asset specificity), entrepreneurs make choices consistent with the assumptions of the RBV.*

3.7. Theoretical framework of the SME growth process

An integrated RBV-TCT theoretical framework of the SME growth process complements the general theoretical framework of the expansion process proposed in Section 1.9. This general framework needed completion with adequate structural elements that represent entrepreneurs' self-reflexive evaluation, i.e., their perceptions affecting "why" and "how" issues regarding growth.

We applied the theoretical framework of the RBV and TCT according to the methodology described in Section 3.1. This deductive approach enabled the identification of the major "why" and "how" issues in terms of motives, rationale, mechanisms, and modes. Furthermore, the alternative RBV and TCT theories were confronted, and the meta-synthesis of boundary studies integrating them was performed to identify the logics of this integration and to select the most appropriate logic for explaining the structuration of the SME growth process. Finally, we matched the logic of integration from the boundary literature with the entrepreneurship literature on SME growth to hypothesize the entrepreneurs' perceptions about the structural elements identified. The integrated RBV-TCT theoretical framework of the SME growth process builds upon the earlier efforts to accumulate the knowledge on firm growth from the boundary studies, including the expansion option, that was developed in economics, strategic management and entrepreneurship literature (Figure 6).

The general framework of the growth process included the structuration of varied growth patterns and the flow of events as entrepreneurial decisions and actions about new products, services, and processes. The structuration covered the entrepreneur's self-reflexive evaluation and artifacts related to feedback effects and jointly affecting the flow of events (decisions and actions).

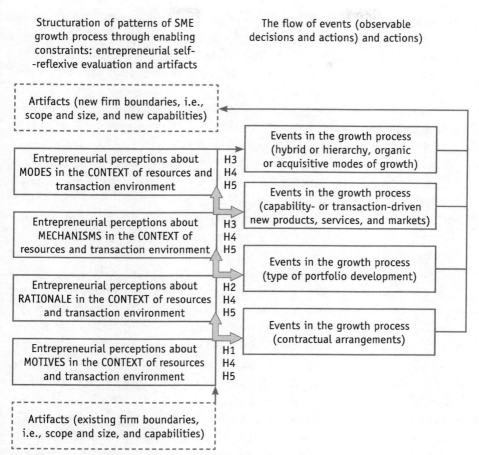

Figure 6. The integrated RBV-TCT theoretical framework of SME growth process
Source: own work.

The current integrative RBV-TCT framework specifies the object of entrepreneurial self-reflexive evaluation, i.e., his or her perceptions about "why" and "how" issues. These objects are structural elements of the growth process as theorized in the RBV and TCT, i.e., motives and rationale for "why" issues, and mechanisms and modes for "how" problems. Additionally, the framework hypothesizes about the way entrepreneurs perceive these elements (Hypotheses 1–3), and how the context affects these perceptions (adequate moderators asserted in Hypotheses 4–5). Causal relations among structural elements represent theory-driven and intuitively convincing inferences. Although it is a simplified causality, there are possible feedback loops among the elements such as modes implying a certain level of transaction costs and thus a perceived rationale for growth. The entrepreneurs' self-reflexive evaluation, i.e., the way they perceive motives, rationale, mechanisms, and modes will affect the pattern of growth. Although we hypothesize the specific course of these perceptions based on the literature review (Hypotheses 1–3), we also acknowledge a heterogeneity of growth and thus posit the influences of capability (resource advantage) and environmental (transaction environment) influence on this course (Hypotheses 4 and 5). Therefore, the framework admits diverse patterns of SME growth depending on contextual issues.

The entrepreneurs' perceptions about structural elements are a basis for observable decisions and actions. These, in turn, result in artifacts that affect the firm owner's perceptions and evaluations. Motives, rationale, mechanisms, and modes as perceived by entrepreneurs play the role of enabling constraints. They structure reality to enable the flow of events, and at the same, they limit the range of accessible options. The perceptions about the motives of agents in economic exchange (trust versus opportunism) will influence how contractual arrangements are conducted by adopting adequate types of contracts and safeguards. The perceived rationale for growth (value creation or transaction cost avoidance) will affect the type of portfolio developed. This development may respond to the opportunities for value creation (a portfolio diversified according to opportunities and capabilities) or to the need for lowering transaction costs (a portfolio developed around a customer or supplier, based on vertical integration). Mechanisms of growth describe the sources of new products, services, processes, and markets, which are driven by capabilities or by transaction requirements stemming from customer and supplier needs. The modes of growth result from mechanisms adopted as hierarchy, hybrid, organic, or acquisitive expansion. Overall, the flow of events (observable decisions and actions) stems from the unobservable entrepreneurial sense-making and leads to the emergence of artifacts in the form of new firm size and scope as well as new capabilities.

Artifacts (a specific scope and size and capabilities) result from the entrepreneur's decisions and actions, but also affect these decisions as well as the entrepreneur's self-reflexive evaluation. Like this evaluation, they are enabling constraints that give a foundation to the owner's sense-making and future actions. However, they also limit the opportunities that can be exploited based on these artifacts (such as strategic plan, extant products and services, and personnel competencies), and thus, they constrain the range of future decisions and actions.

The model can be tracked as a relationship between the structuration through enabling constraints and the observable flow of decisions and actions resulting from this structuration. The research implication is that it is necessary to investigate the structuration of the growth process, since it underpins or even determines decisions and actions. Another informative relationship that can be inferred from the model relates to observable and unobservable elements of the growth process. The observable elements, namely, decisions and actions, as well as artifacts, are founded on the unobservable entrepreneurial self-reflexive evaluation (perceptions and opinions). For future research, it implies an in-depth exploration of the entrepreneur's sense-making that is less obvious and more difficult to objectivize than tangible and observed phenomena, but is crucial to understanding how these phenomena emerge.

To complete the general framework of the firm's growth process, a deductive approach is proposed based on the integration of the RBV and TCT. At this stage of theorizing on the fuzzy and idiosyncratic expansion phenomenon, it provides a well-rooted approach to expanding the firm's boundaries (broadening them compared with the current scope and size). Adopting an inductive approach to fulfilling the general schema presents the hazard of varied and incomparable evidence that would be difficult to generalize. We recognize the threat of losing the uniqueness of this explorative theme when employing already available theoretical approaches. However, this peril was offset with the adoption of a comprehensive perspective that combines two differing theories, thus following the alternative template approach (Langley, 1999). Moreover, we drew upon both theoretical and empirical integrative efforts to nuance and match the original assumptions of each theory. Eventually, we discussed these findings in the context of the literature on SME expansion to generate research hypotheses that clarify the structuration of expansion patterns.

Considering the extent of the literature review, the hypotheses are built upon the accumulation of knowledge from the research on economics, strategic management, and entrepreneurship. They address growth predominantly through the lens of boundary studies that consider hierarchy or hybrid expansion as diversification and vertical integration, or hybrid forms, such as joint ventures, outsourcing, and alliances. However, only a portion of this research was conducted explicitly in the context of high-growth SMEs. Therefore, the assumptions included in the hypotheses require verification in the empirical research focused specifically on high-growth SMEs.

4. METHODOLOGY OF EMPIRICAL RESEARCH ON THE GROWTH PROCESS OF SMES

4.1. Empirical research framework

As indicated in the introduction, the general methodology adopted in this book for building a model of the SME growth process consists of (1) confronting and empirical testing of RBV and TCT theoretical perspectives on firm growth, and then (2) integrating them to build a new theoretical framework, which is a descriptive model of the SME growth process. This idea is developed on both conceptual and empirical grounds. The previous chapters elucidated the conceptual efforts to synthesize the core of the firm growth process and to elaborate a theoretical framework of the SME growth process based on the integration of both approaches.

The current empirical research is intended to test the theoretical framework presented in Figure 7. Thus, the research framework for empirical investigations presented here is primarily directed at the operationalization of the theoretical framework. It is focused on testing the assumptions of five hypotheses as to structural elements of SME growth process regarding motives, rationale, mechanisms, and modes, including the contextual influences (moderators) from the firm's capabilities and the transactional environment. The structural elements were described with the use of constructs of the RBV and TCT to follow the alternative template approach (Langley, 1999; Lee, 1989). Table 12 presents the links among particular elements of the growth process, the major RBV and TCT constructs, and the hypotheses to be tested.

Table 12. The links among structural elements of the growth process, the major RBV and TCT constructs, and research hypotheses

Structural elements of the growth process	TCT constructs	The RBV constructs	Hypotheses tested
Motives	Opportunism	Trust	Hypothesis 1
Rationale	Reduction of transaction costs	Value creation	Hypothesis 2
Mechanisms and modes	Aligning a new activity and its mode with trans-action characteristics	Aligning a new activity and its mode with a firm's core competencies	Hypothesis 3
Moderators of the RBV's and TCT's influence	Asset specificity	Resource advantage	Hypothesis 4 Hypothesis 5

Source: own work.

Moreover, the empirical research aimed to reveal how these structural elements act as enabling constraints of entrepreneurial decision-making, i.e., how they enable and constrain the flow of decisions and actions. Therefore, we match the hypotheses about the structural elements and their moderators with research questions about how they affect the entrepreneur's choices (Figure 7).

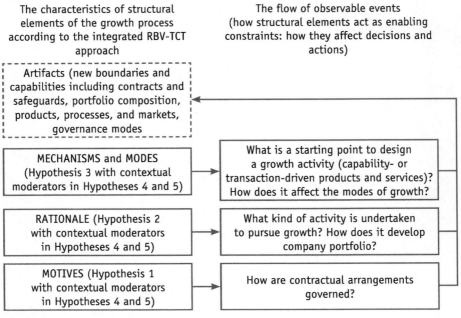

Figure 7. Empirical research framework

Source: own work.

In the theoretical discussion leading to the development of the hypotheses and the theoretical model of the SME growth process, it was proposed that the importance of entrepreneurs' perceptions lies in their influence on specific decisions that structure the growth process (Adamus & Gręda, 2005). The empirical investigations will be guided by the questions that disentangle how the entrepreneurial perceptions about structural elements affect specific decisions and actions and thus the emergence of artifacts. Namely, we will research how the perception of motives is associated with the decisions about contractual relationships and the adopted kinds of contracts and safeguards. Another question to be answered is how will a particular activity undertaken to pursue growth and the resulting portfolio be related with the rationale for growth. The mechanisms and modes of growth will be examined in association with the questions about a starting point to design a growth activity, a resulting capability, or transaction-driven products and services. We emphasize this perspective of the theoretical model that focuses on the interactions between the unobservable entrepreneurial perceptions of structural elements (entrepreneurial sense-making) and the observable phenomena (decisions, actions, and artifacts).

4.2. Methods and sources of data

Research methods

The main methodological challenge for the empirical research on the SME growth process lies in the requirements of process analysis. This kind of research assumes the availability of data in long-term horizons, the delineation of cause-effect relationships, and the conditions that make the case study method the most appropriate (Yin, 2009; Silverman, 2006; Eisenhardt & Graebner, 2007). The case study method is justified by the explorative nature of the firm growth theme, since extant studies focus primarily on growth determinants and predictors. The case study will facilitate deep qualitative analyses of the complex relationships among factors, including their changes over time and during differing conditions of company resources and operating environment (Woodside & Wilson, 2003; Larsson, 1993). The case method does not differentiate by attempting to control the context. Instead, boundaries between the phenomena and the context tend to be blurred (Yin, 2009). The contextual issues form a set of independent variables besides those directly planned as independent. This is well suited to this research, which hypothesizes the moderating effect of the environment and the firm's capability on the explanatory power of RBV and TCT. Therefore, in the empirical experiment, it is planned to adopt a multiple case study method.

A multiple case approach based on deliberate and theory-driven sampling enables qualitative, analytic generalization (Eisenhardt, 1989). Despite explorative nature of approaching SME growth through process lenses, there are established theoretical approaches to firm scope and size such as the RBV and TCT, which supports the idea of case-based, qualitative deductive testing (Yin, 2009). Our approach differentiates by adopting a prospective case study design (Bitektine, 2008). The prospective case study provides a structured way of addressing empirical phenomena based on the existing theory and to-date empirical verifications. It represents the integration and refinement of to-date qualitative and case-based deductive theory testing, namely, the pattern-matching approach and alternative theoretical template strategy (Langley, 1999; Lee, 1989). The pattern matching approach involves comparing the expected, theory-based outcomes with the real-life phenomena (Campbell, 1966; Trochim, 1989; Yin, 2009). Alternative template approach confronts the competing theories to prune (reduce) the theoretical landscape (Langley, 1999; Leavitt, Mitchell, & Peterson, 2010).

The prospective case study design consists of (1) the systematic formulation of hypotheses based on the extant theory and (2) testing them in the case study to achieve analytical generalization (Bitektine, 2008). Analytical generalization enables falsification testing (Eisenhardt, 1989). The falsification test rejects theories that do not explain the empirical findings and sustains theories that do. Sometimes there is a basis for combining theories into one theoretical framework (Popper, 1968). As such, the falsification test does not have the capacity to confirm theories by proof, but only to reject, sustain, expand, or combine them based upon the evidence from the case study. Falsification is especially appropriate for the case study method, where generalization cannot be achieved by 'proof' due to the non-random design and small sample size. Instead, it focuses on rejection of theoretical assumptions that are inadequate to explain actual phenomena.

The deductive approach seems contradictory to the explorative theme of the research. However, relying on a deductive, well-structured conceptual framework limits the risk of subjectivity in the case study method. The prospective case study design avoids the shortcomings of most current qualitative deductive testing, such as the ambiguity of hypotheses or proposals derived from testing extant theories and the selective bias of the researcher (Bitektine, 2008). In the traditional, case-based analyses, hypotheses or proposals are the outcomes of empirical analysis. However, case study analysis often results in ambiguous hypotheses, i.e., more than one hypothesis can be derived from the findings. In the prospective case study design, hypotheses are derived from the theory and then subjected to qualitative testing. Deductive case studies enable the formulation of both research questions and hypotheses at the start of the research. The selective bias of the researcher consists of his or her awareness of the qualitative outcomes at the start of the analysis and linking the results to the assumptions or vice-versa. In the prospective case study, hypotheses are formulated at the start, before the analysis is undertaken, which helps to avoid biased selection.

A possible bias of deductive theory testing is *post-hoc* reasoning; the propensity to accept or reject specific assumptions. This deficiency is in place when using only one case study and one theory to which empirical observations and conclusions are adjusted. In the current research, this bias is avoided by applying a multi-case study approach and by combining two theoretical perspectives instead of relying upon only one theory. Confronting two or more alternative theories opens an analyst to a variety of interpretations. This helps to expand the options of interpreting the phenomena and, in the presence of some competing theoretical assumptions, it makes the researcher resolve contradictory statements of the theories by observing the real processes in several case studies, instead of sticking to only one approach. Moreover, the bias of *post-hoc* reasoning is avoided due to the thematic focus. Namely, the research is not intended to explain determinants that lead to growth as an outcome, which would be known to the researcher at the start. It is rather to explore how firms pursue growth and what the growth process is, regarding its modes, rationale, motivation, and mechanisms. The nature and content of this process is not known to the researcher at the start, but is revealed by the investigation.

The case studies were explored with the use of a mixed method approach to achieve triangulation. The sources of data for case study development were of primary and secondary nature. The primary sources included two-staged direct interviews by the principal researcher with owner-managers supplemented by natural observation. Data triangulation was accomplished through confronting the primary sources with secondary sources, such as company reports, webpages, newsletter releases, and press articles.

The major source of data were two-staged interviews with entrepreneurs conducted by the principal investigator, and recorded and transcribed by the principal investigator and an associate researcher. The interviews were retrospective, covering the last 4 years of the company expansion. The advantage of retrospection was the focus on the past experiences and the possibility to evaluate past choices based on objective outcomes. The limitation of retrospection consists of the difficulty to recall the past decisions and activities. The information obtained from the interviews was validated by additional methods such as natural observation, analyzing the company records, and other secondary data, as well by the two-staged plan of interviews to give the possibility of information adjustments.

The first, structured interview was intended to test the theoretical assumptions of the RBV and TCT. The first questionnaire for the interview was based on operationalizing the RBV and TCT approaches to explain the process of growth. Differing theoretical assumptions about motives, rationale, mechanisms, and modes were tested with the use of the structured questionnaire to assure rigor in using terms and describing variables. Based on the findings from the first-stage interview, an initial model of the SME growth process that integrates the RBV and TCT assumptions was conceptualized and operationalized to provide a questionnaire for the second, semi-structured interview.

The second, semi-structured interview was intended to test and refine the initial conceptualization of the integrated RBV and TCT approaches. The questionnaire consisted of open-ended questions to focus more on the proper identification of causal relationships in the growth process than on the variables themselves. The causal relationships referred to the influence of structural elements of the growth process (enabling constraints) on decisions and actions referring to contractual arrangements, portfolio development, sources of new activities leading to growth, and the resulting modes of growth. Attention was given to mechanisms and modes of growth, as they proved to be the most complex constructs with many variables and interdependencies that needed clarification after the first wave of structured interviews. This second phase of interviewing also provided for validation of data from the first phase. Before the second wave of interviews, the entrepreneurs were provided with reports from the first wave results to review them and to validate the aggregation and interpretation of findings.

Analytical methods

The multi-case study design provides rich data for comprehensive and nuanced reasoning based on common and idiosyncratic characteristics of the cases and opens a researcher to a variety of inferences and interpretations (Eisenhardt & Graebner, 2007; Gibbert & Ruigrok 2010; Hoon, 2013). Moreover, it is particularly useful to assume that a social phenomenon under study does not follow only one path, but that different paths are possible. The growth phenomenon demonstrates such characteristics as revealed in earlier empirical research on growth determinants and the properties of gazelles in the first chapter of this book.

On the other hand, the relatively high number of cases we used (14 case studies of high-growers plus 2 case studies of moderate growers as control cases) represents two considerable challenges.

One challenge is processing and structuring the data obtained when there are many cases, and consequently many variables and their interdependencies need to be examined. Recently, multi-case study research has been directed toward increasing the number of cases, presuming that more research evidence enables more possibilities to explore the phenomenon revealed in a variety of contexts and thus provide analytical generalization (Souitaris & Zebernati, 2014; Reymen et al., 2015; Daniel, Di Domenico & Sharma, 2015; Muñoz & Dimov, 2015). The number of cases used in the present research is similar to those in recent studies focused on SMEs and entrepreneurial ventures that used 9 cases (Reymen et al., 2015), 13 cases (Souitaris & Zebernati, 2014), 23 interviews (Daniel, Di Domenico & Sharma, 2015), and 45 case studies (Muñoz & Dimov, 2015) to perform case-based investigations.

We used Qualitative Comparative Analysis (QCA) to structure the cross-case comparison and to identify growth patterns as well as deviants from the major patterns observed. QCA enables comparing how different decisional approaches combine in specific cases, forming different paths of growth process and not competing against each other (Greckhamer et al., 2008; Greckhamer, 2011; Kent & Argouslidis, 2005). This method helps to derive equifinal approaches to the growth process, instead of looking for one "general" or "average" solution that might not exist in reality (Kogut & Ragin, 2006). QCA combines the qualitative and quantitative treatment of data, appropriate for both small sets of cases (2 to 15) and larger sets as well (Berg-Schlosser et al., 2009). Regardless of the sample size, it does not fulfill all of the requirements for quantitative statistical analysis and positivist generalization. Statistical validity is normally precluded due to an insufficient number of cases and non-random sampling. Some subjectively determined steps and operations in the procedure adjust the outcomes to theoretical and logical interpretations and need to be highlighted in the research reports, but it questions the complete objectivity of reasoning from quantitative data. Instead, QCA attempts to attain scientific rigor by processing and structuring a large set of variables. This rigor effectively supports the achievement of external research validity (replicability, transparency, and trustworthiness) and integrity through a detailed audit trail, i.e., reporting on interpretations and decisions leading to the synthesis of results (Weed, 2005). In this sense, the method will be closer to interpretative phenomenological analysis than to positivistic objectivity (Smith, Flowers, & Osborn, 1997). The specific steps of the method will be provided in the presentation of the findings in the next sections. The analytical tool associated with this method is fsQCA 2.5 software used to process the data.

The QCA analytical method was used to test a set of research hypotheses about the RBV and TCT assumptions to distinguish sub-groups of cases representing differing profiles in this regard and thus varying patterns of growth process (Hypotheses 1–3). The hypotheses assuming the influence of moderator variables were further tested in relation to groups representing given patterns of growth to learn how the influence of moderators is associated with different patterns of growth (Hypotheses 4 and 5). Hypothesis testing in this instance does not claim statistical confirmation and generalization. It rather aims at falsification of the assumptions for individual cases to identify different configurations among them and to form clusters of similar configurations to achieve generalizations about differing paths of the growth process. The major source of data for processing through QCA was based on the first wave of structured interviews, and it is applied to a cross-case analysis.

The other challenge stemming from a large set of data is a comprehensive and in-depth utilization of data richness. Thus, the large number of cases is less manageable for a within-case study investigation. QCA supports the aggregation and structuring of data by using a semi-quantitative, robust, transparent, and trustworthy procedure (Legewie, 2013). However, when it is applied as the only method, it can lead to losing some nuanced but relevant information. Therefore QCA was planned to organize the cross-case analysis to be followed by an in-depth, within-case study investigation of growth patterns identified through QCA. The data source for the within-case study analysis will predominantly come from the second wave of interviews, which were semi-structured. In accordance with the theoretical assumptions about the importance of the entrepreneur's perceptions for shaping the pattern of growth, the design of interviews and questionnaires was based on the owner-managers' self-reporting about decisions, actions, opinions, values, and experiences. Such an approach is a double hermeneutic (tangible and intangible phenomena filtered by the perceptions of interviewees and further by the researcher) (Weed, 2005; Smith, Jarman, & Osborn, 1997). The information from the semi-structured interviews was less strictly organized than the information from the first, structured interviews, strengthening the challenge of double hermeneutic. The citations and paraphrases enable a more objective and transparent treatment of reports from interviewees. To code and interpret data, we utilized text mining and content analysis supported by Statistica 10 software.

We also employed some supplementary methods in the process of sampling cases and aggregating the information from the interviews, such as the statistical analysis of high-grower profiles included in the database 'Gazelles of Business.' Table 13 presents the overview of methods and analytical methods adopted in the empirical research.

The major research method, the multiple-case study, will be developed based on specific methods serving as sources of data to case studies. These specific methods include structured and semi-structured interviews, natural observation and analysis of secondary sources. There are

Table 13. The research and analytical methods

Research methods		Analytical methods and tools	
The major method	Specific methods as sources of data for case studies	Methods	Tools
Multiple-case study	Structured interviews	QCA (Hypotheses 1–3); Comparative analysis of growth patterns (Hypotheses 4 and 5)	fsQCA 3.5
	Semi-structured interviews	Text mining, content analysis, descriptive statistics (non-parametric tests, such as chi-square and concordance tests)	Statistica 10 software for text mining
	Natural observation		
	Analysis of secondary data		

Source: own work.

interrelationships among sources of data as per the triangulation rule, i.e., they mutually inform one another to adjust for gaps or inconsistencies and to validate the information and inference. Analytical methods serve processing and structuring data and information obtained based on the research methods. QCA is matched with structured interviews, while text mining and content analysis are tailored to semi-structured interviews. However, this is only a general division, since the inference from data was an iterative process, during which both analytical and research methods mutually validated and facilitated one another, providing for adjustments and new highlights. For instance, natural observation and secondary data were helpful in coding and structuring data from both waves of interviews, while QCA and content analysis mutually highlighted the findings.

4.3. Variables

Within the elements of growth, the constructs of TCT and the RBV were operationalized into research variables.

Motives

During the interviews, the entrepreneurs declared their level of agreement with a set of five statements reflecting their perceived motives of trust versus opportunism in business relationships, using a 5-point Likert scale (Table 14).

Respondents are normally reluctant to openly reveal their attitudes towards trust and opportunism, and they demonstrate the social desirability bias in this regard (Wathne & Heide, 2000; Levi, 2000). Therefore, in the structured interviews, the measure of perceived motives in business exchange emphasized the perceptions of opportunistic behaviors. Furthermore, during the semi-structured interviews, the respondents were additionally asked to evaluate their views as either trust- or opportunism-oriented or balanced. The results did not show any considerable inconsistency with the five-statement measure.

As earlier assumed, the perceived motives of partners in business exchange will affect how cooperative relationships are governed. Therefore, we examined the types of contracts and safeguards applied by the entrepreneurs. The measures of cooperation governance were derived from

Table 14. The statements of opinions about the role of trust and opportunism in business relationships rated by using a 5-point Likert scale

Statement	Interpretation
1. Trust and mutuality are the primary basis for business relationships	1, 2 – support for TCT 3 – in between 4, 5 – support for the RBV
2. Each party in business relationships demonstrates opportunism (self-interest seeking with guile)	1, 2 – support for the RBV 3 – in between 4, 5 – support for TCT
3. Trust in business relationships is limited and should be supported with adequate safeguards	1, 2 – support for the RBV 3 – in between 4, 5 – support for TCT
4. Opportunism is present before signing a contract, but its influence is particularly evident after signing a contract (*ex-post*)	1, 2 – support for the RBV 3 – in between 4, 5 – support for TCT
5. *Ex-post* opportunism is caused by incomplete contracts, as after they are signed dependency of partners exists and the incomplete terms encourage rent seeking at the cost of the partner	1, 2 – support for the RBV 3 – in between 4, 5 – support for TCT

Source: own work.

TCT and operationalized based on pilot studies (Williamson, 1975; 1989; 1991; Macneil, 1986; Williamson, 1991). The type of contracts included spot contracts, formal long-term contracts, and relational contracts based on repetitive commissions (Williamson, 1975; 1989; 1991; Macneil, 1986; Williamson, 1991). The safeguards (incentives) that can be included in contracts are sections dealing with the pledge, prepayment, bank insurance, bank guarantee, the loss of reputation, the threat of terminating a contract, mutuality, and prospects for future business. The importance and frequency of adopting these contracting arrangements were investigated to identify a dominant type of governance for a given company.

Rationale

The rationales of value and transaction costs were reformulated into research variables. The empirical analysis focused on transaction costs as the perceived total costs of exchange stemming from the bargaining position relative to buyers and suppliers. The rationale of value increase was considered at both the business and personal levels.

The main research question to investigate the rationale for expansion included eight options, of which four denoted value considerations (profit increase, better exploitation of the existing resource and scale economies, utilizing market opportunities, business success, and personal satisfaction). The remaining four options acted as proxies for transaction cost savings implied by the bargaining position (reducing market uncertainty on the part of buyers and suppliers, increasing market power relative to buyers and suppliers, reducing dependence on suppliers and buyers, and decreasing costs of purchasing goods). The entrepreneurs were to select the relevant options and rank them according to the hierarchy of importance.

We also investigated how the adopted rationale affects the kind of activity undertaken to achieve growth (a new product or service, new process, organizational or marketing solution, penetration of the existing or development of new local or international markets, finding a new customer, or discovering a market niche). Furthermore, the scope of the innovativeness of these activities was examined (new to the firm, its market/industry, or to the world) and the impact on portfolio development (portfolio development through diversification or vertical integration into new or modified products, or volume increase only through market penetration or launching a new market with existing products).

Mechanisms and modes of growth

The mechanisms of growth were explored during the structured interviews, but more specifically during the semi-structured interviews, due to the complex nature of these constructs. The alignment with transaction characteristics was acknowledged if the new activity as a source of growth was driven by customer or supplier requirements or needs (Williamson, 2005). Launching the new activity based on the recognition to either exploit or expand a capability denoted its alignment with capabilities (Silverman, 1999).

The resulting modes of growth were investigated as organic, acquisitive, or hybrid options (Penrose, 1959; Williamson, 2005). We checked the coherence of these modes with the RBV and TCT alignment logics, depending on the starting point of growth activities (products, processes, markets). These were either capabilities and opportunities (support for the RBV) or business partner requirements (support for TCT). The coherence with the RBV alignment logic was additionally checked, based on the consistency or inconsistency of growth activities with a firm's core competencies (industry, employee skills, market, or technology). It was expected that the perceived consistency in at least two aspects of the core competencies would result in the organic mode, while full inconsistency or consistency in only one aspect generated the external mode, other things being equal. The coherence with the TCT alignment logic was further explored to assess the impact of idiosyncratic investments, the complexity and frequency required in the new, growth activities on either hierarchy growth (the internalization of these activities) or hybrid growth (joint ventures, licensing, franchising). The internalization was expected when among the factors of asset specificity, transaction complexity, and transaction frequency at least two variables demonstrated high levels. Hybrid modes were assumed when at least two factors demonstrated medium levels or all the factors were at different levels (a mixture of low, medium and high levels of the three factors).

Moderators – contextual factors

The entrepreneurs were to assess the level and type of asset specificity understood as the level (low, medium, high) of idiosyncratic investment (in physical infrastructure, personnel competence, location, logistics, etc.) related to transactions with three major suppliers and buyers before the growth occurred. Additional features were obtained by investigating the connections between asset specificity and the perceived dependence from customers (low, moderate, high). The variable of asset specificity as a moderator differs from the earlier researched idiosyncratic investments that affect the modes of growth. Namely, here it is a general characteristic of a firm's transactions with key exchange partners, while earlier (the analysis of mechanisms and modes) it was a characteristic of an individual transaction, considering the new activity as a source of growth.

Resource advantage was identified by the entrepreneurs by the level (low, medium, high) and type of resource that gives their firms an advantage over competitors (technology, marketing and customer relationships, human resource management, experience, routines, etc.) (Mayer & Salomon, 2006).

The prevalence of either of these factors is expected to support the impact of the theory to which it belongs. However, the influence of asset specificity and resource advantage as core determinants of the two theories should be considered as an interaction rather than as an individual impact. The nature of moderators requires that they are tested either in quantitative research or based on the groups of cases reflecting some common patterns (a cross-case study analysis) and not based on the falsification test performed for individual cases (a within-case study analysis).

4.4. Case selection criteria, characteristics of the research sample, and data collection procedure

The deliberate (purposeful), theory-driven sampling process embraced predominantly companies listed in the ranking of Polish Gazelles 2013, a contest with a 10-year history, run every year by an economic weekly *Puls Biznesu* [The Pulse of Business]. The database contains records of approximately 4,000 Polish companies that increased their sales within the last three consecutive years. Three-year sales are the basis for the ranking, and the 2013 edition covered the years 2010–2012. Enterprises participate in the ranking on a voluntary basis and the data provided by them (industry, employment in 2012, as well as sales, equity, and gross and net profit in the years 2010–2012) are validated by an independent consulting company. Databases of gazelles from country-wide or international contests were also utilized in other research studies, a notable example is by Barringer, Jones, and Neubaum (2005).

As discussed in the first chapter, the selection criteria for gazelles focus on employment and sales, due to the relative accessibility and objectivity in demonstrating the size dynamics. Extant studies were used to adopt different measures of growth. One option is to define high-growth firms as those demonstrating at least 20 to 25% size increase per annum during 3 to 4 consecutive years, assuming relatively stable dynamics every year. Another option is to choose the criterion of the overall size increase of at least 100% during 3 to 4 years, if that growth is irregular and unstable (Davidsson & Wiklund, 2000; Moreno & Casillas, 2007). The latter method better responds to SME reality (Coad, 2009) and it was chosen in the project. The selection criteria below acknowledge sales growth as the major criterion, since it is the most objective with regard to data sourcing and interpretation. Sales growth is also the most widespread measure, which enhances the comparability of the study with other research. The selection criteria also acknowledge employment growth as the best indicator of the entrepreneur's conviction of a stable and sustainable size increase that justifies hiring and taking on the responsibility and costs of additional human resources. Although some authors note a considerable overlap between these two measures in statistical analysis (Coad, 2009), others often find them independent and caused by different factors (Chandler, McKelvie, & Davidsson, 2009). This controversy represents additional justification for including the high-growers of employment in the sample.

The sampling process was directed at the micro, small, and medium-sized enterprises that increased sales by at least 100% within four years and the firms with considerable employment growth during this period. The OECD sampling method focuses on firms that employ at least 10 people (OECD, 2007; 2010). However, we included micro-firms in the sample, because there are arguments that ignoring them would bias the characteristics of high-growers (Cieślik, 2014). First, the smallest companies demonstrate the most dynamic relative growth, since they are pressured to improve their economies of scale and market bargaining power (Storey, 1994). Second, although relative (percentage) expansion of micro-firms is not considerable in individual terms, considering their dominant share in the population of start-ups and young firms, this group significantly contributes to economic growth (Stam et al., 2006) and was included in the previous studies (Acs, Parsons, & Tracy, 2008).

We also intended to select a sample with substantial variation in size, age, technological level, and type of industry. This diversity of features aimed to capture different conditions for testing the RBV and TCT propositions and to find common patterns of growth within this heterogeneity.

The final set of selection criteria was as follows:
- at least 100% increase in employment and/or sales during the last four consecutive years;
- micro, small, or medium size as per the criteria of the EU Commission Recommendation 2003/361/EC, which states that the category of SMEs comprises the enterprises that employ fewer than 250 persons, with an annual turnover not more than EUR 50 million, and/or an annual balance sheet total not more than EUR 43 million (the same criteria apply to Polish Law on Economic Freedom of 2004); or micro, small, or medium size in the base year;
- at least one year of operations before the base year;
- differing size in the sample as measured by employment and sales as an indicator of resource differences;
- differing levels of industry technology in the sample as an indicator of capability differences (a representation of companies from high, medium-high, medium-low, and low technology sectors, as per Eurostat (2008);
- differing levels of performance in terms of profitability;
- differing levels of maturity (start-ups, young, and mature companies).

Based on the statistical analysis of the database, the cohorts of companies were systematically addressed to accomplish the required representation. Figure 8 presents the data collection procedure.

Transcribing and organizing data and development of the final model of SME growth process

↑

Development of a research tool (a semi-structured questionnaire)

↑

The second wave of semi-structured, tape-recorded interviews, accompanied by natural observation and secondary data analysis

↑

Structuring and coding the data, processing data with the use of adequate methods; developing the initial model of SME growth process

↑

The first wave of direct structured, tape-recorded interviews, accompanied by natural observation and secondary data analysis

↑

A pilot study to test the structured questionnaire (direct pilot interviews with entrepreneurs) and adjustments to the questionnaire

↑

Establishing case selection criteria and sampling of companies for case studies based on the ranking database, contacting companies via e-mails and phone calls

↑

Establishing an empirical research framework, operationalization of variables and development of a research tool (a structured questionnaire)

Figure 8. Data collection procedure

Source: own work.

The sampling process was iterative, since the database does not directly enable selecting the companies with a four-year history of growth. Moreover, the entrepreneurs were moderately responsive to the invitation to participate in the research. The firms were addressed directly through e-mail and telephone calls. To increase their representation, entrepreneurs were contacted via some trustful entrepreneurs and business organizations, (Polish Chamber of Commerce, regional and city chambers of commerce, and technology parks). These endeavors resulted in 20 positive responses from entrepreneurs, who were interviewed during the first stage of the research. Two companies were start-up firms not yet included in the ranking.

Two-stage interviews were preceded by a pilot study to test the structured questionnaire. After refining and revising the questionnaire, the first wave of direct, structured interviews was held from August to December 2014. The interviews were held directly by the researcher and lasted from 2.5 to 3.5 hours each. During the visits to companies, other sources of data were exploited, including natural observation by the researcher and secondary data collection in the form of company reports and documents.

After the first wave of interviews was followed by the coding, transcribing, and structuring of data, the first analyses were performed based on the sample of 19 companies, as one case had to be skipped due to incomplete data. Two of the 19 companies were medium-growers with 30%–40% sales increase over four years to act as a control group recommended in the QCA method (Ragin, 2000; 2009). The findings were presented and discussed during scientific conferences. The sample of cases was larger than initially planned in order to check their usefulness for the methodology and objectives of the research. Moreover, this surplus avoided the risk of an insufficient number of firms in the second wave of interviews planned for 2015. The reduction of the sample was based on consistency with case selection criteria (industry, size, and variety, long-term growth and at least 100% increase in sales and employment within four years, among others), feedback from conference participants, as well as willingness to participate in the second wave of the research. The second wave of direct, semi-structured interviews was conducted from September to December 2015. The interviews lasted from 1.5 to 3.5 hours each.

The final sample of 16 firms considered in this study was composed of 14 high-growth entrepreneurs with an aggregate sales increase of at least 100% within four consecutive years plus two medium-growers with an aggregate sales increase of 35% and 40%. Growth in employment is much less popular among gazelles. However, the majority of high-growers in sales (eight firms) increased their employment by at least 30% within four consecutive years, and four of them more than doubled their employment in this period. The investigation also searched for companies listed in the ranking more than once, to verify that their expansion was not incidental. Twelve of the 16 firms were recorded in the ranking at least twice within three last editions. Table 15 presents the overview of the characteristics of the research sample.

Table 15. The characteristics of the research sample

Characteristic	Characteristic's distribution			
Sales growth within 2009–2012 or 2010–2013[a]	>100%		30–40%	
Number of firms	14	2		
Employment growth within 2009–2012 or 2010–2013[a]	>100%	>30–70%	>15–30%	0–15%
Number of firms	4	4	5	3
Industry technology	High technology products and knowledge-intensive services	Medium-high technology products	Medium-low technology products	Low technology products and less knowledge intensive services
Number of firms	6	3	3	4
Sector	Manufacturing	Services		
Number of firms	6	10		
Firm age in 2009 or 2010[a]	Up to 3,5 years	3,5–10 years	11–20 years	>20 years
Number of firms	4	6	5	1
Firm size in 2009 or 2010[b]	Micro	Small	Medium	
Number of firms	4	7	5	

[a] – depending on the year set as a starting point to calculate the four-year period of growth; except for two start-ups established in 2010 and 2012; [b] – depending on the year set as a starting point to calculate the four-year period of growth; except for two start-ups established as micro-firms in 2010 and 2012

Source: own work.

The profiles of individual firms in the sample are shown in Table 16.

Table 16. The profiles of individual companies in the sample

Company	Sales growth within 2009–2012 or 2010–2013 (%)	Employment growth within 2009–2012 or 2010–2013 (%)	Size in 2009 or 2010	The year of establishment	Industry
AutomCo	111	20	Small	1994	IT Services
BikeCo	155	35	Small	1991	Trade and services in sports equipment
Construct-Co	101	23	Medium	2002	Manufacturing of metal construc-tions, construction services
InstalCo	156	12	Small	1999	Electric and elec-tronic services
ITServCo	133	110	Medium	2005	IT services
LineCo	102	50	Small		Manufacturing of industrial ropes
MediaCo	450[a]	250[b]	Micro[c]	2010	Media marketing services
NutriCo	258	31	Small	1991	Infant formula manufacturing
OilCo	136	0	Micro	2009	Vegetable oil trade
SafetyCo	35	16	Small	1991	Wholesale of spe-cialized electronic equipment, safety and monitoring services
SoftCo	270	102	Medium	2000	Software develop-ment
SpedCo	590	70	Medium	2008	Transporting and shipping services
SportSoft-Co	800[d]	800[e]	Micro[f]	2012	IT services for gym-nastic facilities
TransCo	175	20	Micro	2007	Transporting ser-vices
VacuumCo	40	20	Medium	1968	Manufacturing of pumps and com-pressors
WasteCo	170	10	Small	2005	Waste management (construction, consulting, and design)

[a] – sales growth in the years 2011–2014; [b] – employment growth in the years 2011–2014; [c] – size in 2011; [d] – sales growth in the years 2013–2015 (an early start-up company); [e] – employment growth in the years 2013–2015; [f] – size in 2012

Source: own work.

In the sampling procedure, we did not intend to match growers with non-growers, since our focus was on the actual process of growth. Thus non-growers' characteristics do not provide relevant information (Achtenhagen, Naldi, & Melin, 2010). Matching high-growers and non-growers is required when the aim is to explore growth determinants – to explain why some firms expand while others do not.

We utilized QCA version 3.5 and Statistica software for coding, structuring, and processing information, including text mining. Two independent researchers were engaged in coding, calibrating and synthesizing data from the interviews and the secondary sources of information in the form of company reports, records, and press releases.

4.5. Scientific validity of the research methodology

The qualitative nature of the case study method sets specific requirements to ensure scientific rigor of concept validity, internal validity, external validity (generalizability), and reliability (Eisenhardt & Graebner, 2007; Gibbert & Ruigrok, 2010).

Concept validity refers to the appropriateness of the research procedure and to the accuracy of observations (proper data collection). In the present research, this is ensured by combining an extensive literature review of narrative and systematic natural and qualitative meta-analysis with a two-stage empirical research design, using a mixed-method approach and data triangulation.

Internal validity (logical validity) has been attained when the data analysis reflects proper causal relationships between the variables and reliable results (Yin, 2009). Adopting a well-structured theoretical framework, where the causal mechanism for growth was clearly stated enabled the required consistency. It was a sound starting point to use falsification testing to explore the real processes of expansion. The falsification tests were performed for individual case studies with the use of comprehensive data treatment using qualitative and quantitative analytical methods and deviant-case analysis.

External validity (generalizability) is the transferability of the knowledge achieved in the particular study to other contexts. Applicability in other contexts is especially difficult to achieve with the case study method. At least a weak form of generalization applies to results from case studies (naturalistic generalization), i.e., the relevance of knowledge generated through research for cases similar to those in the study. This form of validity was strengthened with the use of the multiple-case approach with a maximum variety of contexts. The case study method offers analytical generalization, i.e., generalization from empirical observations to theory building (unlike statistical generalization that translates empirical findings to population behavior) (Eisenhardt, 1989). This study aimed at analytical generalization for building a new integrated theoretical framework of RBV and TCT relating to the SME growth process. Generalization was dependent on the appropriateness and accuracy of the sampling method. Here the purposeful sampling was aimed at maximizing the variety of research objects. External analytical validity is additionally strengthened by the multiple-case approach and some quantitative data analysis.

Reliability is precision and transparency of the implementation of the research plan, so that the methodology can be replicated with the same result by different researchers (Silverman, 2013). It was secured by audio recording the interviews, transcribing them, and coding them by using the appropriate software.

5. PATTERNS OF THE SME GROWTH PROCESS: RESULTS OF THE MULTI-CASE STUDY RESEARCH

5.1. Results of the cross-case study analysis

The cross-case analysis will include testing Hypotheses 1, 2, and 3 (the structural elements of the SME growth process in the integrative view of the RBV and TCT) and Hypotheses 4 and 5 (the contextual influences on the characteristics of these elements) with the use of the falsification approach to each case study. Through testing these hypotheses, the cross-case study analysis is directed at identifying the characteristics of entrepreneurs' perceptions about structural elements of motives, rationale, mechanisms, and modes of expansion. Hypotheses 1, 2, and 3 reflect the extant research evidence about the validity of the RBV and TCT in explaining the structural elements of the growth process and about different patterns followed by the entrepreneurs in this regard. Considering the empirically revealed heterogeneity of SME expansion, we predict that there will be differing growth patterns that stem from the context, including the firm's capabilities and the transaction environment. Therefore, Hypotheses 4 and 5 detect possible contextual influences that might generate differing profiles of the growth process as marked by its structural elements.

To test Hypotheses 1, 2, and 3, the QCA method was adopted. This method investigates configurations (solutions) of factors (conditions) that are necessary and sufficient for a specific outcome in the evolution of a given phenomenon (Ragin, 2008b; Legewie, 2013)[1]. In this research,

---

[1] In the QCA terminology, interrelated *factors*, also called *conditions*, combine to form *configurations* (also called *solutions*) that denote processes or evolution of some social phenomena to produce a specific *outcome*. In this research, factors or conditions will be particular *structural elements of the growth process*, while configurations or solutions will be synonymous with *patterns of the growth process*. Finally, the outcome is *firm growth expressed as size increase*.

the expected outcome is high SME growth, while the structural elements are interrelated factors (conditions) for the outcome to happen. The understanding of the structural elements as factors or conditions is justified by their earlier conceptualization as enabling constraints that both constrain (structure in some predetermined way) and assist decisions and actions (give a tangible and intangible basis and framework for entrepreneurs to act). The characteristics of these factors are expected to form different configurations (also called solutions), which will denote differing pathways of the growth process that result in size and scope increases and the appropriate learning effects. This logic of adopting QCA to identifying patterns of the growth process is consistent with the earlier theoretical inference. Namely, differing configurations of structural elements form different patterns of the growth process through impacting decisions and actions (the flow of events) eventually leading to SME expansion.

Hypotheses 4 and 5 will be verified based on the comparative analysis of growth patterns identified by the QCA method. The comparative analysis should reveal the contextual influences of the firm's capabilities and the transaction environment on the emergence of distinctive patterns of growth. This will be accomplished by checking whether these contextual factors are associated with patterns of growth as per the logic of the RBV, TCT, or both approaches combined.

QCA is based on combinatory logic requiring that all research variables are standardized into binary values: either 1 as present (confirmed in the research), or 0 as absent (rejected in the research). This QCA approach is called *crisp-set analysis*. A more nuanced approach, the so-called *fuzzy-set analysis,* is also possible when results are mixed (Ragin, 2008a; 2009). This approach requires qualifying a particular factor as fully present (completely in) or fully absent (completely out) or in-between (a crossover point). Data are calibrated in this fashion to assign them with values corresponding to these states on the scale from 0 to 1 (Ragin, 2008b).

We have employed the crisp set analysis due to its suitability for hypothesis verification. It is also favored due to its straightforward way of delimiting the final sets of configurations and in presenting the results. The binary qualification denoted approval (1) or rejection (0) of a given hypothesis to maintain the falsification logic for individual case studies.

However, to utilize the richness of data and ensure the possibility of a more nuanced approach typical of the case study method, we also assigned three states denoting the level of agreement with Hypotheses 1, 2, and 3. Namely, fully approved was recorded as 1 and rejected or in-between were aggregated and recorded as 0. This enabled additional interpretations of findings during the within-case study analysis.

Motives

We transformed the ranks attributed to the statements about trust versus opportunism to the scale ranging from 0 to 1 (the closer the average score to 1, the higher the level of agreement with the RBV; the closer the average score to 0, the higher the level of agreement with TCT). As a result, we found nine cases supporting Hypothesis 1 that trust has more explanatory power about the perceived motives of exchange partners in the process of growth, limited by the perceived opportunism (average scores from 0.6 to 0.9). Three cases attributed a balanced approach to trust and opportunism in business exchange (average score of 0.5). Three cases emphasized the opportunistic behavior (average scores from 0.1 to 0.4). Applying the logic of Popper's falsification test to 10 of the cases, Hypothesis 1 cannot be rejected, but for the remaining 6 cases, this hypothesis was rejected.

Rationale

We computed weighted average scores of factors describing the rationale by using their ranks (from 1 as the least important to 5 as the most important). Then they were transformed to values from 0 to 1: the closer the average score to 1, the higher the level of agreement with the RBV; the closer the average score to 0, the higher the level of agreement with TCT. Eight cases supported exclusively the value rationale for growth (score of 1) and in eight cases the predominant rationale was value supplemented by transaction costs considerations (scores from 0.6 to 0.8). The latter eight cases supported Hypothesis 2, while the remaining eight cases rejected Hypothesis 2.

Mechanisms and modes of growth

Due to the complex, interrelated nature of mechanisms and modes of growth, these constructs were approached with comprehensive evidence from both stages of interviews, but the final verification of hypotheses was performed based on the semi-structured interviews. The variables in the structured interviews, and primarily the qualitative accounts from the entrepreneurs, enabled inferences about the mechanisms. The mechanisms of the alignment of the new activity with the transaction characteristics (buyer/supplier requirements and needs) and the firm's capabilities were revealed in five cases. These cases support Hypothesis 3, i.e., it cannot be rejected by the falsification test. The remaining 11 cases stipulate the rejection of Hypothesis 3. They either follow exclusively the RBV mechanism of aligning the new activity with a firm's capability (6 cases) or the TCT mechanism of aligning with transacting with buyers and suppliers (5 cases).

In some cases, hybrid growth, internalization, organic, and acquisitive growth were combined in the growth process. The observed connections between the levels of asset specificity, transaction frequency, transaction uncertainty and expansion through either internalization (16 cases) or hybrid modes (three cases) comply with the TCT rules. Organic growth was adopted as the only option or as one of the options by the entire sample of cases. Consequently, all the cases revealed bonding to the core competencies (exploitation mechanism) when growing organically. There were six cases when the new activity was not related to existing employee skills or technology and these cases were associated with the external method through mergers or acquiring new employees, which complies with the RBV rules about the acquisitive mode of growth when the explorative mechanism is adopted. The general conclusion about decisions on growth mode is that the entrepreneurs' choices were consistent with both theoretical approaches. Namely, regardless of the dominant mechanism of growth, TCT provides explanations of the choice between the internalization (hierarchy growth) or hybrid modes, while the RBV clarifies the choice between external and internal (organic) modes.

Verification of Hypotheses 1–3

Table 17 summarizes the verification of the research hypotheses. Due to non-random sampling and a limited number of observations, only the statements derived from Popper's falsification test are possible (Popper, 1968). Consequently, a hypothesis can be supported (i.e., it cannot be rejected) or can be rejected, but it cannot be confirmed by proof (Popper, 1968; Bitektine, 2008).

Table 17. Verification of the research hypotheses based on the falsification test

Hypothesis	Verification	
	Cannot be rejected (*n* cases)	Rejected (*n* cases)
1	9	7
2	8	8
3	5	11

Source: own work.

Falsification may provide a simple tallying of cases that results in listing the instances when some assumptions hold, while others do not. QCA goes one step further towards a synthesis that does not claim to be a statistical generalization (Legewie, 2013). It is rather a logical, analytical generalization about configurations or patterns of how hypotheses are verified. The method goes beyond tallying of the cases towards an analytical generalization. This ensures a synthesis, but due to acknowledging the diverse patterns of growth, it does not simplify the observed heterogeneity (Ragin & Sonnett, 2005).

Table 18. Summary of the verification of research hypotheses for each case study

Case	H1	H2	H3	Outcome
AutomCo	0	1	0	1
BikeCo	1	1	1	1
ConstructCo	0	1	0	1
InstalCo	0	1	0	1
ITServCo	1	0	0	1
LineCo	0	0	1	1
MediaCo	1	0	0	1
NutriCo	1	1	1	1
OilCo	1	1	1	1
SafetyCo	0	0	1	0
SoftCo	1	1	0	1
SpedCo	0	1	0	1
SportSoftCo	0	1	0	1
TransCo	1	0	0	1
VacuumCo	1	0	0	0
WasteCo	1	0	0	1

Hypothesis (H) supported (not rejected) – 1, hypothesis rejected by falsification – 0; outcome 1 – aggregate sales increase of at least 100% within four consecutive years, outcome 0 – aggregate sales increase of 35% and 40% within four consecutive years

Source: own work.

The QCA combinatory logic and the falsification test of individual hypotheses require that each case is described with dichotomous variables of 1 or 0. This approach fits well with the analytical step we achieved, i.e., verified research hypotheses. Table 18 presents a summary of the verification of research hypotheses in each case associated with growth process outcome, which is either high (more than 100% within four consecutive years) or moderate (35% and 40% within four consecutive years) increase in sales.

Identifying patterns of SME growth

The next step of the analytical procedure was to construct a so-called "truth table," a presentation of results that shows all the possible configurations of factors; grouping the cases demonstrating the same configuration of factors (in this research – a verification of hypotheses) (Ragin, 2000; 2008b; 2009). These configurations (patterns, solutions) denote alternative, equifinal pathways of the growth process (Table 19). The essence of the pattern are motives, rationale, mechanisms, and modes that have distinctive characteristics to be described in the following paragraphs.

Table 19. Truth table with all possible configurations and the sets of cases demonstrating the same configurations relative to the outcome

Configuration	H1	H2	H3	N (%)	Consistency	Outcome
1	1	0	0	6 (38%)	86%	1
2	0	1	0	5 (69%)	100%	1
3	1	1	1	3 (88%)	100%	1
4	0	0	1	2 (100%)	50%	0
5	1	1	0	0		
6	1	0	1	0		
7	0	1	1	0		
8	0	0	0	0		

Hypothesis (H) supported (not rejected) – 1, hypothesis rejected by falsification – 0; outcome 1 – relevant configuration to describe the growth process, 0 – not relevant solution to describe the growth process

Source: own work.

The truth table (Table 19) presents 8 possible patterns (solutions) that result from introducing three independent variables in the form of the verified research hypotheses (2^k algorithm[2]), while 4 configurations are represented by the data. The relevant configurations that describe the process of expansion by high-growers are coded as 1 in the outcome column. They were determined by referring to the criteria of frequency and consistency. Relevant frequency was defined to be at least one case representing a given configuration, a rule recommended for small N samples by Ragin (2008b). Consistency measures how close the specific pattern is to the process of high (instead of moderate) growth. It is measured by computing the share of cases producing the outcome 1 (high growth) in all cases representing a given configuration. The recommended consistency threshold is 0.75, and we used the threshold level of 0.83 for configuration 1 (Ragin, 2008b). It was therefore accepted as producing an outcome of high-growth marked as 1 in the outcome table. Configuration 4 with a consistency of 0.50 was excluded from further analysis, since it did not meet the consistency threshold. One of the excluded cases was a moderate grower acting as a control case study, while the other one belonged to the group of high-growers.

The analysis of the truth table based on the criteria of frequency and consistency produced three relevant configurations, namely solutions 1, 2, and 3. The next step involved the minimization procedure to identify the final sufficient patterns for describing the high growth process. The sufficient solution is a configuration that always produces the outcome in question, i.e., high growth, therefore, it needs to demonstrate relevant consistency (Berg et al., 2009). In the present results, all three configurations demonstrate relevant consistency (above 0.75). Moreover, they were not reduced upon the minimization procedure and represent sufficient conditions for high growth. The minimization procedure consists in combining solutions that differ in only one condition (one hypothesis) and removing this condition does not change the required outcome (Ragin, 2008b). The differences among the cases representing specific solutions justified abandoning more minimization, since the three conditions differed in at least two factors (two hypotheses). This procedure is continued when configurations differ on only one factor (hypothesis) (Ragin, 2008b). In Table 20, the final patterns are listed according to their share in all high-growth cases (unique coverage) and the consistency with the outcome of high growth.

---

[2] 2^k denotes binary option of 2 (0 or 1) with k features/conditions – a part of the QCA combinatory logic (Ragin, 2000; 2009).

Table 20. Final patterns (solutions) of the SME growth process

Solution	Unique coverage (share in all high-growth cases)	Consistency
1.	36%	83%
2.	36%	100%
3.	21%	100%
Solution coverage 93% (three combined solutions represent 93% of all high growth cases) Solution consistency 93% (combined consistency of all three solutions)		

Source: own work.

Description of the SME growth patterns

Table 19 displays more detailed characteristics of each pattern of entrepreneurial perceptions in decision-making as to motives, mechanisms, and modes of growth combined with moderators, i.e., the level of resource advantage (differentiating and rare capabilities relative to competitors) and of asset specificity (adjustment to transaction (customer or supplier) requirements. The first feature represents the core construct of the RBV, namely the nature of capabilities for competitive advantage relative to those of competitors. It reflects a company's internal context for entrepreneurial decision making. The second feature is the TCT construct that implies the level of dependence in business relationships. It represents an external, contractual context for the entrepreneurs' decisions in the process of growth.

The three patterns differentiate in the characteristics of structural elements and their moderators (Table 21).

More detailed profiles of the above patterns of the growth process are described below with the use of the exemplary evidence from the respondents' accounts and explanations given during the interviews.

Pattern 1 – a capability-based process of growth

The entrepreneurs following this pattern perceive the motives in business exchange as dominated by trust and mutuality but limited by some level of opportunism. The respondents acknowledged a high level of agreement with the importance of trust as a basis of business relationships. However, trust is perceived as limited, and safeguards are deemed moderately

Table 21. Patterns of growth process – structural elements and their moderators

Pattern	Case	Structural elements of growth process			Moderators (firm-level and transaction-level context)	
		Perceived motives in a business exchange	Rationale for growth	Mechanisms and modes of growth	Resource advantage (level and type)	Asset specificity
1. Capability-based process of growth (growth and value achieved due to development of capabilities)	WasteCo SoftCo MediaCo ITServCo VaccumCo TransCo	Dominated by trust with some level of opportunism	Value and competitive advantage	Based on the alignment to capabilities	High due to technology superiority	Medium asset specificity raising moderate dependence
2. Transactional process of growth (growth and value achieved due to effective managing transaction costs)	ConstructCo SpedCo AutomCo SportSoftCo InstalCo	Opportunism dominates, or trust and opportunism are balanced	Value and competitive advantage supplemented by transaction cost considerations	Based on the alignment to customers/ suppliers	Medium to high due to non-technological advantages (human resources, marketing, routines, experience, and quality)	High asset specificity raising high dependence
3. A capability and market opportunity-oriented process of growth (growth due to capability development and constraining transaction costs)	OilCo NutriCo BikeCo	Trust dominates, but is strongly limited by opportunism	Value and competitive advantage supplemented by transaction cost considerations	Based on the alignment to capabilities and to customers/ suppliers	Low	Medium asset specificity raising moderate dependence

Source: own work.

important. Generally, the entrepreneurs questioned ex-post opportunism due to incomplete contracts. The excerpts from their accounts show how they cope with the threat of opportunism and how they perceive trustful relationships.

'Problems can be resolved by mutual consent and understanding of common and individual interests, negotiation skills, and flexible adaptation...' (TransCo)

'When there are fringes to earlier agreements, we terminate cooperation. Customers used their position when we were starting up; when our products were not recognized in the market. They even did not want to hear about paying for our products. But now, we have excluded unfair partners from the business. Now we can choose among partners. If we do not see a potential for mutual consent and cooperation, we switch to another partner... But we do not use our superior technological position against partners; we do not take advantage of this position looking for a fair balance.' (SoftCo)

'The older generation of entrepreneurs probably thinks about some unfair steps to secure its position this way. The new wave of entrepreneurs, the younger generation, puts emphasis on competencies, capabilities and trustful relationships.' (MediaCo)

'We build fair relationships with high-quality suppliers who guarantee our quality. We do not pursue ad hoc contracting.' (WasteCo)

Value and competitive advantage are exclusive growth rationale for the entrepreneurs following this solution, and they do not see any need to treat expansion as a way to improve their bargaining position and reduce transaction costs in the exchange with customers and suppliers. The rationales for growth reported by this group of respondents were predominantly focused on value and included an increase of income, exploitation and exploration of market opportunities, and better utilization of surplus resources through scale and scope economies. Beside direct pointing to these options in the structured interviews, the entrepreneurs also provided their comments about rationales for expansion.

'The improvement in the bargaining, transacting position is not our rationale for growth, we seek for profitable growth. We search for profitable niches and withdraw from unprofitable ones.' (WasteCo)

'We just wanted to be a Polish, global, large company. We knew that there are huge niches that can be exploited over there. We wanted to build a global brand.' (SoftCo)

'Income and satisfaction were of primary relevance for us.' (VaccumCo)

The mechanisms of growth applied in this pattern follow the logic of aligning a new, growth activity (product, service, process, market) with capabilities. The level of consistency with core competence determines either an organic or acquisitive mode of expansion.

'Our products are very much specialized, and they overreach customer needs; therefore we follow our ideas rather than customer expectations. [...] Quite new competencies were needed to explore another opportunity. Therefore, we acquired a company, in which we had earlier minority shares.' (SoftCo)

'We are first in the market; therefore, we focus on own capabilities and resources as there are no similar technologies in Poland.' (MediaCo)

The above characteristics of the structural elements of growth process point to the RBV-oriented entrepreneurial decision-making.

The views of entrepreneurs can be explained by contextual factors (moderators). Considering contextual factors (moderators) at the firm- and transaction levels, the companies included in this subsample demonstrate *high resource advantages, due to technological superiority and moderate levels of asset specificity that invoke moderate dependence from key suppliers and buyers, as initial conditions of their capabilities and transaction environment.* Such characteristics of contextual factors strengthen these firms' bargaining position and inhibit opportunistic behaviors from partners. This advantageous position does not force the entrepreneurs to consider transaction costs as a rationale. They are a source of innovations for their customers; therefore, their mechanisms of growth are driven by their capabilities rather than by their customer or supplier requirements. Therefore, they treat the superiority of their technologies as the most powerful guarantee of customer loyalty that hinders unfair behaviors. The companies in this subgroup are all technological innovators at least at the country level, with two exceptions. One company demonstrates high flexibility and excellence in customer relationships rather than in technology. The advantages of the other firm are highly efficient personnel management and contracting, while its technology is based on external standards from large corporations. The entrepreneurs of both firms report high levels of capabilities compared to competitors. Moreover, they consider their business relationships with key customers and suppliers as predominantly balanced and not raising dependence. The moderate level of dependence from customers means that they address their needs, but the assets they devote to this cooperation are not fully adjusted (can be redeployed after some additional investment). They are not dependent on suppliers, but they raise dependence on the part of their suppliers.

'*Our suppliers are superior and adjust to our requirement, benefitting from unique knowledge. We pursue long-term relationships.*' (MediaCo)

Our suppliers are providers of standardized products and services; we can easily change them; the contracts are ad hoc.' (ITServCo)

Pattern 2 – a transactional process of growth is aimed at achieving growth and value by effectively managing transaction costs. The entrepreneurs see opportunism dominating in a business exchange with some level of trust, or they perceive trust and opportunism as balanced motivations.

The respondents were more skeptical and cautious in evaluating the motives in a business exchange. Exemplary evidence also shows that growth was deliberately planned to strengthen their transacting position and enable the exclusion of unreliable partners. Before growth occurred, smaller capability and inadequate experience exposed the entrepreneurs to opportunistic behaviors. These were still experienced in the very early stages of the firm's life cycle. Therefore, the respondents stressed these issues in the structured responses to the questionnaire. Here is some exemplary evidence from their interview transcripts.

'*The level of dependence among companies in our field is so high that opportunism is unavoidable raising high transaction costs. Companies blame one another and want to pass responsibility to someone else.*' (AutomCo)

'*Opportunism and taking advantage over us was a common thing.*' (SportSoftCo)

'*There are many hold backs, cheating, and concealing the information to sign a contract and engage somebody. The problems arise after the contract is signed*'. (InstalCo)

Considering the rationale for growth, their major target is value increase supplemented by the goal of strengthening their bargaining position to reduce the costs of transacting.

'*We wanted to build a large international firm and obtain a satisfying income. Growth was also conducive for a better position in relation to competitors, to effectively bid for commissions, and in relation to public agencies.*' (SpedCo)

'*Transaction costs are overwhelming in our field – all these diverse and interrelated activities need to be linked, and we do it for our customers. This is also why we employ architects instead of outsourcing such activities.*' (ConstructCo)

The mechanisms of growth in these cases stem from the requirements and expectations of customers or suppliers.

'*The product idea was customer-driven. A friend-manager of sports facility approached me after the market research and said there was a demand for software tailored to the specific needs of the owners of sports facilities.*' (SportSoftCo)

'*Our business depends on customers, and we follow their requirements in terms of decreasing the costs of transacting.*' (ConstructCo)

'*Growth ideas and directions depend on some groups of our customers. It is for them that we learn and acquire new technologies.*' (AutomCo)

'*A customer expects from us new solutions and activities. They say: just do it for us.*' (SpedCo)

As to contextual factors, the entrepreneurs following this pattern describe their businesses as featuring medium to high resource advantage due to non-technological capabilities, such superiority of human resources, marketing, quality, routines, and experience. The specificity of assets devoted to their main customers and buyers is rather high, which leads to the high perceived dependence from these partners. The characteristics of moderators make the entrepreneurs acknowledge the threat of opportunism in seeing motives in business exchange. This may be driven by their dependence on key buyers and/or suppliers, as well as by a lower resource position (advantage) than in Pattern 1. Consequently, their mechanism of growth aligns primarily with customer/supplier requirements and then considers the behaviors of competitors. This pattern of entrepreneurial decisional rules in the process of growth is oriented toward managing transactions with key partners. Transaction cost reasoning was strongly present in the entrepreneurs' thinking and activities. They also acknowledged the face validity of transaction costs as a significant issue in growing their firms. High asset specificity exposes them to opportunism and necessitates both the growth rationale of alleviating transaction costs and developing new activities (product, processes, market entrance) by adjusting to customer requirements.

'*The companies need to adjust tightly to one another in our field of activity and requirements are very idiosyncratic. This raises opportunism and the costs of transacting.*' (AutomCo)

'*We continuously adjust products and services to a group of loyal customers. We make improvements based on their specific needs and in a very close and continuous communication.*' (SportsSoftCo)

'*We adjust to large, few, long-term customers who set specific requirements about the rules of cooperation.*' (InstalCo)

One deviant case relative to the characteristics of moderators in Pattern 2 is an early start-up company showing a high resource advantage in technological terms (a proprietary and unique in the market solution) that is highly tailored to the customer needs and requires adequate adjustments of the assets. However, the entrepreneur does not perceive a high dependence on customers, seeing them as largely reliant upon cooperating with his company as a service provider. He assesses these relationships as mutual dependence, with a moderate advantage on the part of his firm. This outlier case may be explained by the early life cycle of the company that experiences behavioral uncertainty in business exchange and sees transaction costs as an important, supplementary rationale due to the liabilities of newness and smallness. However, with continuing capability development in the advanced phases of its life cycle, it may acquire the characteristics typical of the capability-based cases of the growth process in Pattern 1.

Pattern 3 – a capability and market opportunity-oriented process of growth is aimed at expansion through capability development and constraining transaction costs. The entrepreneurs following this pattern consider trust to dominate business relationships, but they see themselves more strongly limited by opportunism than in Pattern 1.

'Trust is a basis, and without it one cannot pursue any relationships. However, business is a game and who would like to reveal the information that would be harmful to him or her? When I see that prices go down, and the buyer says that they rise... Opportunism is present particularly before the contract is signed.' (OilCo)

'Opportunism occurs ex-ante, but ex-post we just deal with the contract execution and possible sanctions if contract terms are not kept. The contract is an effective safeguard. It takes time to develop trust and trustful relationships with selected partners while excluding those untrustworthy.' (BikeCo)

'Trust is an important condition, but it should be strongly supported with safeguards. Deceiving and concealing information or other forms of unfair play is present ex-ante, but definitely not after the contract was signed. Generally, our contracts are rarely incomplete and can be specified.' (NutriCo)

The entrepreneurs consider value and competitive advantage as the major rationale for growth supplemented by transaction cost considerations, i.e., they aim at improving their bargaining position to reduce the costs of transacting.

'Our rationales for growth are exploitation of market opportunities, income, and better utilization of resources; however, the improvement in transacting position relative to customers and suppliers is also crucial.' (NutriCo)

'*First, we want to utilize market chances and accomplish scale economies, but strengthening our position in relation to business partners and lowering dependence on suppliers due to their opportunism are also important.*' (BikeCo)

The mechanism of growth in this sample complies with the logic of aligning a new activity with the firm's capabilities and with transaction characteristics (requirements of customers or suppliers) at the same time.

'*We develop new products considering market risks (risk reduction) and own capabilities to develop products ourselves (we develop proprietary technologies which we patent).*' (NutriCo)

'*Flexible, fast reaction to market opportunities and environment scanning are our strengths, but we explore the chances considering extant capabilities.*' (OilCo)

Regarding moderator variables, their technological capabilities are not directed at differentiation and product or service uniqueness (they represent low resource advantage), but at standardization, which avoids high asset specificity (medium asset specificity) and thus alleviates the dependence on their customers. In this instance, the companies cannot fully control opportunistic behaviors based on the resource uniqueness, but these behaviors are limited by moderate dependence. The latter results from medium asset specificity, due to standardization of their offerings associated with adjusting to requirements of key buyers regarding the terms of supplies and institutional conditions (permits, certificates).

'*Our product is strictly standardized in accordance with external food safety regulations. However, we are flexible in terms of supplies and other terms of the contract.*' (NutriCo)

'*It is a first-need and standard product, therefore we do not adjust its features. But we try to be responsive to customers in organizational terms.*' (OilCo)

The impact of contextual variables and verification of Hypotheses 4 and 5

The three patterns differ in their characteristics of entrepreneurs' perceptions about motives, rationale, mechanisms, and modes of expansion. At the same time, we have observed a logical connection between these characteristics and the characteristics of moderators, i.e., the contextual factors of resource advantage and asset specificity. Based on the observation of distinctive features of moderators for each of the growth patterns considered, we state that *Hypothesis 4 is sustained (cannot be rejected). Namely, the moderators of resource advantage and asset specificity affect entrepreneurial perceptions about motives, rationales, and mechanisms of growth.* The predominance of either of these moderators is associated with a stronger impact from the theory it represents. The higher level of resource advantage over asset specificity in Pattern 1 corresponds with the dominance of the RBV approach. The higher level of asset specificity over resource advantage in Pattern 2 shows the dominance of the TCT approach. Moderate and low levels of the moderators in Pattern 3 enable the RBV and TCT determinants to overlap in the entrepreneurs' perceptions. These *findings confirm Hypothesis 5 in its assumption that the explanatory power of the RBV and TCT towards the SME growth process depends on the contextual characteristics of SMEs' capabilities and the transactional environment.*

However, the detailed assumptions of Hypothesis 5 regarding specific levels of moderators that support the validity of the RBV and TCT are only partially supported. In generally favorable conditions of company potential (high resource advantage) and transactional environment (moderate asset specificity not raising dependence), the RBV is more valid than TCT. Also, in generally less favorable conditions of company potential (moderate to high resource advantage) and transactional environment (asset specificity), TCT is more valid than the RBV.

Detailed assumptions about the levels of resource advantage and asset specificity were not supported, which may be caused by two reasons. One reason is that our findings did not reveal such configurations of firm potential and environment. However, we cannot preclude the existence of such contextual characteristics. The growth patterns we identified embrace only three out of eight possible configurations – patterns of the growth process that may exist in reality and feature such contextual characteristics. The other reason is that capability-based and transactional patterns of growth do not represent "ideal" types as per the theoretical assumptions, but generally conform to the principles of the RBV and TCT, accordingly. Therefore, the contextual characteristics we identified are not "ideally" compliant with the theoretical assumptions.

All in all, it needs to be admitted that the verifications of Hypotheses 4 and 5, alike earlier Hypotheses 1–3 are not statistical generalizations, but they serve analytical generalizations about possible causes and explanations of cause-effect relationships in the growth process.

5.2. Results of the within-case study analysis

The within-case study analysis highlights how specific patterns of the growth process (configurations of motives, rationale, mechanisms, and modes) associate with the entrepreneurs' decisions and actions (Table 22). This reflects the idea that structural elements of growth processes act as enabling constraints to entrepreneurial decision-making.

The capability-based process of growth is centered around developing the firm's resources to achieve value. The motives perceived as trustful are associated with cooperative governance based on relational contracting and soft, positive incentives substituting for hard, formal safeguards. The entrepreneurs do not see any need to draft detailed contracts. Due to the knowledge advantage (unique technology, often new to the world), they are not threatened by contract gaps. The rationale for growth focuses exclusively on value with no need to constrain transaction costs, which enables the development of a horizontal, diversified portfolio by exploiting the existing core competencies or exploring new areas. The growth mechanism is driven by the development of capabilities. Depending on the affinity to the existing portfolio, they adopt either organic or hybrid or acquisitive growth.

The transactional growth process is oriented towards managing relations with partners in the value chain (customers and suppliers). If the entrepreneur assumes opportunism to either dominate or balance trust in the business exchange, the governance of this exchange relies upon hard informal and formal incentives and careful, detailed contract drafting. The growth rationale of increasing value and improving the transaction position is associated with the portfolio developing around key customers, based on vertical integration that leads to upgrading the value chain. The mechanism of growth starts from the needs and requirements of customers and suppliers and competitors' moves are considered. This often leads to loosely related technological activities to supply customers with complementary products and services. The internalization of transaction-specific assets is a mode of growth limited by the contractual complexity to cover the range of activities.

Table 22. Structural elements of growth processes as enabling constraints to entrepreneurial decisions and actions

Pattern	Structural elements and kinds of decisions and actions they affect		
	Perceived motives: *How to govern cooperation (contractual) relationships?*	**Rationale:** *What kind of activity to undertake to pursue growth? How does it develop the company portfolio?*	**Mechanisms and modes:** *What is a starting point to design a growth activity (customer/supplier or capability recognition)? How does it affect the modes of growth?*
Pattern 1 Capability-based process of growth	The hierarchy of governance tools: Relational contracts based on trust and repetitive commissions, few instances of formal long-term contracts. *'[Formal long-term contracts] protect a customer not us, we are more aware of technology and might take advantage of contract gaps.'* (ITServCo) Soft and informal, positive incentives such as maintaining reputation and cooperation, mutuality, looking for future business. *'Relations are important - independence and partnership.'* (WasteCo) Hard, formal safeguards in short-term contracts (bank guarantee, pledge, prepayment) alike informal threat of losing reputation or terminating relational contracts are not considered important. *'The older generation entrepreneurs threaten with penalties, courts, and lawyers; the new generation demonstrates high trust and low formalization. In this industry, it is impossible to specify a broad range of issues; therefore trust needs to regulate these things.'* (MediaCo)	A dominant idea is developing new products and services for new markets to form a horizontal, diversified portfolio; products and services new to the industry and even to the world. *'We were setting up standards and technologies in the industry.'* (MediaCo) *'We are barbarians and we colonize niches. We set up proprietary solutions, and we don't want to follow someone else's standards.'* (SoftCo)	A starting point is the development of capabilities. They apply exploitation of core competencies that leads to organic growth. The firms exploring new activities acquire new employees or establish hybrid forms such as joint ventures, eventually leading to mergers. *'We follow our own ideas and competencies and do not bother about specific customers – we are so innovative that large firms just have to buy these solutions not to be crowded out of the market.'* (SoftCo)

Structural elements and kinds of decisions and actions they affect

Pattern			
Pattern 2 Transactional process of growth	The hierarchy of governance tools: Informal hard safeguards: the threat of losing reputation and the threat of terminating a contract, a systematic customer rating, excluding unreliable customers, informal search for information about partners in a narrow business community. *'A customer is trustworthy to the extent we check it.'* (AutomCo) Formal hard safeguards in short-term contracts become important: bank insurance, bank guarantee, prepayment, pledge. Relational contracts are more popular than long-term ones. However, when asset specificity increases among partners, they tend to choose long-term contracts. *'As our products and services became more specialized we demanded more adjustments from our suppliers. These changes were followed by the adoption of long-term contracts to specify mutual responsibilities.'* (AutomCo)	A dominant idea is 1) vertical integration to provide clients with complementary products and services and 2) volume increase by penetrating the existing markets supplemented by new markets. This often results in upgrading in value chain into higher value adding activities. Products and services are new to the industry and market, not to the world. *'Customers look for the company to coordinate everything and to help them avoid transacting and monitoring.'* (ConstructCo) *'We want to increase volume to be stronger relative to customers and to avoid corruptive behavior of the officials.'* (SpedCo)	A starting point is transaction characteristics, i.e. requirements from the major customers or suppliers to introduce products and services for the existing markets and, in some cases, to expand into new markets; idiosyncratic and transaction-related activities are internalized to the limits imposed by the contract complexity. *'The range of our portfolio is limited by the ability to specify the terms of contracts with customers we serve.'* (AutomCo)
Pattern 3 A capability- and market opportunity-oriented process of growth	The hierarchy of governance tools: Beside relational contracting, strong presence of formal long-term contracts required by customers. Formal contract safeguards – hard financial and legal measures and reputation-related incentives. The incentives are more formal, simpler and effective than in Pattern 2. Informal incentives: the threat of losing reputation or terminating a contract, looking for future business. *'If a customer does not have a bank guarantees or insurance, we do not cooperate, or we require pledges and advance payments before goods are delivered.'* (OilCo)	A dominant idea is to increase in volume and number of permits and certificates to penetrate markets or to enter new markets, based on identifying market trends and gaps. Other options to increase volume are refocusing from final to intermediate goods in the same industry or introducing a product unrelated to the existing portfolio to reduce uncertainty. *'We look for chances and opportunities tracking market changes and niches; we are hunters.'* (OilCo) *'We want to grow in volume, and we want to grow in the number of [foreign governments'] permits to sell in the new markets.'* (NutriCo)	A starting point is the development of capabilities, a key product. At the same time, they match resources with requirements of key buyers regarding terms of supplies and institutional conditions (permits, certificates). The result is organic growth. Reduction of external uncertainty drives unrelated diversification that involves acquisitions and hybrid modes. *'We do not adjust our products to customers' requirements. We develop the core products, and we adjust our certificates and permits to markets to which these products would fit.'* (NutriCo)

Source: own work.

The capability- and market opportunity-oriented process of growth is featured by relational, reputational, and trust-based contracts, formal long-
term agreements, and some strong, formal incentives to govern cooperation. The entrepreneurs can utilize these incentives in a very effective way
due to their lower dependence than in Pattern 2. The utilization of hard
safeguards corresponds with the motives in business exchange perceived
by the entrepreneurs as trustful, but with a stronger component of opportunism than in Pattern 1. Aiming to increase value and improve their
transaction position, they pursue growth by volume increase, by developing core products, or by extending the portfolio with products unrelated
to the existing ones in order to avoid uncertainty. Their major mechanism
of growth starts from the core competencies as a basis for product development, since the standardized products they develop need to comply with
external institutions rather than with individual customer expectations. At
the same time, being alert to trends and market niches, they adjust to key
customers with regard to supplies and institutional environments by in-
vesting in adequate certificates and permits. This leads to organic growth.
Hybrid and acquisitive modes are associated with unrelated diversification
adopted to avoid uncertainty.

5.3. A model of the SME growth process

The final model of the SME growth process is based on the integration of
the RBV and TCT to address the major aim of the research presented in this
book. This model is an outcome of both conceptual and empirical endeavors to contribute to the emerging stream of studies in the firm's growth
process with the theory of this process adapted specifically to small and
medium-sized enterprises. The conceptual efforts were marked with the stages of developing a model. It started from the proposal of a general framework
of the firm's growth process, based on adapting the structuration theory of
the entrepreneurial process by Sarason, Dean and Dillard (2006) and the concept of enabling constraints by Selden and Fletcher (2015). The merit of this
framework is a conceptualization of firms' growth as a unique process within
the entrepreneurial process perspectives that has a dual nature as a structuration and the flow of decisions and actions. The general framework required
specification by explaining how the entrepreneurial self-reflexive evaluation structures decisions and actions, i.e., how it acts as an enabling constraint. This task was implemented by synthesizing the boundary literature

integrating the RBV and TCT and the entrepreneurship literature to elaborate a theoretical framework of the SME growth process. The theoretical framework proposed structural elements of this process as motives, rationale, mechanisms, and modes. Moreover, it hypothesized how SME entrepreneurs decide and act depending on their perceptions of these structural elements.

Finally, in the empirical research, the hypothesized characteristics and influence of the structural elements of the SME growth process were verified, which resulted in the identification of three distinctive patterns of SME growth. These findings complete the model of SME growth process as depicted in Figure 9.

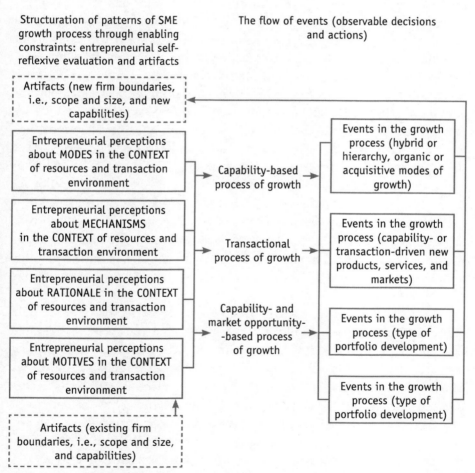

Figure 9. The model of the SME growth process based on the integration of the resource-based view of the firm and transaction cost theory

Source: own work.

The current integrative RBV-TCT framework specifies the SME growth patterns as determined by the entrepreneur's self-reflexive evaluation, i.e., his or her perceptions about the structural elements. The emerged patterns, in turn, affect the flow of decisions and actions that eventually follow one of these paths and shape the artifacts – new firm size and scope and new capabilities.

The cause-effect relationships and feedback loops in the proposed model are as follows. The entrepreneur's perceptions about structural elements of growth (motives, rationale, mechanisms, and modes) are conducive to observable decisions and actions. The structuring of the process is based on the entrepreneurial self-reflexive evaluation and the artifacts that act as enabling constraints in generating the flow of events. The entrepreneurial evaluation of opportunities is at the core, i.e., his or her perceptions about structural elements. The perceptions are also context-specific, since they demonstrate differing features depending on the moderating effect from the firm's potential and the transactional environment. The perceptions about the structural elements may assume three distinct characteristics of capability-based, transactional, and capability- and market opportunity-oriented patterns that affect the decisions and actions that follow one of these patterns. The emergent flows of events differ in the way that contractual arrangements are governed, in the type of portfolio that is developed, in the adopted sources of new activities, and in the governance structures for expansion. Finally, from differing sets of decisions and action, new artifacts are generated in the form of new scope and size and new capabilities. These artifacts, along with the entrepreneur's self-reflexive evaluation, will also act as enabling constraints for future decisions and actions in the growth process.

In this model, the central importance is assigned to the unobservable entrepreneurial sense-making that forms a pattern affecting observable decisions and actions that result in artifacts. Artifacts, which include new firm size and scope as well as new capabilities, are essentially the outcomes of the growth process. Following the growth patterns shaped by entrepreneurial perceptions, they are represented by distinct types of contracts, portfolio composition, and capability-driven or customer- and supplier-driven new products, processes, and markets. Different governance modes, such as hierarchy or hybrid, and organic or acquisitive structures are used to pursue expansion. Therefore, the model reflects the heterogeneity of the SME growth pathways that are equifinal in leading to the same outcome, i.e., expanding size and scope, and capability development.

DISCUSSION AND CONCLUSION

Contribution and implications of the research

The research presented in this book accomplished the aim of the elaboration of the model of the SME growth process based on the integration of the resource-based view of the firm and transaction cost theory. Consequently, the major research hypothesis and corresponding research question about the possibility of the integration of the RBV and TCT to develop the model of SME growth process, were positively verified. Moreover, the identification of three distinct properties of motives, rationale, mechanisms, and modes as patterns of the SME growth process addressed the research question about the characteristics of these structural elements.

The study explored an emerging, under-researched area of the firm growth process on both theoretical and empirical grounds. The challenging aim of developing the model of SME growth process required the adoption of new theoretical and methodological approaches. It also demanded synthesizing the knowledge of growth phenomenon from the entrepreneurship, economics, and strategic management literature. Thus, this study offers three major contributions: the model of SME growth process, methodological advancement, and broadening the integrative RBV-TCT studies. Although the research is basic in nature, it also proposes some practical implications.

The model of the SME growth process

The first contribution of the research is the development of the *model of SME growth process with the use of the deductive approach*. By elaborating this model, this research responded to the call for a broader theoretical and conceptual basis to study the process of entrepreneurial growth and for more empirical verification of these theoretical approaches (McKelvie & Wiklund, 2010; Dobbs & Hamilton, 2007; Koryak et al., 2015; Wright & Stigliani, 2013).

The proposed model advances the emerging stream on the growth process to explain why and how the expansion is achieved. Such a focus is different from extant major research streams about growth, and it complements the studies on growth determinants and the growth stages (life cycle). We investigated why and how growth is achieved instead of identifying growth determinants (Garnsey, Stam & Heffernan, 2006; Dobbs & Hamilton, 2007; McKelvie & Wiklund, 2010; Wright & Stigliani, 2013). The studies on growth factors identified a number of drivers in this area (Storey, 1994; Barringer, Jones & Neubaum, 2005; Gilbert, McDougall, & Audretsch, 2006; Dobbs & Hamilton, 2007; Coad, 2007b; 2009; Macpherson & Holt, 2007). However, they were less efficient in explaining cause-effect relationships among the multitude of factors (Achtenhagen, Naldi, & Melin, 2010; Shepherd & Wiklund, 2009). We investigate these relationships as links between entrepreneurial decisional rules (reflected in their convictions on motives, rationale, mechanisms, and modes), and decisions and actions. Moreover, we point to the relationship between decisional rules and contextual issues. The growth stage models, in turn, focus on how to manage a company that achieved growth as a new development stage (McKelvie & Wiklund, 2010; Dobbs & Hamilton, 2007; Levie & Lichtenstein, 2010). The current study complements the life cycle models by explaining how a company implements its journey towards growth, i.e., how it accomplishes a new development stage.

Moreover, the model advances entrepreneurial process perspectives at large. It builds upon and extends the structuration view (Sarason, Dean & Dillard, 2006) and the idea of enabling constraints (Selden & Fletcher, 2015) to conceptualize the firms' growth as a unique process within the entrepreneurial process. We proposed a dual nature of this process, as a structuration and the flow of decisions and actions. The structuration is the entrepreneur's self-reflexive evaluation that affects decisions and actions (events).

The proposed model has deductive, theoretical origins. However, it also has been verified in the empirical research, which identified three distinct patterns of SME growth process. *This finding is consistent with the idiosyncrasy of SME growth, since it emphasizes a variety of solutions that are equifinal and equally efficient in accomplishing growth* (McKelvie & Wiklund, 2010; Coad, 2009; Muñoz & Dimov, 2015). *Thus, the research responds* to the nature of SME growth as heterogeneous regarding determinants, conditions, and pathways (Coad, 2009; Shepherd & Wiklund, 2009; Dobbs & Hamilton, 2007).

Another merit of the model consists in formulating conclusions as to the entrepreneurial decisional rules and choices in the process of expansion. *The three patterns of growth processes differ in entrepreneurs' perceptions as to motives, rationale(s), mechanisms and modes. Moreover, we show how these structural elements act as enabling constraints, i.e., how they affect the decisions and actions in the process of growth* (Selden & Fletcher, 2015; Muñoz & Dimov, 2015; McMullen & Dimov, 2013).

The three patterns of expansion demonstrate distinct characteristics. In the first, capability-based pattern of the growth process, the entrepreneurs assume trust as the major motive in business exchange and value represents their only rationale for expansion. Considering the mechanism of growth, they follow the logic of aligning capabilities with a new activity (product, service, market) that leads to expansion. *The second, transactional growth process*, features the entrepreneurs' perceptions of motives as either dominated by opportunism in a business exchange with some level of trust or they recognize balanced trust and opportunism. Their major rationale for growth is value increase supplemented by the goal of strengthening the bargaining position to reduce the costs of transacting. The growth mechanism in this pattern stems from the characteristics of transactions, i.e., the new, growth activities are driven by the requirements and expectations of customers or suppliers. Finally, *in the third, capability- and market opportunity-oriented pattern of growth*, the entrepreneurs consider trust as dominating, but more limited by opportunism than in Pattern 1. Value and competitive advantage are their major rationale for growth supplemented by transaction cost considerations. The mechanism of growth is based on aligning a new activity with capabilities and with the transaction characteristics (requirements of customers or suppliers) when developing new products, processes, and entering new markets.

The observed patterns bring the conclusion that growth of small and medium-sized enterprises is achieved either by the focus on capability development (Pattern 1) or by effective managing transaction costs (Pattern 2) or both (Pattern 3). SMEs, by nature, are heavily exposed to handle contracting, since they cannot rely on internal markets as do the large companies (Nooteboom, 1993; Everaert, Sarens, & Rommel, 2010). Consequently, they need to cope with relationships in difficult, hierarchical networks of customers and suppliers (Besser & Miller, 2010). This observation adds to the current studies on growth factors, which were oriented towards drivers and the RBV-related factors of growth (Davidsson, Steffens, & Fitzsimmons, 2009; Garnsey, Stam, & Heffernan, 2006; Storey, 1994; Barringer, Jones & Neubaum, 2005; Gilbert, McDougall, & Audretsch, 2006; Dobbs & Hamilton, 2007; Macpherson & Holt, 2007). However, the entrepreneurship research has increasingly referred to the TCT approach, confirming its validity regarding growth issues as well (Chandler, McKelvie, & Davidsson, 2010; Verwaal et al., 2010). The present study finds TCT assumptions as one of the optional explanations of the growth process, which is reflected in Pattern 2, or at least a substantial component of this process (Pattern 3).

We have identified equally efficient alternative approaches to the growth process, which are framed by differing characteristics of context-specific enabling constraints (Selden & Fletcher, 2015). *These constraints are context-specific as affected by the internal context of company capabilities and external contracting conditions.* Our findings suggest that the level and type of resource advantage, as the RBV determinant, and the level of asset specificity, the key variable of TCT, interact in shaping entrepreneurial perceptions as to motives, rationale, mechanisms, and modes. The predominance of either of these moderators is associated with a stronger impact of the theory it represents (Patterns 1 and 2), while their balanced or lower levels enable the RBV and TCT determinants to overlap in the entrepreneurs' perceptions and subsequent choices (Pattern 3). These findings are consistent with extant studies about firm boundaries and company growth that investigated the moderating effect of firm capability on the TCT validity (Tseng & Chen, 2013; Ray, Xue, & Barney, 2013; Steensma & Corley, 2001; Chandler, McKelvie, & Davidsson, 2009; Verwaal et al., 2010) and the effect of TCT factors on the validity of the RBV (Mutinelli & Piscitello, 1998; Fabrizio, 2012; Jacobides & Hitt, 2005). *The input from the current study is the exploration of how these moderators interact in one research experiment that combines both theories to explain the process of high growth instead of the determinants of the firm's scope and size or growth determinants.*

Moreover, we show how the entrepreneurs' alternative perceptions about motives, rationale, mechanisms, and modes act as enabling constraints, i.e., how they associate with entrepreneurial decisions and actions. Other studies that explored the structural elements of entrepreneurial processes referred to venture creation and to sustainable entrepreneurship characteristics, pointing to varied patterns observed in reality (Muñoz & Dimov, 2015; Selden & Fletcher, 2015; Hansen & Hamilton, 2011). The current findings show that entrepreneurial choices have different characteristics in each pattern as well. Namely, the perceived motives affect the choice of cooperative governance and what kind of safeguards and incentives make the cooperation work and continue. The perceived rationale for growth logically associates with different approaches to designing new activities (products, services, and markets) to pursue expansion and results in alternative directions of portfolio development. Finally, the mechanisms of growth are characterized by distinct drivers or starting points for designing new products, services, or markets, since they stem from either the firm's capability recognition or the requirements and needs of key contractors or from both of these sources. *The modes of growth are not specific to any of the patterns, since hierarchy expansion, including organic and external growth, and hybrid expansion are applied in all three patterns. The logics of their choice proves consistent with the assumptions of both theories.* The choice of hierarchy versus hybrids complies with TCT, and the choice of external versus organic growth conforms to the RBV rules.

Methodological advancement

The second contribution of the research is a theoretical and methodological framework for further studying the growth process of firms, whether focused on SMEs or other types of enterprises, and for future research in the entrepreneurial process. The entrepreneurial process perspectives offer models focused predominantly on venture creation and the subsequent development stages (Muñoz & Dimov, 2015; McMullen & Dimov, 2013; Sarasvathy, 2001; 2009; Venkataraman et al., 2012; Baker & Nelson, 2005; Garud & Karnøe, 2003; Sarason, Dean, & Dillard, 2006). However, to our knowledge, none of them tackles the specificity of the growth process. We address this gap in the entrepreneurial process modeling by approaching the growth process with a focus on SMEs. Moreover, the general framework of the firm's growth process in Chapter 1 can serve future empirical studies on firm growth as a deductive, theory-driven tool. This general theoretical framework can be adapted and complemented with the use of approaches other than RBV and TCT that are relevant for the enterprises and processes under study. The idea that structuration through enabling constraints generates entrepreneurial decisions and actions can guide research in such entrepreneurial processes as venture creation, innovation development, and restructuring of the enterprise.

Moreover, novel methodologies were applied in the study, such as the prospective case study method (Bitektine, 2008) for empirical research, and theory pruning to synthesize results from the integrative RBV-TCT literature (Leavitt, Mitchell, & Peterson, 2010; Hoon, 2013). These methods were consistent with the aim of the study to elaborate a model of the SME growth process based on a deductive approach that takes into account the explorative nature of this theme. The deductive approach to theory building was applied (Bitektine, 2008), due to the preliminary status of research on the firm growth process to ensure a coherent basis for problem conceptualization and for empirical research methodology. Thus, it helps to limit the ambiguity of interpretations that might stem from inductive, empirically-driven theory development (Hoon, 2013). In both cases, the possible bias from extant theories in explaining the explorative research area was alleviated through adopting two alternative theories to interpret the findings, and through ensuring scientific validity from the start of the research.

The methodologies adopted address the characteristics of growth as idiosyncratic and enabled us to identify equifinal patterns with the use of combinatory logic (Ragin, 2008b; 2009). Based on the combinatory method of QCA, the alternative options of expansion were identified instead of only one 'general' or 'average' solution that might not actually exist. The assumption of the 'dominant' or 'average' firm has been implied in extant quantitative studies both on firm boundary (scope and size) decisions and on growth determinants (Coad, 2009). However, these studies explained only a moderate amount of variation in the population, leaving the remaining variation unexplored (Achtenhagen, Naldi, & Melin, 2010; Shepherd & Wiklund, 2009). The current research managed to better capture this variety.

Broadening the integrative RBV-TCT studies

Third, the research broadens the integrative RBV-TCT studies by the inclusion of the specific context of the entrepreneurial growth process, both in theoretical and empirical terms. The integrative RBV-TCT studies in firm boundaries (scope and size) refer to growth as a strategy and governance issue. However, they are almost silent about the context of high-growth firms and entrepreneurial growth (Davidsson, Achtenhagen, & Naldi, 2010; Jacobides & Winter, 2007). Correspondingly, in the entrepreneurship literature, the framework linking both theories to explore growth issues is present only in individual studies, and these studies do not refer to the process of expansion (Chandler, McKelvie, & Davidsson, 2009; Verwaal et al., 2010). The present research places the RBV-TCT approach in the context of high-growth firms, thus broadening these integrative studies both in the firm boundary and entrepreneurship literature. Moreover, we propose the configurational view and method in testing and integrating the RBV and TCT, which has not been applied in extant studies. The results of these studies point to the validity of both perspectives, depending on the context (Combs et al., 2011; Ray, Xue, & Barney, 2013; Leiblein, 2003). The present research provides the evidence and explanation of reciprocal validity of the RBV and TCT in studying one phenomenon (McIvor, 2009). It shows how the RBV and TCT assumptions combine in different configurations, proving their validity in different conditions of entrepreneurial sense-making, and in distinct contexts of the firm's capabilities and asset specificity. Therefore, the current study *contributes to the extant research on the firm's scope and size that aims to combine these approaches, by explaining how they interact in the specific situation of high growth, and in the context of internal (company capabilities) and external (contracting) conditions.*

Since firm growth is an interdisciplinary field of research, this book *bridges the fields of entrepreneurship, micro-economics and strategic management literature,* thus *accumulating knowledge on the growth phenomenon.* In doing so, it responds to recommendations from both the entrepreneurship literature (Davidsson, Achtenhagen, & Naldi, 2010; McKelvie & Wiklund, 2010) and from the strategic management and firm boundary literature (Jacobides & Winter, 2007).

Practical implications

Regarding *practical implications,* the knowledge of rules and cause-effect relationships in pursuing growth decisions and actions aids the management of high-growth firms and the policies directed at supporting them. The patterns of entrepreneurial decisional rules and choices identified in this research are equally effective, so they can be treated as benchmarks for entrepreneurs planning growth. The patterns show how SME entrepreneurs are acting in different contexts of internal potential and environmental transaction conditions, employing adequate cooperation governance, choosing products, services, and markets to build a portfolio. The patterns also show what represents the starting point, a major stimulus for ideas of new activities being a source of expansion. Moreover, these findings are informative for business consultants and decision-makers designing policy measures, helping them to tailor their methods to the specific needs of companies pursuing different patterns of growth. The model of the SME growth process resulting from this research is descriptive, since it explains why and how decisions and actions emerge during the expansion. However, it was tested in the context of high-growth and high-performance firms. Three patterns of growth explain the entrepreneurial decisions and actions giving the normative guidance to practitioners. One of the major messages from these three patterns is that value considerations should be viewed simultaneously with transaction cost considerations in the entrepreneur's choices regarding expansion (Kulkarni & Ramamoorthy, 2005).

Limitations

Finally, the *limitations of the study* need to be acknowledged together with the ways of alleviating them. The limitations refer to the conceptual work based on the literature review and the empirical research.

Literature review

A theoretical integration of the RBV and TCT was implemented based on a limited number of empirical papers with differing methodologies, which impeded quantitative analysis. To increase the scope of analysis, we added theoretical papers to this review. Therefore, a qualitative and stylized approach to analysis was applied. The small number of publications indicates a young but growing literature that integrates both approaches, especially after 2000 (c.f. Tables 9 and 10). Some studies had to be excluded from the review, since they did not meet the criteria of combining the constructs of the RBV and TCT in a systematic way. To minimize the bias from qualitative synthesis, methodological rigor was ensured, i.e., a systematic literature search and analytical steps complying with the methods of meta synthesis combined with the rules of theory pruning (Gancarczyk, 2016). Extant literature reviews conducted for the RBV and TCT separately draw from a broad set of empirical studies and provide a systematic literature review. Some of them use quantitative meta-analysis and claim to not only extend investigations of individual theories but also to integrate RBV and TCT research (Combs et al., 2011). The current study addresses this claim. Moreover, it differs from extant reviews that integrate the RBV and TCT by conducting a systematic literature review, while other such projects are only narrative reviews (please see Table 10).

Another limitation that might stem from the review of the RBV-TCT integrative studies is a propensity of authors to support the joint validity of the theories and to avoid excluding one of them (Bitektine, 2008). The current contribution acknowledged this potential bias by a thorough analysis of the findings reviewed and by identifying mediators and moderators to the major theoretical variables. Thus, we avoided a simplification in joining the theories.

As noted earlier, a deductive approach to building a theory of explorative phenomena may bias the description toward extant theories, losing its real nature (Leavitt, Mitchell, & Peterson, 2010). It also has a potential advantage, considering the threat of ambiguity of findings that rely on only the inductive approach (Lee, 1989). Matching and testing two alternative views prevents adhering to only one perspective that would bias the interpretation of findings (Leavitt, Mitchell, & Peterson, 2010). Another benefit from the deductive design of empirical research would be the coherent replication of methodologies based on recognized constructs.

Empirical research

Adopting a case study method for verifying a research hypothesis has its limitations due to a non-random design and the small number of observations. However, this research does not aim at statistical, but rather at analytical, generalization. Moreover, it is not directed at confirming hypotheses, but it either supports or rejects them based on falsification testing (Bitektine, 2008; Popper, 1968). The validity of case study results is strengthened by the choice of a multi-case approach, data triangulation, and emphasizing firm diversity to avoid the bias of a specific size, industry, age, and technological level (Yin, 2009; Eisenhardt & Graebner, 2007). Moreover, to avoid the ambiguity of theoretical findings from an inductive case study, we adopted a deductive method based on the extant theories (Bitektine, 2008; Langley, 1999). Deductive approaches can also be a source of bias in the case study when only one theory forms a framework, and the researcher is inclined to confirm this theory. Here this concern is avoided by applying two approaches.

Since we rely on interviews to record opinions from entrepreneurs, there is the subjectivity problem of self-reported data as well as information inaccuracy due to retrospective accounts of perceptions, decisions, and actions (Muñoz & Dimov, 2015). However, this threat was mitigated by two-stage interviews so that respondents could reflect on their initial responses interpretations, by employing two independent researchers to code the data, and by comparing the interview data with secondary sources of information, such as company records, press releases, and financial records (Yin, 2009).

The sampling process based on the records from the ranking of high-growth firms requires some explanation as well. Databases from country-wide or international contests were also utilized in other research studies (Muñoz & Dimov, 2015; Barringer, Jones, & Neubaum, 2005). The sampling process in these studies and in the current research was not directed at randomization, but at theory-driven, purposive selection of cases of high-growth enterprises, which aimed at the maximum variety of firms in the sample. Therefore, we can consider the results as relevant for SMEs pursuing growth, but not to the behaviors and characteristics of the remaining population of non-growing or slow-growing small and medium-sized enterprises.

BIBLIOGRAPHY

Acedo, F.J., Barroso, C., & Galan, J.L. (2006). The Resource-Based Theory: Dissemination and Main Trends. *Strategic Management Journal* 27(7), 621–636.

Achtenhagen, L., Naldi, L., & Melin, L. (2010). Business Growth-Do Practitioners and Scholars Really Talk about the Same Thing? *Entrepreneurship Theory and Practice* 34(2), 289–316.

Acs, Z., Parsons, W., & Tracy, S. (2008), *High-Impact Firms: Gazelles Revisited*. U.S. Small Business Administration: Washington DC.

Aldrich, H., & Auster, E.R. (1986). Even Dwarfs Started Small: Liabilities of Age and Size and Their Strategic Implications. *Research in Organizational Behavior* 8(1986), 165–186.

Adamus, W., & Gręda, A. (2005). Wspomaganie decyzji wielokryterialnych w rozwiązywaniu wybranych problemów organizacyjnych i menedżerskich. *Badania operacyjne i decyzje*, (2), 5–36.

Alchian, A.A. (1950). Uncertainty, Evolution, and Economic Theory. *Journal of Political economy* 58(3), 211–221.

Aldrich, H. (1999). *Organizations Evolving*. London: Sage.

Almus, M., & Nerlinger, E.A. (1999). Growth of New Technology-Based Firms: Which Factors Matter? *Small Business Economics* 13(2), 141–154.

Alvarez, S.A. (2007). Entrepreneurial Rents and the Theory of the Firm. *Journal of Business Venturing* 22(3), 427–442.

Alvarez, S.A., & Barney, J.B. (2007). The Entrepreneurial Theory of the Firm. *Journal of Management Studies* 44(7), 1057–1063.

Amit, R., & Schoemaker, P.J. (1993). Strategic Assets and Organizational Rent. *Strategic Management Journal* 14(1), 33–46.

Anderson, E., & Schmittlein, D.C. (1984). Integration of the sales force: An empirical examination. *The Rand Journal of Economics*, 385–395.

Arend, R.J. (2006). Tests of the Resource-Based View: Do the Empirics Have Any Clothes? *Strategic Organization* 4(4), 409–422.

Arend, R.J., & Lévesque, M. (2010). Is the Resource-Based View a Practical Organizational Theory? *Organization Science* 21(4), 913–930.

Argyres, N. (1996). Evidence on the Role of Firm Capabilities in Vertical Integration Decisions. *Strategic Management Journal* 17(2), 129–150.

Argyres, N., & Liebeskind, J.P. (1999). Contractual Commitments, Bargaining Power, and Governance Inseparability: Incorporating History into Transaction Cost Theory. *Academy of Management Review* 24(1), 49–63.

Argyres, N., & Silverman, B.S. (2004). R&D, Organization Structure, and the Development of Corporate Technological Knowledge. *Strategic Management Journal* 25(8–9), 929–958.

Argyres, N. & Zenger, T. (2012). Capabilities, Transaction Costs, and Firm Boundaries. *Organization Science* 23(6), 1643–1657.

Armstrong, C.E., & Shimizu, K. (2007). A Review of Approaches to Empirical Research on the Resource-Based View of the Firm. *Journal of Management* 33(6), 959–986.

Arrow, K.E. (1974). *The Limits of Organization*. New York: Norton.

Audretsch, D.B. (1995). *Innovation and Industry Evolution*. MIT Press.

Audretsch, D.B. (2012). Determinants of High-Growth Entrepreneurship. OECD/DBA report. http://www.oecd.org/cfe/leed/Audretsch_determinants%20of%20high-growth%20firms.pdf. Accessed November 1, 2013.

Autio, E., Arenius, P., & Wallenius, H. (2000). Economic Impact of Gazelle Firms in Finland. *Helsinki University of Technology Working Paper Series*.

Baker, T., & Nelson, R.E. (2005). Creating Something from Nothing: Resource Construction through Entrepreneurial Bricolage. *Administrative Science Quarterly* 50(3), 329–366.

Barney, J.B. (1991). Firm Resources and Sustained Competitive Advantage. *Journal of Management* 17(1), 99–120.

Barney, J.B. (1999). How a Firm's Capabilities Affect Boundary Decisions. *MIT Sloan Management Review* 40(3), 73–81.

Barney, J.B., & Hansen, M.H. (1994). Trustworthiness as a Source of Competitive Advantage. *Strategic Management Journal* 15(S1), 175–190.

Barringer, B., Jones, F., & Neubaum, D. (2005). A Quantitative Content Analysis of the Characteristics of Rapid-Growth Firms and Their Founders. *Journal of Business Venturing* 20(5), 663–687.

Barth, H. (2003). Fit among Competitive Strategy, Administrative Mechanisms, and Performance: A Comparative Study of Small Firms in Mature and New Industries. *Journal of Small Business Management* 41(2), 133–147.

Barzel, Y. (1997). *Economic Analysis of Property Rights.* Cambridge: Cambridge University Press, Cambridge.

Baum, J.R., Locke, E.A., & Smith, K.G. (2001). A Multidimensional Model of Venture Growth. *Academy of Management Journal* 44(2), 292–303.

Baumol, W.J. (1959). *Business Behavior, Value and Growth.* New York: Macmillan.

Bednarczyk, M. (ed.). (2006). *Konkurencyjność małych i średnich przedsiębiorstw na polskim rynku turystycznym.* Kraków: Wydawnictwo Uniwersytetu Jagiellońskiego.

Benham, A., & Benham, L. (2000). Measuring the Costs of Exchange. In: Ménard, C. (ed.), *Institutions, Contracts and Organizations. Perspectives from New Institutional Economics.* Cheltenham: Edward Elgar, 367–375.

Berg-Schlosser, D., De Meur, G., Rihoux, B., & Ragin, C.C. (2009). Qualitative Comparative Analysis (QCA) as an Approach. In: Rihoux, B., & Ragin, C.C. (eds.), *Configurational Comparative Methods: Qualitative Comparative Analysis (QCA) and Related Techniques.* Thousand Oaks, CA: Sage, 1–18.

Besser, T.L., & Miller, N.J. (2010). The Significance of Customer Base in the New Economy: Satisfaction and Perceptions of Success among Small Suppliers and Small Nonsuppliers. *Journal of Small Business Management* 48(1), 1–15.

Birch, D.L. (1979). *The Job Generation Process: Final Report to Economic Development Administration.* Cambridge, MA: MIT Program on Neighborhood and Regional Change.

Birch, D.L. (1987). *Job Creation in America.* New York: Free Press.

Birch, D.L., Haggerty, A., & Parsons, W. (1995). *Who's Creating Jobs?* Cambridge, MA: Cognetics.

Birch, D.L., & Medoff, J. (1994). Gazelles. In: Solmon, L.C., & Levenson, A.R. (eds.), *Labor Markets, Employment Policy and Job Creation.* Boulder and London: Westview Press, 159–167.

Bitektine, A. (2008), Prospective Case Study Design: Qualitative Method for Deductive Theory Testing. *Organization Research Methods* 11(1), 160–180.

Boehlke, J. (2010). *Firma we współczesnej myśli ekonomicznej. Studium teoretyczno–metodologiczne.* Toruń: Wydawnictwo Naukowe UMK.

Borowiecki, R., & Siuta-Tokarska, B. (2010). Challanges Facing Polish SMES in the Face of Globalization Processes. *Folia Oeconomica Stetinensia* 9(1), 52–71.

Bottazzi, G., & Secchi, A. (2003). A Stochastic Model of Firm Growth. *Physica A: Statistical Mechanics and its Applications* 324(1), 213–219.

Brahm, F., & Tarziján, J. (2014). Transactional Hazards, Institutional Change, and Capabilities: Integrating the Theories of the Firm. *Strategic Management Journal* 35(2), 224–245.

Bratnicki, M. (2000). *Kompetencje przedsiębiorstwa: od określenia kompetencji do zbudowania strategii.* Warszawa: Agencja Wydawnicza Placet.

Brewer, B., Ashenbaum, B., & Carter, J. (2014). Understanding the Supply Chain Outsourcing Cascade: When Does Procurement Follow Manufacturing Out the Door? *Journal of Supply Chain Management* 49(3), 90–110.

Brouthers, K.D. (2002). Institutional, Cultural and Transaction Cost Influences on Entry Mode Choice and Performance. *Journal of International Business Studies* 33(2), 203–221.

Brouthers, K.D., & Nakos, G. (2004). SME Entry Mode Choice and Performance: A Transaction Cost Perspective. *Entrepreneurship Theory and Practice* 28(3), 229–247.

Campbell, D.T. (1966). Pattern matching as an essential in distal knowing. In: Hammond, K.R. (ed.), *The psychology of Egon Brunswik.* New York: Holt, Rinehart & Winston, 81–106.

Carter, R., & Hodgson, G. (2006). The Impact of Empirical Tests of Transaction Cost Economics on the Debate on the Nature of the Firm. *Strategic Management Journal* 27(5), 461–476.

Ceccagnoli, M., Graham, S., Higgins, M., & Lee, J. (2010). Productivity and the Role of Complementary Assets in Firms' Demand for Technology Innovations. *Industrial and Corporate Change* 19(3), 839–869.

Chandler, A. (1992). Organizational Capabilities and the Economic History of the Industrial Enterprise. *Journal of Economic Perspectives* 6(3), 79–100.

Chandler, G., McKelvie, A., & Davidsson, P. (2009). Asset Specificity and Behavioral Uncertainty as Moderators of the Sales Growth – Employment Growth Relationship in Emerging Ventures. *Journal of Business Venturing* 24(4), 373–387.

Chen, H., & Chen, T-J. (2003). Governance Structures in Strategic Alliances: Transaction Cost versus Resource-Based Perspective. *Journal of World Business* 38(1), 1–14.

Cher-Hung, T., & Liang-Tu, Ch. (2013). Firm Capabilities as Moderators of Transaction Cost Factors and Subsidiary Domestic Outsourcing. *Management Decision* 51(1), 5–24.

Chowdhury, S. (2011). The Moderating Effects of Customer Driven Complexity on the Structure and Growth Relationship in Young Firms. *Journal of Business Venturing* 26(3), 306–320.

Churchill, N.C., & Lewis, V. (1983). The Five Stages of Small Business Growth. *Harvard Business Review* 61, 30–50.

Cieślik, J. (2014). *Przedsiębiorczość, polityka, rozwój*. Warszawa: Wydawnictwo Akademickie Sedno.

Coad, A. (2007a). A Closer Look at Serial Growth Rate Correlation. *Review of Industrial Organization* 31(1), 69–82.

Coad, A. (2007b). *Empirical Investigations on the Characteristics and Determinants of the Growth Firms*. Paris: S. Anna School of Advanced Studies, Universite Paris 1 Pantheon Sorbonne, Ecole Doctorale.

Coad, A. (2009). *The Growth of Firms: A Survey of Theories and Empirical Evidence*. Cheltenham: Edward Elgar.

Coad, A., & Rao, R. (2008). Innovation and Firm Growth in High-Tech Sectors: A Quantile Regression Approach. *Research Policy* 37(4), 633–648.

Coase, R.H. (1937). The nature of the firm. *Economica* 4(16), 386–405.

Cohen, W., & Levinthal, D. (1990). Absorptive Capacity: A New Perspective on Learning and Innovation. *Administrative Sciences Quarterly* 35(1), 128–152.

Colombo, M.G., Laursen, K., Magnusson, M., & Rossi-Lamastra, C. (2012). Introduction: Small Business and Networked Innovation: Organizational and Managerial Challenges. *Journal of Small Business Management* 50(2), 181–190.

Combs, J.G., & Ketchen, D.J. (1999). Explaining Interfirm Cooperation and Performance: Toward a Reconciliation of Predictions from the Resource-based View and Organizational Economics. *Strategic Management Journal* 20(9), 867–888.

Combs, J.G., Ketchen, D., Crook R., & Roth, Ph. (2011). Assessing Cumulative Evidence within 'Macro' Research: Why Meta-Analysis Should Be Preferred over Vote Counting. *The Journal of Management Studies* 48(1), 178–197.

Commons, J.R. (1932). The Problem of Correlating Law Economics and Ethics. *Wisconsin Law Review* 8(3), 3–26.

Conner, K.R., & Prahalad, C.K. (1996). A Resource-based Theory of the Firm: Knowledge versus Opportunism. *Organization Science* 7(5), 477–501.

Cordes, Ch., Richerson, P., McElreath, R., & Strimling P. (2011). How Does Opportunistic Behavior Influence Firm Size? An Evolutionary Approach to Organizational Behavior. *Journal of Institutional Economics* 7, 1–21.

Cyfert, S. (2012). Metodyczne aspekty definiowania charakterystyk granic. *Prace Naukowe Wałbrzyskiej Wyższej Szkoły Zarządzania i Przedsiębiorczości* 17, 165–179.

Czakon, W. (2010). Zasobowa teoria firmy w krzywym zwierciadle. *Przegląd Organizacji* 4, 8–12.

Dalley, J., & Hamilton, B. (2000). Knowledge, Context and Learning in the Small Business. *International Small Business Journal* 18(3), 51–59.

Daniel, E.M., Domenico, M.D., & Sharma, S. (2015). Effectuation and Home-Based Online Business Entrepreneurs. *International Small Business Journal*, 33(8), 799–823.

Daszkiewicz, N. (ed.). (2007). *Małe i średnie przedsiębiorstwa: szanse i zagrożenia rozwoju*. Warszawa: CeDeWu.

David, R., & Han, S-K. (2004). A Systematic Assessment of the Empirical Support for Transaction Cost Economics. *Strategic Management Journal* 25(1), 39–58.

Davidsson, P., Achtenhagen, L., & Naldi, L. (2010). Towards an Integrative Framework for Future Research on Small Firm Growth. *Foundations and Trends in Entrepreneurship* 6(2), 135–143.

Davidsson, P., & Delmar, F. (2003). Hunting for New Employment: The Role of High-Growth Firms. In: *Small Firms and Economic Development in Developed and Transition Economies: A Reader*. Ashgate, 7–20.

Davidsson, P., Delmar, F., & Wiklund, J. (2006). *Entrepreneurship and the Growth of Firms*. Cheltenham: Edward Elgar.

Davidsson, P., Steffens, P., & Fitzsimmons, J. (2009). Growing Profitable or Growing from Profits: Putting the Horse in Front of the Cart? *Journal of Business Venturing* 24(4), 388–406.

Davidsson, P., & Wiklund, J. (2000). Conceptual and Empirical Challenges in the Study of Firm Growth. In: Sexton, D., & Landström, H. (eds.), *Handbook of Entrepreneurship*. Oxford, Malden: Blackwell Publishers Ltd., 26–44.

Davis, R. (2006). Strong Inference – Rationale or Inspiration? *Perspectives in Biology and Medicine* 49, 238–249.

Dawid, H. (2006). Agent-based Models of Innovation and Technological Change. *Handbook of Computational Economics* 2, 1235–1272.

Deakins, D., & Freel, M. (1998). Entrepreneurial Learning and the Growth Process in SMEs. *The Learning Organization* 5(3), 144–155.

Deeds, D.L., & Hill, C.W. (1999). An Examination of Opportunistic Action within Research Alliances: Evidence from the Biotechnology Industry. *Journal of Business Venturing* 14(2), 141–163.

Delmar, F., Davidsson, P., & Gartner, W.B. (2003). Arriving at the High-Growth Firm. *Journal of Business Venturing* 18(2), 189–216.

Delmar, F., & Wiklund, J. (2008). The Effect of Small Business Managers' Growth Motivation on Firm Growth: A Longitudinal Study. *Entrepreneurship Theory and Practice* 32(3), 437–457.

Dewald, J.R., Hall, J., Chrisman, J.J., & Kellermanns, F.W. (2007). The Governance Paradox: Preferences of Small Vulnerable Firms in the Home-building Industry. *Entrepreneurship Theory and Practice* 31(2), 279–297.

Díez-Vial, I. (2007). Explaining Vertical Integration Strategies: Market Power, Transactional Attributes and Capabilities. *The Journal of Management Studies* 44(6), 1017–1040.

Díez-Vial, I. (2010). Firm Size Effects on Vertical Boundaries. *Journal of Small Business Management* 47(2), 137–153.

Dobbs, M., & Hamilton, R.T. (2007). Small Business Growth: Recent Evidence and New Directions. *International Journal of Entrepreneurial Behaviour & Research* 13(5), 296–322.

Dominiak, P., Wasilczuk, J., & Starnawska, M. (2016). *Przedsiębiorczość nieproduktywna w świetle ekonomii instytucjonalnej. Analiza zjawiska w Polsce*. Warszawa: Wydawnictwo Naukowe PWN.

Dosi, G., & Grazzi, M. (2006). Technologies as Problem-Solving Procedures and Technologies as Input–Output Relations: Some Perspectives on the Theory of Production. *Industrial and Corporate Change* 15(1), 173–202.

Dosi, G., Marsili, O., Orsenigo, L., & Salvatore, R. (1995). Learning, Market Selection and the Evolution of Industrial Structures. *Small Business Economics* 7(6), 411–436.

Downie, J. (1958). *The Competitive Process*. London: Duckworth.

Dyduch, W., & Bratnicki, M. (2010). Exploring, Exploiting and Effective? The Dialectics of Entrepreneurial Learning and Performance in Post-Accession Economy Organizations (Interactive Paper). *Frontiers of Entrepreneurship Research* 30(12), 19.

Dyer, J.H. (1996). Specialized Supplier Networks as a Source of Competitive Advantage: Evidence from the Auto Industry. *Strategic Management Journal*, 271–291.

Dyer, J., & Singh, H. (1998). The Relational View: Cooperative Strategy and Sources of Interorganizational Competitive Advantage. *Academy of Management Review* 23(4), 660–679.

Eisenhardt, K.M. (1989). Building Theories from Case Study Research. *Academy of Management Review* 14(4), 532–550.

Eisenhardt, K.M., & Graebner, M.E. (2007). Theory Building From Cases: Opportunities and Challenges. *Academy of Management Journal* 50(1), 25–32.

Everaert, P., Sarens, G., & Rommel, J. (2010). Using Transaction Cost Economics to Explain Outsourcing of Accounting. *Small Business Economics* 35(1), 93–112.

Eurostat. (2008). *Science, Technology and Innovation in Europe.* Brussels: European Commission.

Fabrizio, K. (2012). Institutions, Capabilities, and Contracts: Make or Buy in the Electric Utility Industry. *Organization Science* 23(5), 1264–1281.

Fiedor, B. (2006). Nowa Ekonomia Instytucjonalna jako podstawa teoretycznej refleksji nad procesem transformacji od gospodarki centralnie sterowanej do rynkowej. In: Kleer, J., & Kondratowicz, A. (eds.), *Wkład transformacji do teorii ekonomii.* Warszawa: CeDeWu, 137–154.

Fink, R.C., Edelman, L.F., Hatten, K.J., & James, W.L. (2006). Transaction Cost Economics, Resource Dependence Theory, and Customer–Supplier Relationships. *Industrial and Corporate Change* 15(3), 497–529.

Forlani, D., Parthasarathy, M., & Keaveney, S.M. (2008), Managerial Risk Perceptions of International Entry-Mode Strategies. *International Marketing Review* 5(3), 292–311.

Foss, K., & Foss, N. (2005). Resources and Transaction Costs: How Property Rights Economics Furthers the Resource-based View. *Strategic Management Journal* 26(6), 541.

Foss, K., & Foss, N. (2008), Understanding Opportunity Discovery and Sustainable Advantage: The Role of Transaction Costs and Property Rights. *Strategic Entrepreneurship Journal* 2, 191–207.

Foss, N.J. (1993). Theories of the Firm: Contractual and Competence Perspectives. *Journal of Evolutionary Economics* 3(2), 127–144.

Foss, N.J., Klein, P.G., Kor, Y.Y., & Mahoney, J.T. (2008). Entrepreneurship, Subjectivism, and the Resource-Based View: Toward a New Synthesis. *Strategic Entrepreneurship Journal* 2(1), 73–94.

Freeman, J., Carroll, G.R., & Hannan, M.T. (1983). The Liability of Newness: Age Dependence in Organizational Death Rates. *American Sociological Review* 48(5), 692–710.

Freiling, J., Gersch, M., & Goeke, C. (2008). On the Path towards a Competence-based Theory of the Firm. *Organization Studies* 29(8/9), 1143–1164.

Freiling, J., & Laudien, S.M. (2013). Sustaining Trust as Informal Governance Mechanism: A Competitive Edge for Family Firms? *Economia Marche-Journal of Applied Economics* 31(2), 9–24.

Freiling, J., Wassermann, R., & Laudien, S.M. (2012). The Broken Product Chain: Rapid Paths of Service Internationalization in Terms of the Service-dominant Logic. *The Service Industries Journal* 32(10), 1623–1635.

Fritsch, M., & Mueller, P. (2004). Effects of New Business Formation on Regional Development over Time. *Regional Studies* 38(8), 961–975.

Gales, L.M., & Blackburn, R.S. (1990). An Analysis of the Impact of Supplier Strategies and Relationships on Small Retailer Actions, Perceptions, and Performance. *Entrepreneurship Theory and Practice* 15(1), 7–21.

Gancarczyk, M. (2010). Oportunizm w relacjach przedsiębiorstw. *Ekonomika i Organizacja Przedsiębiorstwa* 1, 26–32.

Gancarczyk, M. (2015a). Capability and Value vs Uncertainty and Transaction Costs in Explaining the Process of Firm Growth. A manuscript presented at the European Academy of Management Conference, 'Uncertainty is a Great Opportunity', Kozminski University, June, 17–20, ISBN 978-8386437-60-0.

Gancarczyk, M. (2015b). Enterprise- and Industry-level Drivers of Cluster Evolution and Their Outcomes for Clusters from Developed and Less-developed Countries. *European Planning Studies* 23(10), 1932–1952.

Gancarczyk, M. (2015c). Proces wzrostu przedsiębiorstwa w świetle podejścia zasobowego i teorii kosztów transakcyjnych. *Gospodarka Narodowa* 5(279), 5–31.

Gancarczyk, M. (2016). The Integrated Resource-based And Transaction Cost Approach to the Growth Process of Firms. *Journal of Organizational Change Management* 29(7), 1189–1216.

Gancarczyk, M., & Gancarczyk, J. (2011). Wzrost i internacjonalizacja przedsiębiorstw w klastrach. *Organization and Management* 146, 59–75.

Gancarczyk, M., & Gancarczyk, J. (2016). SME Supplier Upgrading during the Cooperation Life Cycle–Evidence from Central and Eastern Europe. *Journal of East European Management Studies* 21(3), 318–351.

Gancarczyk, M., & Gancarczyk, J. (2017). Proactive International Strategies of Cluster SMEs. *European Management Journal* (forthcoming). Doi: https://doi.org/10.1016/j.emj.2017.03.002.

Gancarczyk, M., & Iturriagagoitia-Zabala, J.M. (2015). The Process of the Growth of Small and Medium-Sized Enterprises (SMEs), *Journal of Entrepreneurship, Management and Innovation* 11(4), 3–24.

Garnsey, E., Stam, E., & Heffernan, P. (2006). New Firm Growth: Exploring Processes and Paths. *Industry and Innovation* 13(1), 1–20.

Garud, R., & Karnøe, P. (2003). Bricolage versus Breakthrough: Distributed and Embedded Agency in Technology Entrepreneurship. *Research Policy* 32(2), 277–300.

Gautam, R., Barney, J., & Muhanna, W. (2004). Capabilities, Business Processes and Competitive Advantage: Choosing the Dependent Variable in Empirical Tests of the Resource-based View. *Strategic Management Journal* 25, 23–37.

Gaweł, A. (2013), Proces przedsiębiorczy. Tworzenie nowych przedsiębiorstw. Warszawa: Difin.

Geroski, P.A. (1995). What Do We Know about Entry? *International Journal of Industrial Organization* 13(4), 421–440.

Geroski, P.A. (2001). Exploring the Niche Overlaps between Organizational Ecology and Industrial Economics. *Industrial and Corporate Change* 10(2), 507–540.

Giaoutzi, M., Nijkamp, P., & Storey, D.J. (eds.). (2016). *Small and medium size enterprises and regional development*. Routledge.

Gibb, A., & Davies, L. (1990). In Pursuit of Frameworks for the Development of Growth Models of the Small Business. *International Small Business Journal* 9(1), 15–31.

Gibbert, M., & Ruigrok, W. (2010). The 'What' and 'How' of case Study Rigor: Three Strategies Based on Published work. *Organizational Research Methods* 13(4), 710–737.

Gibrat, R. (1931). *Les In´egalit´es Économiques*. Paris: Librairie du Receuil Sirey.

Gilbert, B., McDougall, P., & Audretsch, D. (2006). New Venture Growth: A Review and Extension. *Journal of Management* 32(6), 926–950.

Glaister, K.W. (2004), The Rationale for International Equity Joint Ventures. *European Management Journal* 2(5), 493–507.

Glinka, B., & Gudkova, S. (2011). *Przedsiębiorczość*. Warszawa: Wolters Kluwer.

Goldberg, V.P., & Erickson, J.R. (1987). Quantity and Price Adjustment in Long-term Contracts: A Case Study of Petroleum Coke. *The Journal of Law and Economics* 30(2), 369–398.

Gorynia, M. (1999). Przedsiębiorstwo w nowej ekonomii instytucjonalnej. *Ekonomista* 6(99), 778–790.

Grant, R.M. (1996). Toward a Knowledge-based Theory of the Firm. *Strategic Management Journal* 17(52), 109–122.

Greckhamer, T. (2011). Cross-Cultural Differences in Compensation Level and Inequality Across Occupations: A Set-Theoretic Analysis. *Organization Studies* 32(1), 85–115.

Greckhamer, T., Misangyi, V.F., Elms, H., & Lacey, R. (2008). Using Qualitative Comparative Analysis in Strategic Management Research: An Examination of Combinations of Industry, Corporate, and Business-Unit Effects. *Organizational Research Methods* 11(4), 695–726.

Greiner, L. (1972). Evolution and Revolution as Organizations Grow. *Harvard Business Review* 50, 37–46.

Grossman, S.J., & Hart, O.D. (1986). The Costs and Benefits of Ownership: A Theory of Vertical and Lateral Integration. *Journal of Political Economy* 94(4), 691–719.

Gulati, R., Lawrence, P., & Puranam, P. (2005). Adaptation in Vertical Relationships: Beyond Incentive Conflict. *Strategic Management Journal* 25, 415–440.

Hamel, G., & Prahalad, C. (1990). The Core Competence of Corporation. *Harvard Business Review* 68(5–6), 600–620.

Hannan, M.T. (2005). Ecologies of Organizations: Diversity and Identity. *The Journal of Economic Perspectives* 19(1), 51–70.

Hannan, M.T., & Freeman, J. (1977). The Population Ecology of Organizations. *American Journal of Sociology* 82(5), 929–964.

Hanoch, G. (1975). The Elasticity of Scale and the Shape of Average Costs. *The American Economic Review* 65(3), 492–497.

Hansen, B., & Hamilton, R.T. (2011). Factors Distinguishing Small Firm Growers and Non-growers. *International Small Business Journal* 29(3), 278–294.

Hardt, L. (2009). The History of Transaction Cost Economics and Its Recent Developments. *Erasmus Journal for Philosophy and Economics* 2(1), 29–51.

Henrekson, M., & Johansson, D. (2010). Gazelles as Job Creators: A Survey and Interpretation of the Evidence. *Small Business Economics* 35(2), 227–244.

Hitt, M.A., Ireland, R.D., Sirmon, D.G., & Trahms, C.A. (2011). Strategic Entrepreneurship: Creating Value for Individuals, Organizations, and Society. *The Academy of Management Perspectives* 25(2), 57–75.

Hodgson, G.M. (1998). Competence and Contract in the Rent Generation in Competence-based Competition. *Journal of Economic Behavior Organization* 35(April), 179–201.

Hodgson, G.M. (2004). Opportunism Is Not the Only Reason Why Firms Exist: Why an Explanatory Emphasis on Opportunism May Mislead Management Strategy. *Industrial and Corporate Change* 13(2), 401–418.

Hoetker, G. (2005). How Much You Know versus How Well I Know You: Selecting a Supplier for a Technically Innovative Component. *Strategic Management Journal* 26(1), 75–96.

Holcomb, T.R., & Hitt, M.A. (2007). Toward a Model of Strategic Outsourcing. *Journal of Operations Management* 25(2), 464–481.

Holmström, B., & Roberts, J. (1998). The Boundaries of the Firm Revisited. *The Journal of Economic Perspectives* 12(4), 73–94.

Hölzl, W., & Friesenbichler, K. (2008). Final Sector Report Gazelles. Europe Innova Sector Report. Vienna: WIFO.

Hoon, Ch. (2013). Meta-synthesis of Qualitative Case Studies: An Approach to Theory Building. *Organizational Research Methods* 16(4), 522–546.

Humphrey, J., & Schmitz, H. (2002). How Does Insertion in Global Value Chains Affect Upgrading in Industrial Clusters? *Regional Studies* 36(9), 1017–1027.

Humphrey, J., & Schmitz, H. (2004). Governance in Global Value Chains. In: Schmitz, H., *Local Enterprises in the Global Economy*. Cheltenham: Edward Elgar, 95–109.

Iacobucci, D., & Rosa, P. (2010), The Growth of Business Groups by Habitual Entrepreneurs: The Role of Entrepreneurial Teams. *Entrepreneurship Theory and Practice* 34(2), 351–377.

Ijiri, Y., & Simon, H.A. (1977). *Skew Distributions and the Sizes of Business Firms*. Amsterdam: North Holland.

Ireland, R.D., Hitt, M.A., & Vaidyanath, D. (2002). Alliance Management as a Source of Competitive Advantage. *Journal of Management* 28(3), 413–446.

Isaksen, A., & Hauge, E. (2002). Regional Clusters in Europe. *Observatory of European SMEs* 3, 5–55.

Jacobides, M.G. (2008). How Capability Differences, Transaction Costs, and Learning Curves Interact to Shape Vertical Scope. *Organization Science* 19(2), 306–326.

Jacobides, M.G., & Hitt, L.M. (2005), Losing Sight of the Forest for the Trees? Productive Capabilities and Gains from Trade as Drivers of Vertical Scope. *Strategic Management Journal* 26(13), 1209–1227.

Jacobides, M.G., & Winter, S.G. (2005), The Co-evolution of Capabilities and Transaction Costs: Explaining the Institutional Structure of Production. *Strategic Management Journal* 26(5), 395–414.

Jacobides, M.G., & Winter, S.G. (2007). Entrepreneurship and Firm Boundaries: The Theory of a Firm. *Journal of Management Studies* 44(7), 1213–1241.

Jap, S.D., & Anderson, E. (2003). Safeguarding Interorganizational Performance and Continuity under Ex Post Opportunism. *Management Science* 49(12), 1684–1701.

Jensen, M.C., & Meckling, W.H. (1976). Theory of the Firm: Managerial Behavior, Agency Costs and Ownership Structure. *Journal of Financial Economics* 3(4), 305–360.

Joskow, P.L. (1987). Contract Duration and Relationship-specific Investments: Empirical Evidence from Coal Markets. *The American Economic Review* 77(1), 168–185.

Juarrero, A. (2000). Dynamics in Action: Intentional Behavior as a Complex System. *Emergence* 2(2), 24–57.

Kang, M.P., Mahoney, J.T., & Tan, D. (2009). Why Firms Make Unilateral Investments Specific to Other Firms: The Case of OEM Suppliers. *Strategic Management Journal* 30(2), 117–135.

Kent, R.A., & Argouslidis, P.C. (2005). Shaping Business Decisions Using Fuzzy-Set Analysis: Service Elimination Decisions. *Journal of Marketing Management* 21(5–6), 641–658.

Kim, S.M., & Mahoney, J.T. (2006). Mutual Commitment to Support Exchange: Relation-specific IT System as a Substitute for Managerial Hierarchy. *Strategic Management Journal* 27(5), 401–423.

Klein, B., Crawford, R., & Alchian, A. (1978). Vertical Integration, Appropriable Rents, and the Competitive Contracting Process. *Journal of Law and Economics* 21(2), 297–326.

Klein, P.G. (2005). The Make-or-buy Decision: Lessons from Empirical Studies. In: *Handbook of New Institutional Economics*. New York: Springer US, 435–464.

Klimczak, B. (2005). Uwagi o powiązaniach między standardową ekonomią i nową ekonomią instytucjonalną. In: Rudolf, S. (ed.), *Nowa ekonomia instytucjonalna*. Kielce: Wydawnictwo Wyższej Szkoły Ekonomii i Administracji.

Kogut, B., & Ragin, C. (2006). Exploring Complexity When Diversity Is Limited: Institutional Complementarity in Theories of Rule of Law and National Systems Revisited. *European Management Review* 3(1), 44–59.

Kogut, B., & Zander, U. (1992). Knowledge of the Firm, Combinative Capabilities, and the Replication of Technology. *Organization Science* 3(3), 383–397.

Koryak, O., Mole, K., Lockett, A., Hayton, J., Ucbasaran, D., & Hodgkinson, G. (2015). Entrepreneurial Leadership, Capabilities and Firm Growth. *International Small Business Journal* 33, 89–105.

Kraaijenbrink, J., Spender, J.C., & Groen, A.J. (2010). The Resource-based View: A Review and Assessment of Its Critiques. *Journal of Management* 36(1), 349–372.

Krzakiewicz, K., & Cyfert, S. (2016). Strategiczny potencjał organizacji uczącej się w aspekcie koncepcji dynamicznych zdolności. *Studia i Prace Kolegium Zarządzania i Finansów/Szkoła Główna Handlowa* 149, 43–59.

Kulkarni, S.P., & Ramamoorthy, N. (2005). Commitment, Flexibility and the Choice of Employment Contracts. *Human Relations* 58(6), 741–761.

Kumar, M.S. (2010). Differential Gains between Partners in Joint Ventures: Role of Resource Appropriation and Private Benefits. *Organization Science* 21(1), 232–248.

Lachiewicz, S., & Matejun, M. (eds.). (2011). *Zarządzanie rozwojem małych i średnich przedsiębiorstw*. Warszawa: Wolters Kluwer Polska.

Lado, A.A., Dant, R.R., & Tekleab, A.G. (2008). Trust-opportunism Paradox, Relationalism, and Performance in Interfirm Relationships: Evidence from the Retail Industry. *Strategic Management Journal* 29(4), 401–423.

Lafontaine, F., & Slade, M.E. (1997). Retail Contracting: Theory and Practice. *The Journal of Industrial Economics* 45(1), 1–25.

Lafontaine, F., & Slade, M.E. (2001). Incentive Contracting and the Franchise Decision. In: Chatterjee, K., & Samuelson, W. (eds.), *Advances in Business Applications of Game Theory*. Boston: Kluwer Academic Press, 133–188.

Lafontaine, F., & Slade, M.E. (2007). Vertical Integration and Firm Boundaries: The Evidence. *Journal of Economic Literature* 45(3), 629–685.

Lai, W.H., & Chang, P.L. (2010). Corporate Motivation and Performance in R&D Alliances. *Journal of Business Research* 63(5), 490–496.

Langley, A. (1999). Strategies for Theorizing from Process Data. *Academy of Management Review* 24(4), 691–710.

Langlois, R.N. (1992). Transaction-cost Economics in Real Time. *Industrial and Corporate Change* 1(1), 99–127.

Larson, A. (1992). Network Dyads in Entrepreneurial Settings: A Study of the Governance of Exchange Relationships. *Administrative Science Quarterly* 37(1), 76–104.

Larsson, R. (1993). Case Survey Methodology: Quantitative Analysis of Patterns across Case Studies. *Academy of Management Journal* 36(6), 1515–1546.

Lasagni, A. (2012). How Can External Relationships Enhance Innovation in SMEs? New Evidence for Europe. *Journal of Small Business Management* 50(2), 310–339.

Lavie, D. (2006). The Competitive Advantage of Interconnected Firms: An Extension of the Resource-based View. *Academy of Management Review* 31(3), 638–658.

Leavitt, K., Mitchell, T., & Peterson, J. (2010). Theory Pruning: Strategies to Reduce Our Dense Theoretical Landscape. *Organizational Research Methods* 13(4), 644–667.

Lee, A.S. (1989). A Scientific Methodology for MIS Case Studies. *MIS Quarterly* 13(1), 33–50.

Legewie, N. (2013, September). An Introduction to Applied Data Analysis with Qualitative Comparative Analysis. *Forum Qualitative Sozialforschung/Forum: Qualitative Social Research* 14(3). https://www.researchgate.net/publication/291177551_An_introduction_to_applied_data_analysis_with_qualitative_comparative_analysis_QCA. Accessed July 16, 2017.

Leiblein, M. (2003). The Choice of Organizational Governance Form and Performance: Predictions from Transaction Cost, Resource-based, and Real Options Theories. *Journal of Management* 29(6), 937–961.

Leiblein, M., & Miller, D. (2003). An Empirical Examination of Transaction- and Firm-level Influences on the Vertical Boundaries of the Firm. *Strategic Management Journal* 24(9), 839–859.

Leitch, C., Hill, F., & Neergaard, H. (2010). Entrepreneurial and Business Growth and the Quest for a 'Comprehensive Theory': Tilting at Windmills? *Entrepreneurship Theory and Practice* 34(2), 249–260.

Lensink, R., Van Steen, P., & Sterken, E. (2005). Uncertainty and Growth of the Firm. *Small Business Economics* 24(4), 381–391.

Lepak, D.P., & Snell, S.A. (1999). The Human Resource Architecture: Toward a Theory of Human Capital Allocation and Development. *Academy of Management. The Academy of Management Review* 24(1), 31–48.

Levi, M. (2000). When Good Defences Make Good Neighbors: A Transaction Cost Approach to Trust, the Absence of Trust and Distrust. In: Mènard, C., *Institutions, Contracts and Organizations. Perspectives from New Institutional Economics*. Cheltenham: Edward Elgar, 137–157.

Levie, J., & Lichtenstein, B. (2010). A Terminal Assessment of Stages Theory: Introducing a Dynamic States Approach to Entrepreneurship. *Entrepreneurship Theory and Practice* 34(2), 317–350.

Lewicki, R.J., & Bunker, B.B. (1996). Developing and Maintaining Trust in Work Relationships. In: Kramer, R.M., & Tyler, T.R. (eds.), *Trust in Organizations: Frontiers of Theory and Research*. Thousand Oaks, CA: Sage, 114–139.

Lichtenstein, B.B. (2009). Moving Far from Far-from-equilibrium: Opportunity Tension as the Catalyst of Emergence. *Emergence: Complexity and Organization* 11(4), 15–25.

Lisowska, R. (2012). Uwarunkowania rozwoju małych i średnich przedsię-biorstw w regionach zmarginalizowanych na przykładzie województwa łódzkiego. *Prace Naukowe Uniwersytetu Ekonomicznego we Wrocławiu* 244, 416–424.

Lisowska, R. (2015). External Determinants of the Development of Small- and Medium-sized Enterprises – Empirical Analysis. *Journal of Entrepreneurship, Management and Innovation* 11(4), doi: 10.7341/20151145.

Littunen, H., & Tohmo, T. (2003). The High Growth in New Metal-based Manufacturing and Business Service Firms in Finland. *Small Business Economics* 21(2), 187–200.

Lo, D. (Ho-Fu), Frias, K., & Ghosh, M. (2012). Price Formats for Branded Components in Industrial Markets: An Integration of Transaction Cost Economics and the Resource-based View. *Organization Science* 23(5), 1282–1297.

Lockett, A., & Thompson, S. (2001). The Resource-based View and Economics. *Journal of Management* 27(6), 723–754.

Lockett, A., Thompson, S., & Morgenstern, U. (2009). The Development of the Resource-based View of the Firm: A Critical Appraisal. *International Journal of Management Reviews* 11(1), 9–28.

Lockett, A., Wiklund, J., Davidsson, P., & Girma, S. (2011). Organic and Acquisitive Growth: Re-examining, Testing and Extending Penrose's Growth Theory. *Journal of Management Studies* 48(1), 48–74.

Love, J.H., & Roper, S. (2005). Economists' Perceptions versus Managers' Decisions: An Experiment in Transaction-cost Analysis. *Cambridge Journal of Economics* 29(1), 19–36.

Lumpkin, G.T., & Dess, G.G. (2001). Linking Two Dimensions of Entrepreneurial Orientation to Firm Performance: The Moderating Role of Environment and Industry Life Cycle. *Journal of Business Venturing* 16(5), 429–451.

Lyons, B.R. (1994). Contracts and Specific Investment: An Empirical Test of Transaction Cost Theory. *Journal of Economics & Management Strategy* 3(2), 257–278.

Macher, J.T. (2006). Technological Development and the Boundaries of the Firm: A Knowledge-based Examination in Semiconductor Manufacturing. *Management Science* 52(6), 826–843.

Macher, J.T., & Richman, B. (2008). Transaction Cost Economics: An Assessment of Empirical Research in the Social Sciences. *Business and Politics* 10(1), 1–63.

Macneil, I.R. (1986). Exchange Revisited: Individual Utility and Social Solidarity. *Ethics* 96(3), 567–593.

Macpherson, A. (2005). Learning How to Grow: Resolving the Crisis of Knowing. *Technovation* 25(10), 1129–1140.

Macpherson, A., & Holt, R. (2007). Knowledge, Learning and Small Firm Growth: A Systematic Review of the Evidence. *Research Policy* 36(2), 172–172.

Madhok, A. (1997). Cost, Value and Foreign Market Entry Mode: The Transaction and the Firm. *Strategic Management Journal* 18, 39–61.

Madhok, A. (2002). Reassessing the Fundamentals and Beyond: Ronald Coase, the Transaction Cost and Resource-based Theories of the Firm and the Institutional Structure of Production. *Strategic Management Journal* 23(6), 535–550.

Madhok A., & Tallman S.B. (1998). Resources, Transactions and Rents: Managing Value through Interfirm Collaborative Relationships. *Organization Science* 9(3), 326–339.

Magala, S. (2000). Critical Complexities: From Marginal Paradigms to Learning Networks. *Journal of Organizational Change Management* 13(4), 312–333.

Mahoney, J.T. (2001). A Resource-Based Theory of Sustainable Rents. *Journal of Management* 27(6), 651–660.

Majocchi, A., Mayrhofer, U., & Camps, J. (2013). Joint Ventures or Non-equity Alliances? Evidence from Italian Firms. *Management Decision* 51(2), 380–395.

Marris, R. (1963). A Model of the 'Managerial' Enterprise. *The Quarterly Journal of Economics* 77(2), 185–209.

Marris, R. (1964). *The Economic Theory of "Managerial" Capitalism.* London: Macmillan.

Marris, R. (1999). Edith Penrose and Economics. *Contributions to Political Economy* 18(1), 47–65.

Masten, S.E., Meehan, J.W., & Snyder, E.A. (1991). The Costs of Organization. *Journal of Law, Economics, & Organization* 7(1), 1–25.

Masten, S.E., & Saussier, S. (2000). Econometrics of Contracts: An Assessment of Developments in the Empirical Literature on Contracting. *Revue d'Économie Industrielle* 92(1), 215–236.

Mayer, J.H., Davis, F.D., & Shoorman, A. (1995). An Integrative Model of Organizational Trust. *Academy of Management Review* 20(3), 709–734.

Mayer, K., & Salomon, R. (2006). Capability, Contractual Hazards, and Governance: Integrating Resource-based and Transaction Cost Perspectives. *Academy of Management Journal* 49(5), 942–959.

McIvor, R. (2009). How the Transaction Cost and Resource-based Theories of the Firm Inform Outsourcing Evaluation. *Journal of Operations Management* 27(1), 45–63.

McKelvey, B. (2004). Toward a Complexity Science of Entrepreneurship. *Journal of Business Venturing* 19(3), 313–341.

McKelvie, A., & Wiklund, J. (2010). Advancing Firm Growth Research: A Focus on Growth Mode Instead of Growth Rate. *Entrepreneurship Theory and Practice* 34(2), 261–288.

McMullen, J.S., & Dimov, D. (2013). Time and the Entrepreneurial Journey: The Problems and Promise of Studying Entrepreneurship as a Process. *Journal of Management Studies* 50(8), 1481–1512.

Meyer, K.F., Wright, M.W., & Pruthi, S. (2009). Managing Knowledge in Foreign Entry Strategies: A Resource-based Analysis. *Strategic Management Journal* 30(5), 557–574.

Michael, S.C. (2007). Transaction Cost Entrepreneurship. *Journal of Business Venturing* 22(3), 412–426.

Monteverde, K., & Teece, D.J. (1982). Supplier Switching Costs and Vertical Integration in the Automobile Industry. *The Bell Journal of Economics* 13(1), 206–213.

Moore, F.T. (1959). Economies of Scale: Some Statistical Evidence. *The Quarterly Journal of Economics* 73(2), 232–245.

Moreno, A., & Casillas, J. (2007). High-growth SMEs versus Non-high-growth SMEs: A Discriminant Analysis. *Entrepreneurship and Regional Development* 9(1), 1–30.

Muller, P., Caliandro, C., Gagliardi, D., & Marzocchi, C. (2015). *Annual Report on European SMEs 2014/2015 (SMEs Start Hiring Again)*. Luxembourg: European Union.

Muller, P., Devnanim S., Julius, J., Gagliardi, D., & Marzocchi, C. (2016). *Annual Report on European SMEs 2015/2016 (SME Recovery Continues)*. Brussels: European Commission.

Muñoz, P., & Dimov, D. (2015). The Call of the Whole in Understanding the Development of Sustainable Ventures. *Journal of Business Venturing* 30(4), 632–654.

Murphy, P.J., Wu, Z., Welsch, H., Heiser, D.R., Young, S.T., & Jiang, B. (2012). Small Firm Entrepreneurial Outsourcing: Traditional Problems, Nontraditional Solutions. *Strategic Outsourcing: An International Journal* 5(3), 248–275.

Mutinelli, M., & Piscitello, L. (1998), The Entry Mode Choice of MNEs: An Evolutionary Approach, *Research Policy* 27(5), 491–506.

Najda-Janoszka, M. (2016). *Dynamic Capability-based Approach to Value Appropriation*. Cracow: Jagiellonian University Press.

Nandialath, A., Dotson, J., & Durrand, R. (2014). A Structural Approach to Handling Endogeneity in Strategic Management: The Case of RBV. *European Management Review* 11(1), 47–62.

Nelson R.R., & Winter S.G. (1982). *An Evolutionary Theory of Economic Change*. Cambridge: Harvard Business School Press.

Newbert, S. (2007). Empirical Research on the Resource-based View of the Firm: An Assessment and Suggestions for Future Research. *Strategic Management Journal* 28, 121–146.

Noblit, G.W., & Hare, R.D. (1988). *Meta-ethnography: Synthesizing Qualitative Studies*. London: Sage.

Noga, A. (2009). *Teorie przedsiębiorstw*. Warszawa: Polskie Wydawnictwo Ekonomiczne.

Nooteboom, B. (1992). Towards a Dynamic Theory of Transactions. *Journal of Evolutionary Economics* 2(4), 281–99.

Nooteboom, B. (1993). Firm Size Effects on Transaction Costs. *Small Business Economics* 5(4), 283–295.

Obłój, K. (2007). Pułapki teoretyczne zasobowej teorii strategii. *Przegląd Organizacji* 5, 7–10.

OECD (2005). *Oslo Manual. The Measurement of Scientific and Technological Activities. Proposed Guidelines for Collecting and Interpreting Innovation Data*. Paris: OECD Publishing.

OECD-Eurostat, E.O. (2007). *Manual on Business Demography Statistics*. Paris: OECD Publishing.

OECD. (2010). *High-growth Enterprises: What Governments Can Do to Make a Difference*. Paris: OECD Publishing.

Okoń-Horodyńska, E., Wisła, R., & Sierotowicz, T. (2011). Business strategy of innovative enterprises – the case of IBM. *Transformation in Business & Economics*, 10(2A), 357–366.

Okoń-Horodyńska, E., & Zachorowska-Mazurkiewicz, A. (eds.). (2007). *Innowacje w rozwoju gospodarki i przedsiębiorstw: siły motoryczne i bariery*. Warszawa: Instytut Wiedzy i Innowacji.

Ordanini, A., & Silvestri, G. (2008). Recruitment and Selection Services: Efficiency and Competitive Reasons in the Outsourcing of HR Practices. *The International Journal of Human Resource Management* 19(2), 372–391.

Panzar, J.C., & Willig, R.D. (1977). Economies of Scale in Multi-output Production. *The Quarterly Journal of Economics* 91(3), 481–493.

Paterson, B.L., Thorne, S.E., Canam, C., & Jillings, C. (2001). *Meta-study of Qualitative Health Research: A Practical Guide to Meta-analysis and Meta-synthesis*. Thousand Oakes: Sage.

Penrose, E. (1959). *The Theory of the Growth of the Firm*. Oxford: Oxford University Press.

Peteraf, M. (1993). The Cornerstones of Competitive Advantage: A Resources-Based View. *Strategic Management Journal* 14(3), 179–191.

Pfeffer, J., & Salancik, G.R. (1978). *The External Control of Organizations*. New York: Harper & Row.

Piasecki, B. (1997). *Przedsiębiorczość i mała firma: teoria i praktyka*. Łódź: Wydawnictwo Uniwersytetu Łódzkiego.

Piasecki B. (2001). *Ekonomika i zarządzanie małą firmą*. Warszawa–Łódź: Wydawnictwo Naukowe PWN.

Piasecki, B., Rogut, A., & Smallbone, D. (1997). *Mocne i słabe strony małych i średnich przedsiębiorstw produkcyjnych w Polsce w 1995 roku oraz rekomendacje dla polityki*. *Łódź*–Londyn: USAID GEMINI-PEDS Project.

Pitelis, C.N., & Pseiridis, A.N. (1999). Transaction Costs versus Resource Value? *Journal of Economic Studies* 26(3), 221–240.

Pitelis, C.N., & Teece, D.J. (2009). The (New) Nature and Essence of the Firm. *European Management Review* 6(1), 5–15.

Popper, K. (1968). *The Logic of Scientific Discovery*. New York: Harper Torchbooks.

Poppo, L., & Zenger, T. (1995). Opportunism, Routines, and Boundary Choices: A Comparative Test of Transaction Cost and Resource-based Explanations for Make-or-buy Decisions. *Academy of Management Journal* 42, 42–46.

Ragin, C.C. (1987). *The Comparative Method: Moving Beyond Qualitative and Quantitative Strategies*. Berkeley: University of California Press.

Ragin, C.C. (2000). *Fuzzy-Set Social Science*. University of Chicago Press.

Ragin, C.C. (2008a). Measurement versus Calibration: A Set-theoretic Approach. In: *The Oxford Handbook of Political Methodology*. Retrieved 8 Aug. 2017, from http://www.oxfordhandbooks.com/view/10.1093/oxfordhb/9780199286546.001.0001/oxfordhb-9780199286546-e-8.

Ragin, C.C. (2008b). *User's Guide to Fuzzy-Set/Qualitative Comparative Analysis*. Mimeo. Retrieved 23 July 2015, from http://www.u.arizona.edu/~cragin/fsQCA/download/fsQCAManual.pdf. Accessed January 14, 2015.

Ragin, C.C. (2009). Qualitative Comparative Analysis Using Fuzzy Sets (fsQCA). In: Rihoux, B., & Ragin, C.C., *Configurational Comparative*

Methods: Qualitative Comparative Analysis (QCA) and Related Techniques. Thousand Oaks, CA: Sage, 87–121.

Ragin, C.C., & Sonnett, J. (2005). Between Complexity and Parsimony: Limited Diversity, Counterfactual Cases, and Comparative Analysis. In: *Vergleichen in der Politikwissenschaft*. VS Wiesbaden: Verlag für Sozialwissenschaften, 180–197.

Ratajczak, M. (2011). Popularność ekonomii instytucjonalnej. Moda czy trwała zmiana? *Zeszyty Naukowe/Polskie Towarzystwo Ekonomiczne* 9, 29–42.

Ratajczak-Mrozek, M. (2010). *Sieci biznesowe a przewaga konkurencyjna przedsiębiorstw zaawansowanych technologii na rynkach zagranicznych*. Poznań: Wydawnictwo Uniwersytetu Ekonomicznego w Poznaniu.

Ray, G., Xue, L., & Barney, J. (2013). Impact of Information Technology Capital on Firm Scope and Performance: The Role of Asset Characteristics. *Academy of Management Journal* 56(4), 1125–1147.

Reymen, I.M., Andries, P., Berends, H., Mauer, R., Stephan, U., & Burg, E. (2015). Understanding Dynamics of Strategic Decision Making in Venture Creation: A Process Study of Effectuation and Causation. *Strategic Entrepreneurship Journal* 9(4), 351–379.

Rindfleisch, A., & Heide, J.B. (1997). Transaction Cost Analysis: Past, Present, and Future Applications. *The Journal of Marketing* 61(October), 30–54.

Rindfleisch, A., Antia, K., Bercovitz, J., Brown J., & Cannon, J. (2010). Transaction Costs, Opportunism, and Governance: Contextual Considerations and Future Research Opportunities. *Marketing Letters* 21(3), 211–222.

Rindova, V.P., Yeow, A., Martins, L.L., & Faraj, S. (2012). Partnering Portfolios, Value-creation Logics, and Growth Trajectories: A Comparison of Yahoo and Google (1995 to 2007). *Strategic Entrepreneurship Journal* 6(2), 133–151.

Ring, P.S., & Van de Ven, A.H. (1994). Developmental Processes of Cooperative Interorganizational Relationships. *Academy of Management Review* 19(1), 90–118.

Rodríguez-Gutiérrez, M.J., Moreno, P., & Tejada, P. (2015). Entrepreneurial Orientation and Performance of SMEs in the Services Industry. *Journal of Organizational Change Management* 28(2), 194–212.

Romanowska, M. (2001). Kształtowanie wartości firmy w oparciu o kapitał intelektualny. In: Borowiecki, R., & Romanowska, M. (eds.), *System informacji strategicznej. Wywiad gospodarczy a konkurencyjność przedsiębiorstwa*. Warszawa: Difin, pp. 24–27.

Ryoo, J. (2012). Technology Sourcing Decision Making for New Technology Development Projects: An Empirical Study of South Korean Hightech Small Firms. *Asian Business & Management* 11(4), 445–469.

Safizadeh, H., Joy, M., Field, M., & Ritzman, L. (2008). Sourcing Practices and Boundaries of the Firm in the Financial Services Industry. *Strategic Management Journal* 29(1), 79–91.

Sampson, R.C. (2004). The Cost of Misaligned Governance in R&D Alliances. *Journal of Law, Economics, and Organization* 20(2), 484–526.

Sandelowski, M., Docherty, S., & Emden, C. (1997). Focus on Qualitative Methods. Qualitative Metasynthesis: Issues and Techniques. *Research in Nursing and Health* 20(4), 365–372.

Sarason, Y., Dean, T., & Dillard, J.F. (2006). Entrepreneurship as the Nexus of Individual and Opportunity: A Structuration View. *Journal of Business Venturing* 21(3), 286–305.

Sarasvathy, S.D. (2001). Causation and Effectuation: Toward a Theoretical Shift from Economic Inevitability to Entrepreneurial Contingency. *Academy of Management Review* 26(2), 243–263.

Sarasvathy, S.D. (2009). *Effectuation: Elements of Entrepreneurial Expertise*. Cheltenham: Edward Elgar Publishing.

Schilling, M., & Steensma, K. (2002). Disentangling the Theories of Firm Boundaries: A Path Model and Empirical Test. *Organization Science* 13(4), 387–401.

Schreyer, P. (2000). High-growth Firms and Employment. *OECD Science, Technology and Industry Working Papers*, 2000/03, Paris: OECD Publishing.

Scott, B.R., & Bruce, R. (1987). Five Stages of Growth in Small Business. *Long Range Planning* 20(3), 45–52.

Selden, P.D., & Fletcher, D.E. (2015). The Entrepreneurial Journey as an Emergent Hierarchical System of Artifact-creating Processes. *Journal of Business Venturing* 30(4), 603–615.

Shane, S., & Venkataraman, S. (2000). The Promise of Entrepreneurship as a Field of Research. *Academy of Management Review* 25(1), 217–226.

Shareff, R. (2007). Want Better Business Theories? Maybe Karl Popper Has the Answer. *Academy of Management Learning & Education* 6(2), 272–280.

Shelanski, H.A. (1991). *A Survey of Empirical Work in Transaction Cost Economics*. Working paper, University of California, Berkeley.

Shelanski, H.A., & Klein, P.G. (1995). Empirical Research in Transaction Cost Economics: A Review and Assessment. *Journal of Law, Economics & Organization* 11(2), 335–361.

Shepherd, D., & Wiklund, J. (2009). Are We Comparing Apples with Apples or Apples with Oranges? Appropriateness of Knowledge Accumulation across Growth Studies. *Entrepreneurship Theory and Practice* 33(1), 105–123.

Shervani, T., Frazer, G., & Challagalla, G. (2007). The Moderating Influence of Firm Market Power on the Transaction Cost Economic Model: An Empirical Test in a Forward Channel Integration Context. *Strategic Management Journal* 28(6), 635–652.

Silverman, B. (1999). Technological Resources and the Direction of Corporate Diversification: Toward an Integration of the Resource-based View and Transaction Cost Economics. *Management Science* 45(8), 1109–1124.

Silverman, D. (2006). *Interpreting Qualitative Data: Methods for Analyzing Talk, Text and Interaction.* Sage.

Silverman, D. (2013). *Doing Qualitative Research: A Practical Handbook.* London: Sage.

Sirén, C.A., Kohtamäki, M., & Kuckertz, A. (2012). Exploration and Exploitation Strategies, Profit Performance, and the Mediating Role of Strategic Learning: Escaping the Exploitation Trap. *Strategic Entrepreneurship Journal* 6(1), 18–41.

Smallbone, D., Leigh, R., & North, D. (1995). The Characteristics and Strategies of High-growth SMEs. *International Journal of Entrepreneurial Behavior & Research* 1(3), 44–62.

Smith, J.A., Flowers, P., & Osborn, M. (1997). Interpretative Phenomenological Analysis and the Psychology of Health and Illness. In: Yardley, L. (ed.), *Material Discourses of Health and Illness.* London–New York: Routledge, 68–91.

Smith, J.A., Jarman, M., & Osborn, M. (1997). Doing Interpretive Phenomenological Analysis. In: Murray, M., & Chamberlain, K. (eds.), *Qualitative Health Psychology: Theories and Methods.* London: Sage, 218–240.

Souitaris, V., & Zerbinati, S. (2014). How Do Corporate Venture Capitalists Do Deals? An Exploration of Corporate Investment Practices. *Strategic Entrepreneurship Journal* 8(4), 321–348.

Stam, E. (2008), Entrepreneurship and Innovation Policy. https://ssrn.com/abstract=1115262. Accessed December 13, 2017.

Stam, E. (2010). Growth beyond Gibrat: Firm Growth Processes and Strategies. *Small Business Economics* 35(2), 129–135.

Stam, E., & Garnsey, E. (2006). New firms Evolving in the Knowledge Economy; Problems and Solutions around Turning Points. In: Dolfsma,

W., & Soete, L. (eds.), *Understanding the Dynamics of a Knowledge Economy*. Cheltenham, UK and Northampton, MA, USA: Edward Elgar, 102–128.

Stam, E., Suddle, K., Hessels, J., & Van Stel, A. (2006). High-growth Entrepreneurs, Public Policies and Economic Growth. Zoetermeer: EIM Business & Policy Research, SCALES: Scientific Analysis of Entrepreneurship and SMEs.

Stawasz, E. (2011). Innowacyjność a wzrost przedsiębiorstw z sektora MSP w dziedzinach wysokiej technologii w kontekście ich wewnętrznej zdolności innowacyjnej. In: Zakrzewska-Bielawska, A. (ed.), *Wyzwania rozwojowe małych i średnich przedsiębiorstw. Innowacje. Technologie. Kryzys*. Warsaw: Difin.

Steensma, K., & Corley, K. (2001). Organizational Context as a Moderator of Theories on Firm Boundaries for Technology Sourcing. *Academy of Management Journal* 44(2), 271–291.

Steffens, P., Davidsson, P., & Fitzsimmons, J. (2009). Performance Configurations over Time: Implications for Growth- and Profit-oriented Strategies. *Entrepreneurship Theory and Practice* 33(1), 125–148.

Steyaert, C. (2007). 'Entrepreneuring' as a Conceptual Attractor? A Review of Process Theories in 20 Years of Entrepreneurship Studies. *Entrepreneurship and Regional Development* 19(6), 453–477.

Storey, D. (1994). *Understanding the Small Business Sector*. London: Routledge.

Sutton, J. (1997). Gibrat's Legacy. *Journal of Economic Literature* 35(1), 40–59.

Tatum, D. (2007). *No Man's Land: Where Growing Companies Fail*. Penguin.

Teece, D. (2007). Explicating Dynamic Capabilities: The Nature and Microfoundations of (Sustainable) Enterprise Performance. *Strategic Management Journal* 28(13), 1319–1350.

Teece, D., Pisano, G., & Shuen, A. (1997). The Dynamic Capabilities of Firms: An Introduction. *Industrial and Corporate Change* 3(3), 537–556.

Thwaites, A., & Wynarczyk, P. (1996). The Economic Performance of Innovative Small Firms in the South East Region and Elsewhere in the UK. *Regional Studies* 30(2), 135–149.

Trochim, W.M.K. (1989). Outcome Pattern Matching and Program Theory. *Evaluation and Program Planning* 12(4), 355–366.

Tsang E. (2000). Transaction Cost and Resource-based Explanations of Joint Ventures: A Comparison and Synthesis. *Organization Studies* 21(1), 215–242.

Tsang, E. (2006). Behavioral Assumptions and Theory Development: The Case of Transaction Cost Economics. *Strategic Management Journal* 27(11), 999–1011.

Tseng, C.H., & Chen, L.T. (2013). Firm Capabilities as Moderators of Transaction Cost Factors and Subsidiary Domestic Outsourcing. *Management Decision* 51(1), 5–24.

Un, C.A., & Montoro-Sanchez, A. (2010). Innovative Capability Development for Entrepreneurship: A Theoretical Framework. *Journal of Organizational Change Management* 23(4), 413–434.

Van de Ven, A.H., & Engleman, R.M. (2004). Event- and Outcome-driven Explanations of Entrepreneurship. *Journal of Business Venturing* 19(3), 343–358.

Van de Ven, A.H., & Poole, M.S. (1995). Explaining Development and Change in Organizations. *Academy of Management Review* 20(3), 510–540.

Venkataraman, S., Sarasvathy, S.D., Dew, N., & Forster, W.R. (2012). Reflections on the 2010 AMR Decade Award: Whither the Promise? Moving Forward with Entrepreneurship as a Science of the Artificial. *Academy of Management Review* 37(1), 21–33.

Verwaal, E., Bruining, H., Wright, M., Manigart, S., & Lockett, A. (2010). Resources Access Needs and Capabilities as Mediators of the Relationship between VC Firm Size and Syndication. *Small Business Economics* 34(3), 277–291.

Wach, K. (2012). *Europeizacja małych i średnich przedsiębiorstw: rozwój przez umiędzynarodowienie*. Warszawa: Wydawnictwo Naukowe PWN.

Wagner, J. (2001). A Note on the Firm Size-export Relationship. *Small Business Economics* 17(4), 229–237.

Wasilczuk, J. (2000). Advantageous Competence of Owner/Managers to Grow the Firm in Poland: Empirical Evidence. *Journal of Small Business Management* 38(2), 88.

Wasilczuk, J. (2005). *Wzrost małych i średnich przedsiębiorstw: aspekty teoretyczne i badania empiryczne*. Gdańsk: Wydawnictwo Politechniki Gdańskiej.

Wathne, K.H., & Heide J.B. (2000). Opportunism in Interfirm Relationships: Forms, Outcomes, and Solutions. *Journal of Marketing* 64(10), 36–51.

Watson J. (2007). Modeling the Relationship between Networking and Firm Performance. *Journal of Business Venturing* 22(6): 852–874.

Weaver, K.M., & Dickson, P.H. (1998). Outcome Quality of Small- to Medium-sized Enterprise-based Alliances: The Role of Perceived Partner Behaviors. *Journal of Business Venturing* 13(6), 505–522.

Weed, M. (2005, January). "Meta Interpretation": A Method for the Interpretive Synthesis of Qualitative Research. *Forum Qualitative Sozialforschung/ Forum: Qualitative Social Research* 6(1). http://www.qualitative-research. net/index.php/fqs. Accessed July 10, 2017.

Weinzimmer, L.G., Nystrom, P.C., & Freeman, S.J. (1998). Measuring Organizational Growth: Issues, Consequences and Guidelines. *Journal of Management* 24(2), 235–262.

Wernerfelt, B. (1984). A Resource-based View of the Firm. *Strategic Management Journal* 5(2), 171–180.

Wiklund, J., Davidsson, P., & Delmar, F. (2003). What Do They Think and Feel about Growth? An Expectancy-value Approach to Small Business Managers' Attitudes toward Growth. *Entrepreneurship Theory and Practice* 18(3), 247–270.

Wiklund, J., & Shepherd, D. (2003). Aspiring for, and Achieving Growth: The Moderating Role of Resources and Opportunities. *The Journal of Management Studies* 40(8), 1919–1941.

Williamson, O.E. (1964). *The Economics of Discretionary Behavior: Managerial Objectives in a Theory of the Firm*. Englewood Cliffs, New York: Prentice-Hall.

Williamson, O.E. (1975). Markets and Hierarchies: Analysis and Antitrust Implications. New York: The Free Press.

Williamson, O.E. (1979). Transaction-cost Economics: The Governance of Contractual Relations. *Journal of Law and Economics* 22(2), 231–266.

Williamson, O.E. (1989). Transaction Cost Economics. In: Schmalensee, R., & Willig, R. (eds.), *Handbook of Industrial Organization*, vol. 1. Amsterdam: Elsevier Science Publishers, 135–182.

Williamson, O.E. (1991). Comparative Economic Organization: The Analysis of Discrete Structural Alternatives. *Administrative Science Quarterly* 36(2), 269–296.

Williamson, O.E. (1993). Transaction Cost Economics and Organization Theory. *Industrial and Corporate Change* 2(1), 107–156.

Williamson, O.E. (1998). Transaction Costs Economics: How It Works, Where It Is Headed. *De Economist* 146(1), 23–58.

Williamson, O.E. (1999). Strategy Research: Governance and Competence Perspectives. *Strategic Management Journal* 20(12), 1087–1108.

Williamson, O.E. (2002). The Theory of the Firm as Governance Structure: From Choice to Contract. *Journal of Economic Perspectives* 16(3), 171–195.

Williamson, O.E. (2005). The Economics of Governance. *The American Economic Review* 95(2), 1–18.

Wojtyna, A. (2004). Bank centralny w świetle teorii agencji. *Gospodarka Narodowa* 9, 1–22.

Woodside, A.G., & Wilson, E.J. (2003). Case Study Research Methods for Theory Building. *Journal of Business & Industrial Marketing* 18(6/7), 493–508.

Wright, M., & Stigliani, I. (2013). Entrepreneurship and Growth. *International Small Business Journal* 31(1), 3–22.

Yin, R.K. (2009). *Case Study Research: Design and Methods*, 3rd edition. Los Angeles, London: Sage.

Zajac, E.J., & Olsen, C.P. (1993). From Transaction Cost to Transactional Value Analysis: Implications for the Study of Interorganizational Strategies. *Journal of Management Studies* 30(1), 131–145.

Zakrzewska-Bielawska, A. (2011). *Relacje między strategią a strukturą organizacyjną w przedsiębiorstwach sektora wysokich technologii*. Łódź: Wydawnictwo Politechniki Łódzkiej.

Ząbkowicz, A. (2003). „Współczesna ekonomia instytucjonalna wobec głównego nurtu ekonomii." *Ekonomista*, (6), 795–824.

Ząbkowicz, A. (2015). Instytucjonalny kontekst funkcjonowania rynku i organizacyjne formy koordynacji jako elementy nowego paradygmatu w ekonomii. *Research Papers of the Wroclaw University of Economics/ Prace Naukowe Uniwersytetu Ekonomicznego we Wrocławiu* 405, 9–22.

Zbierowski, P. (2012). *Orientacja pozytywna organizacji wysokiej efektywności*. Wolters Kluwer.

Zott, C., & Amit, R. (2007). Business Model Design and the Performance of Entrepreneurial Firms. *Organization Science* 18(2), 181–199.

LIST OF TABLES

Table 1. The major measures of growth and implications of using them
in empirical research 26

Table 2. Methodological choices regarding the identification of high-growers 31

Table 3. Theoretical approaches to firm growth and their suitability for research
in SME growth 37

Table 4. The research streams in firm growth – the major research questions
and the relevant theoretical background 46

Table 5. Research streams in firm growth and their prospective
cross-fertilizations 48

Table 6. The structural elements of the firm growth process according to the RBV
approach and its critiques 64

Table 7. The structural elements of the firm growth process according to the TCT
approach and its critiques 69

Table 8. The RBV and TCT alternative approaches to the structural elements
of the growth process and the resulting research problems 71

Table 9. The empirical studies that integrate the RBV and TCT in exploring
firm boundary decisions 85

Table 10. The theoretical studies that integrate the RBV and TCT in exploring
firm boundary decisions 94

Table 11. Three logics of integrating the RBV and TCT in the boundary literature   103

Table 12. The links among structural elements of the growth process, the major
RBV and TCT constructs, and research hypotheses 122

Table 13. The research and analytical methods 129

Table 14. The statements of opinions about the role of trust and opportunism
in business relationships rated by using a 5-point Likert scale 131

Table 15. The characteristics of the research sample 138

Table 16. The profiles of individual companies in the sample 139

Table 17. Verification of the research hypotheses based on the falsification test 147

Table 18. Summary of the verification of research hypotheses for each case study 147

Table 19. Truth table with all possible configurations and the sets of cases demonstrating the same configurations relative to the outcome 148

Table 20. Final patterns (solutions) of the SME growth process 150

Table 21. Patterns of growth process – structural elements and their moderators 151

Table 22. Structural elements of growth processes as enabling constraints to entrepreneurial decisions and actions 160

LIST OF FIGURES

Figure 1. The phases of the elaboration of the model of SME growth process and the structure of the book 16

Figure 2. A general framework of the firm's growth process 54

Figure 3. The evolution of the research testing the validity of the RBV and TCT and its results 75

Figure 4. The expansion and convergence of the theoretical foci of the RBV and TCT 76

Figure 5. A methodological procedure to develop a theoretical framework of the growth process of SMEs based on the integration of the RBV and TCT 83

Figure 6. The integrated RBV-TCT theoretical framework of SME growth process 117

Figure 7. Empirical research framework 122

Figure 8. Data collection procedure 136

Figure 9. The model of the SME growth process based on the integration of the resource-based view of the firm and transaction cost theory 163

TECHNICAL EDITOR   *Karolina Wąsowska*

PROOFREADER   *Magdalena Bielska*

TYPESETTER   *Jerzy Najder*

Jagiellonian University Press
Editorial Offices: Michałowskiego 9/2, 31-126 Kraków, Poland
Phone: +48 12 663 23 80, +48 12 663 23 82, Fax +48 12 663 23 83